STARGATE™
VALA MAL DORAN

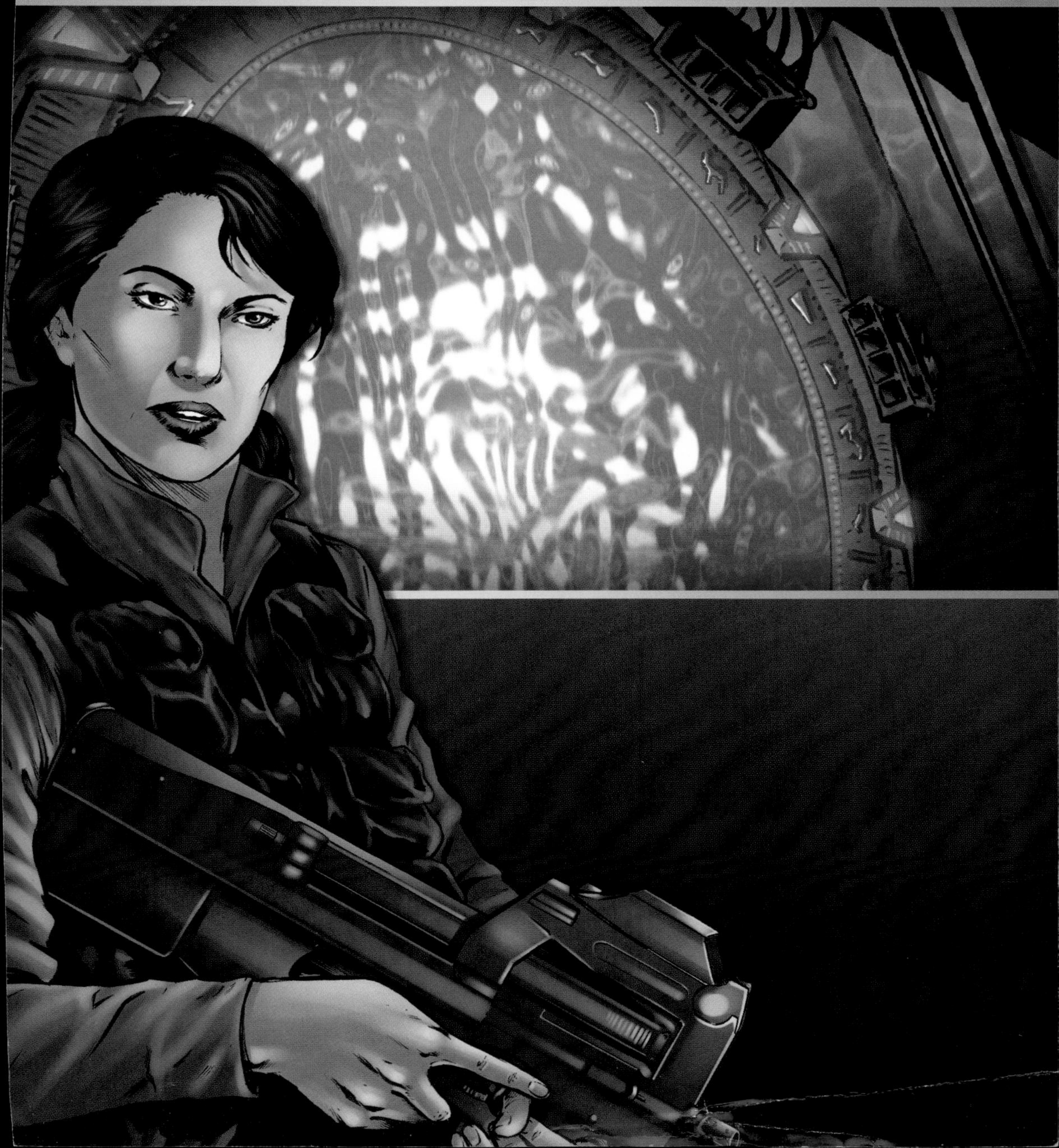

STARGATE
VALA MAL DORAN

WRITTEN BY
BRANDON JERWA

ILLUSTRATED BY
CEZAR RAZEK

COLORED BY
SALVATORE AIALA

LETTERED BY
SIMON BOWLAND

COLLECTION COVER BY
BRETT BOOTH

COLLECTION DESIGN BY
BILL TORTOLINI

ISBN13: 978-1-60690-153-3   ISBN10: 1-60690-153-2

10 9 8 7 6 5 4 3 2

Dynamite Entertainment:

NICK BARRUCCI	· PRESIDENT
JUAN COLLADO	· CHIEF OPERATING OFFICER
JOSEPH RYBANDT	· EDITOR
JOSH JOHNSON	· CREATIVE DIRECTOR
RICH YOUNG	· BUSINESS DEVELOPMENT
JASON ULLMEYER	· GRAPHIC DESIGNER

www.dynamiteentertainment.com

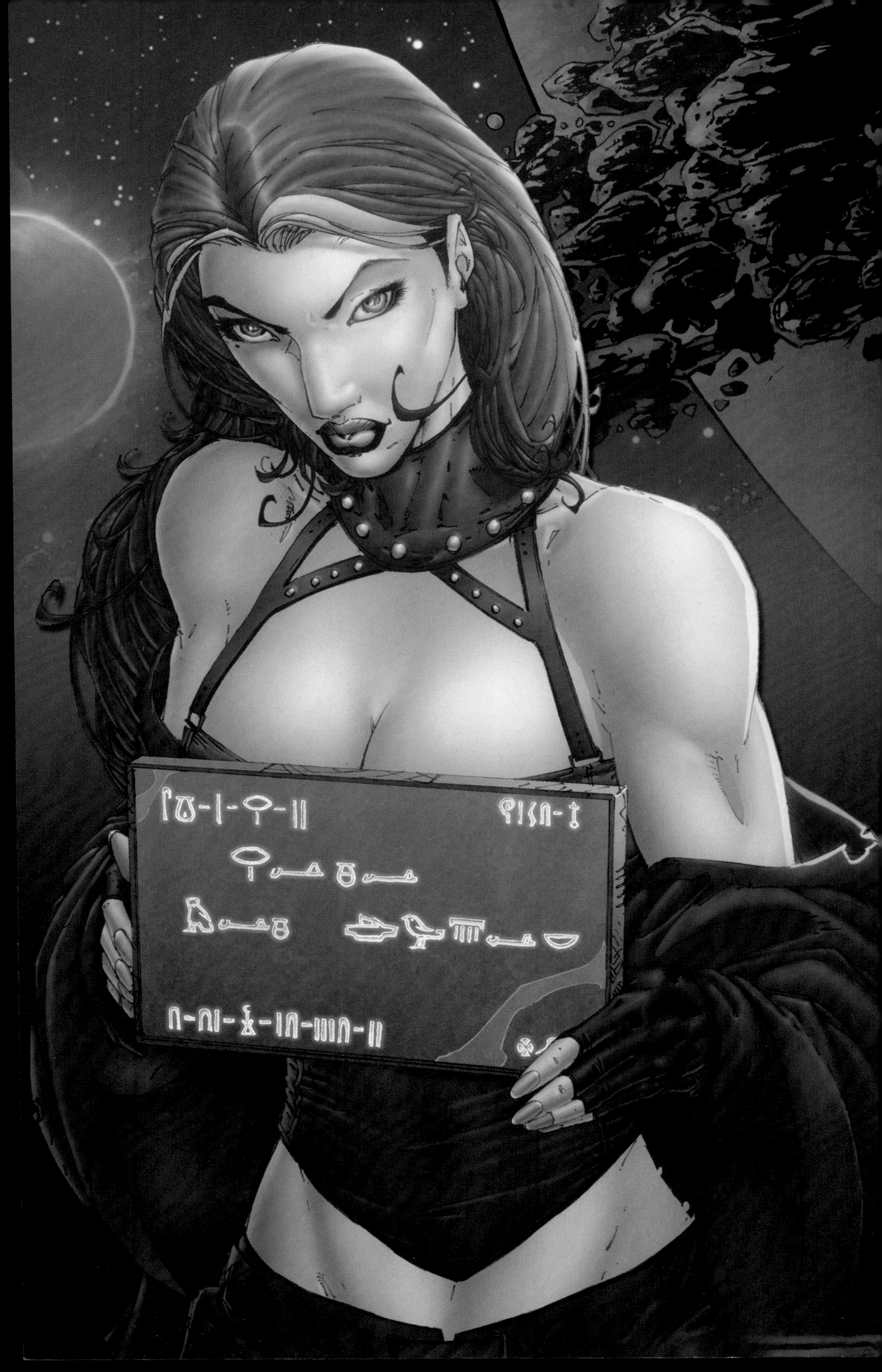

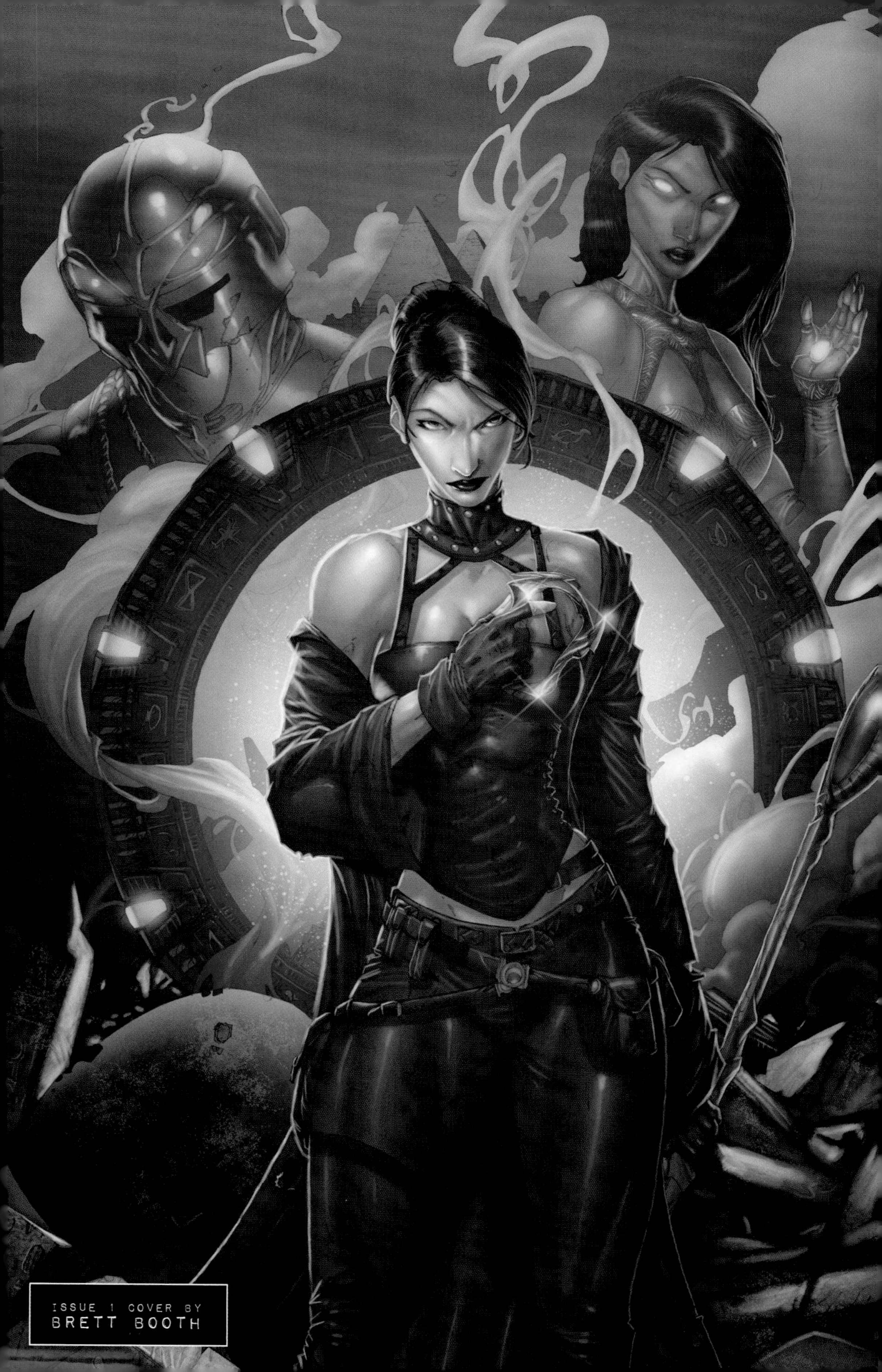

ISSUE 1 COVER BY
BRETT BOOTH

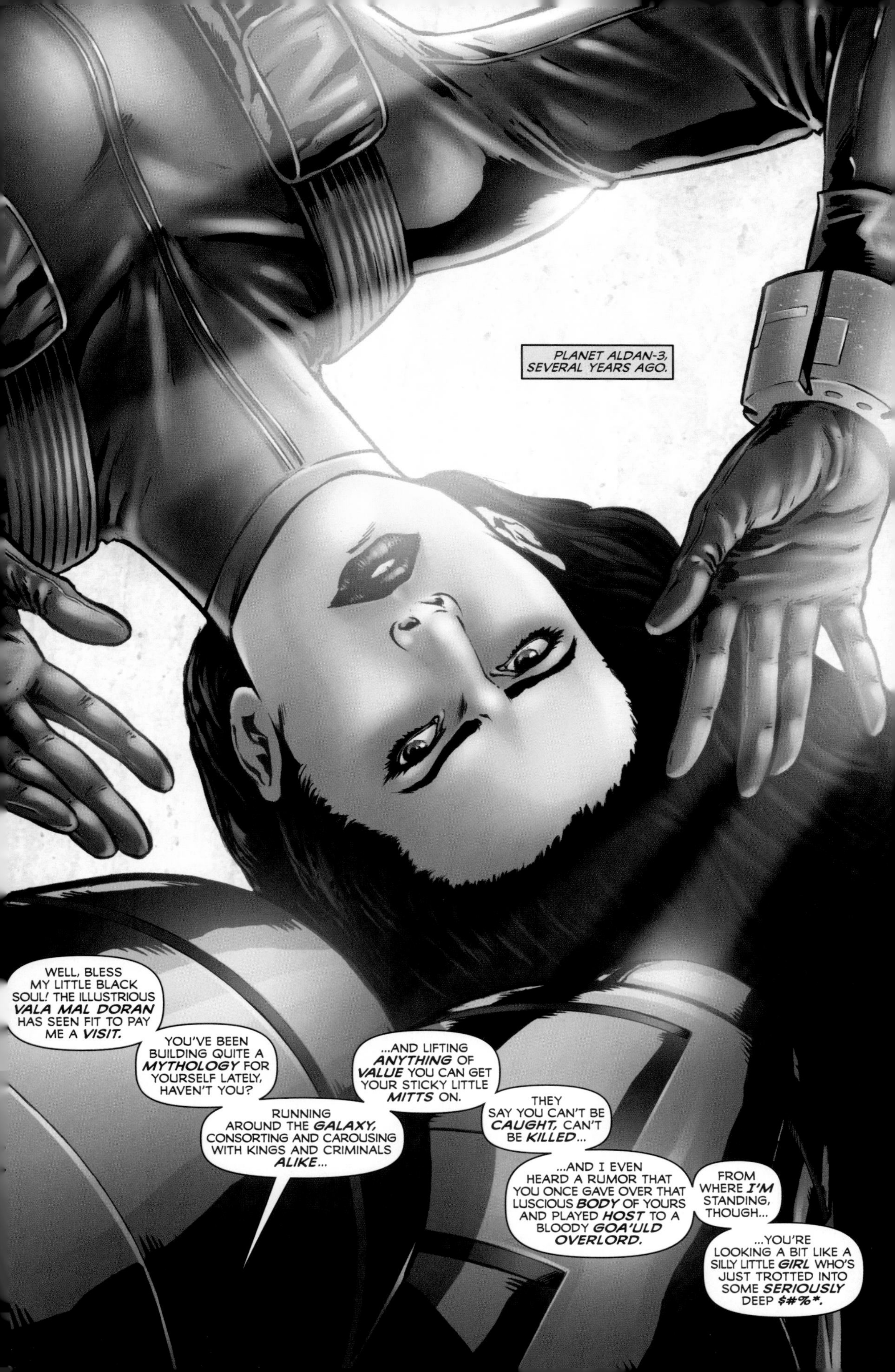
PLANET ALDAN-3, SEVERAL YEARS AGO.
WELL, BLESS MY LITTLE BLACK SOUL! THE ILLUSTRIOUS VALA MAL DORAN HAS SEEN FIT TO PAY ME A VISIT.
YOU'VE BEEN BUILDING QUITE A MYTHOLOGY FOR YOURSELF LATELY, HAVEN'T YOU?
RUNNING AROUND THE GALAXY, CONSORTING AND CAROUSING WITH KINGS AND CRIMINALS ALIKE...
...AND LIFTING ANYTHING OF VALUE YOU CAN GET YOUR STICKY LITTLE MITTS ON.
THEY SAY YOU CAN'T BE CAUGHT, CAN'T BE KILLED...
...AND I EVEN HEARD A RUMOR THAT YOU ONCE GAVE OVER THAT LUSCIOUS BODY OF YOURS AND PLAYED HOST TO A BLOODY GOA'ULD OVERLORD.
FROM WHERE I'M STANDING, THOUGH...
...YOU'RE LOOKING A BIT LIKE A SILLY LITTLE GIRL WHO'S JUST TROTTED INTO SOME SERIOUSLY DEEP $#%*.

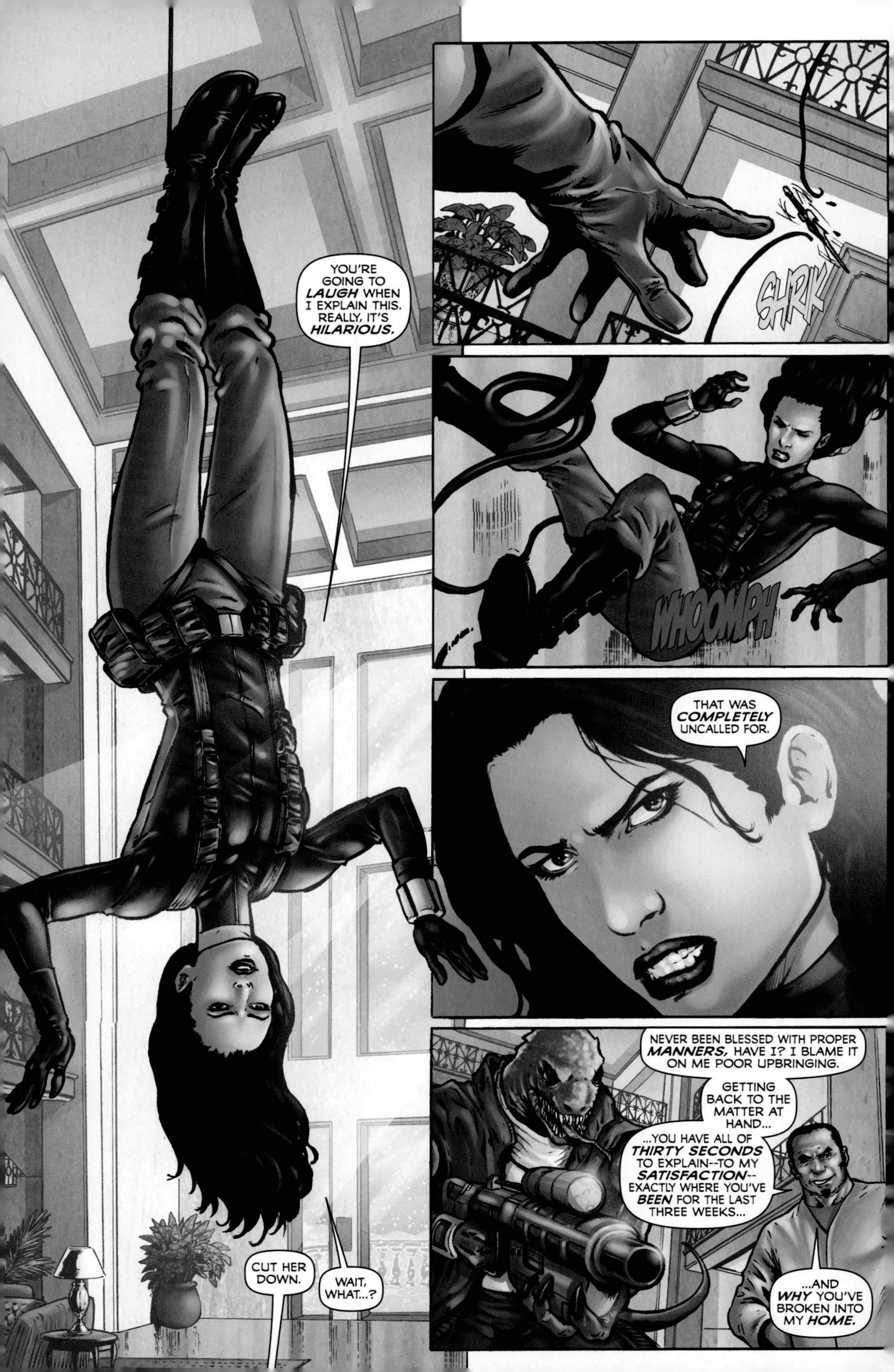
YOU'RE GOING TO LAUGH WHEN I EXPLAIN THIS. REALLY, IT'S HILARIOUS.
CUT HER DOWN.
WAIT, WHAT...?
SHRK
WHOOMPH
THAT WAS COMPLETELY UNCALLED FOR.
NEVER BEEN BLESSED WITH PROPER MANNERS, HAVE I? I BLAME IT ON ME POOR UPBRINGING.
GETTING BACK TO THE MATTER AT HAND...
...YOU HAVE ALL OF THIRTY SECONDS TO EXPLAIN--TO MY SATISFACTION--EXACTLY WHERE YOU'VE BEEN FOR THE LAST THREE WEEKS...
...AND WHY YOU'VE BROKEN INTO MY HOME.

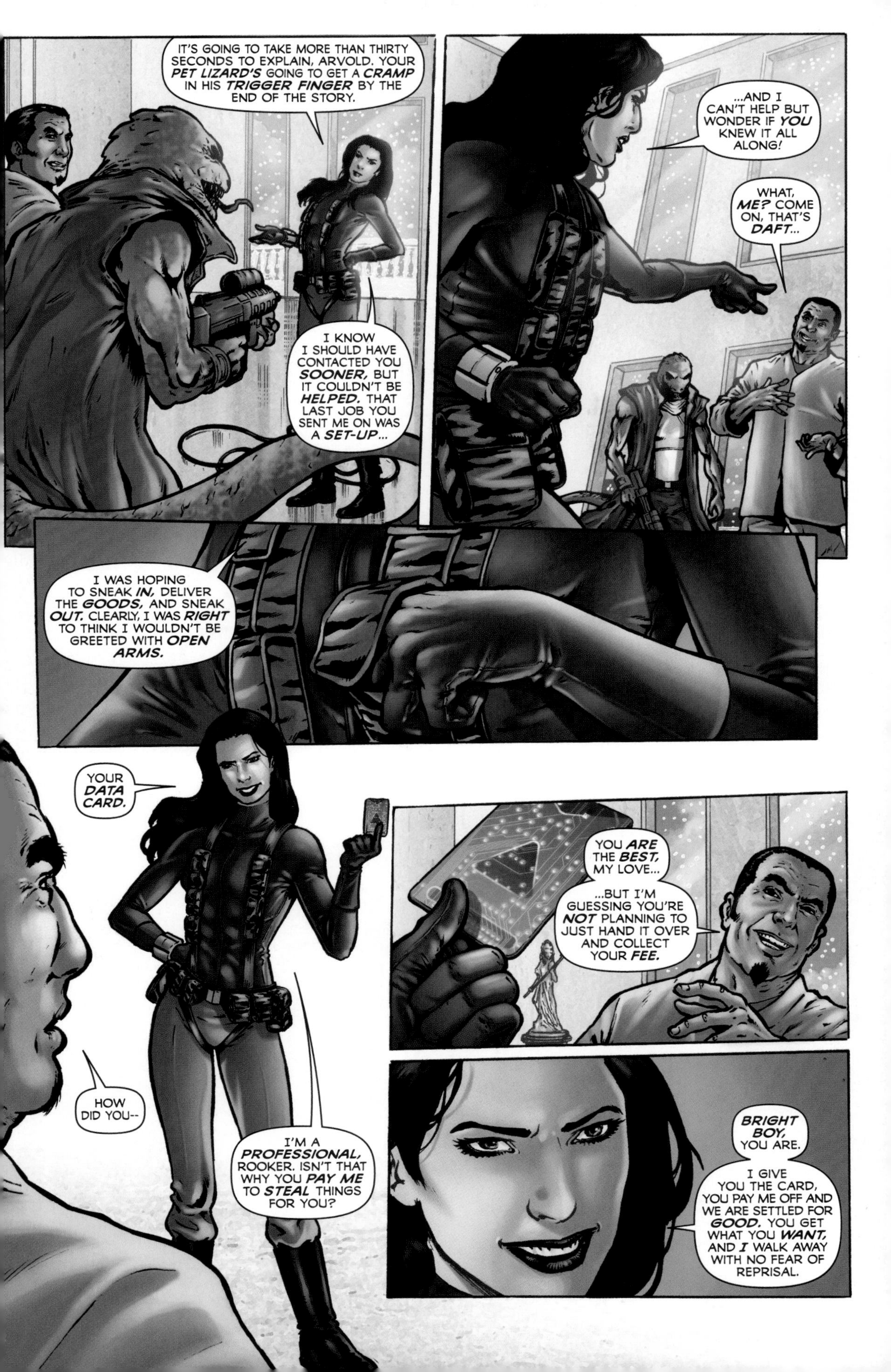
IT'S GOING TO TAKE MORE THAN THIRTY SECONDS TO EXPLAIN, ARVOLD. YOUR PET LIZARD'S GOING TO GET A CRAMP IN HIS TRIGGER FINGER BY THE END OF THE STORY.
I KNOW I SHOULD HAVE CONTACTED YOU SOONER, BUT IT COULDN'T BE HELPED. THAT LAST JOB YOU SENT ME ON WAS A SET-UP...
...AND I CAN'T HELP BUT WONDER IF YOU KNEW IT ALL ALONG!
WHAT, ME? COME ON, THAT'S DAFT...
I WAS HOPING TO SNEAK IN, DELIVER THE GOODS, AND SNEAK OUT. CLEARLY, I WAS RIGHT TO THINK I WOULDN'T BE GREETED WITH OPEN ARMS.
YOUR DATA CARD.
HOW DID YOU--
I'M A PROFESSIONAL, ROOKER. ISN'T THAT WHY YOU PAY ME TO STEAL THINGS FOR YOU?
YOU ARE THE BEST, MY LOVE...
...BUT I'M GUESSING YOU'RE NOT PLANNING TO JUST HAND IT OVER AND COLLECT YOUR FEE.
BRIGHT BOY, YOU ARE.
I GIVE YOU THE CARD, YOU PAY ME OFF AND WE ARE SETTLED FOR GOOD. YOU GET WHAT YOU WANT, AND I WALK AWAY WITH NO FEAR OF REPRISAL.

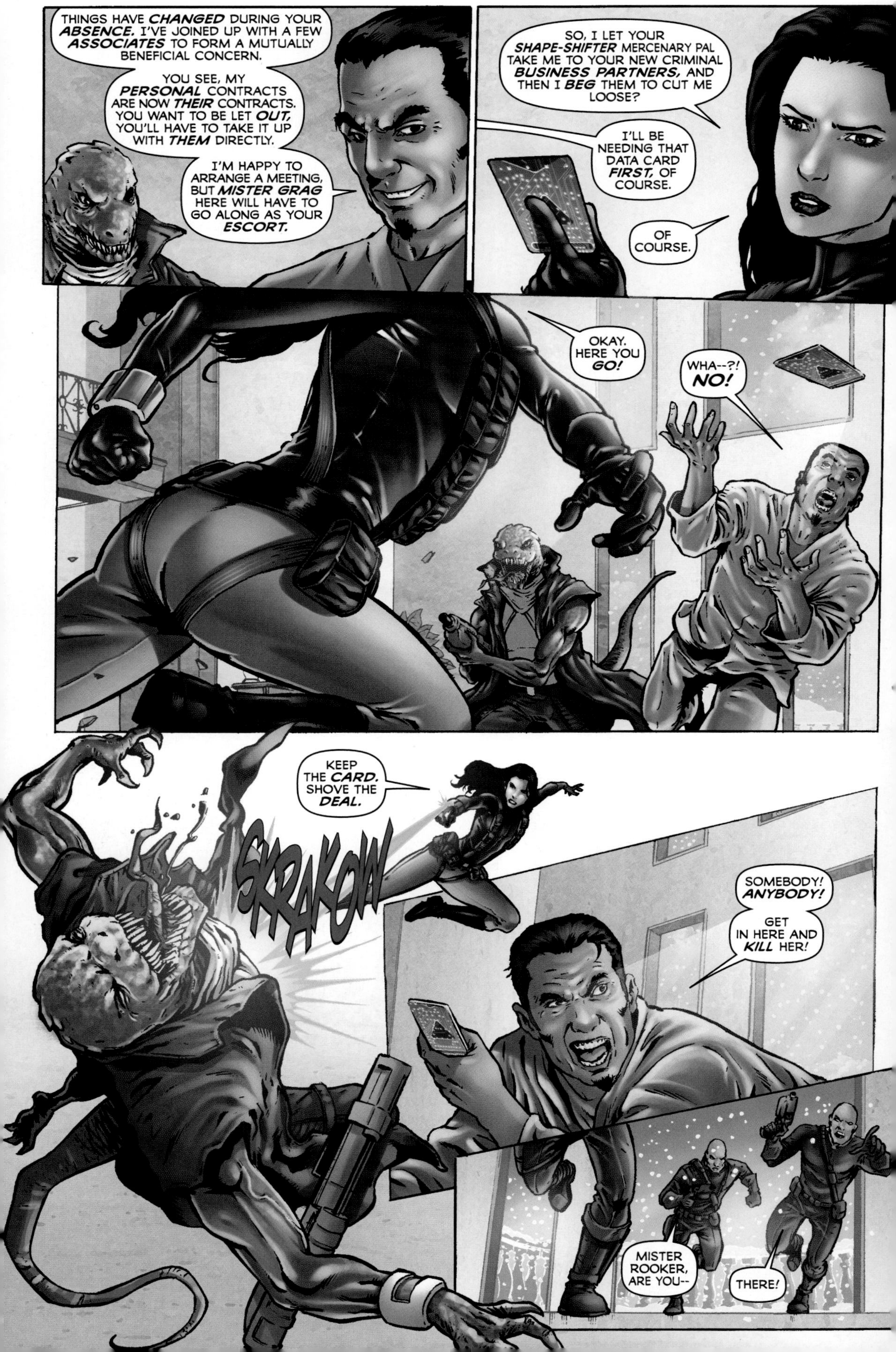
THINGS HAVE CHANGED DURING YOUR ABSENCE. I'VE JOINED UP WITH A FEW ASSOCIATES TO FORM A MUTUALLY BENEFICIAL CONCERN.
YOU SEE, MY PERSONAL CONTRACTS ARE NOW THEIR CONTRACTS. YOU WANT TO BE LET OUT, YOU'LL HAVE TO TAKE IT UP WITH THEM DIRECTLY.
I'M HAPPY TO ARRANGE A MEETING, BUT MISTER GRAG HERE WILL HAVE TO GO ALONG AS YOUR ESCORT.
SO, I LET YOUR SHAPE-SHIFTER MERCENARY PAL TAKE ME TO YOUR NEW CRIMINAL BUSINESS PARTNERS, AND THEN I BEG THEM TO CUT ME LOOSE?
I'LL BE NEEDING THAT DATA CARD FIRST, OF COURSE.
OF COURSE.
OKAY. HERE YOU GO!
WHA--?! NO!
KEEP THE CARD. SHOVE THE DEAL.
SKRAKOW
SOMEBODY! ANYBODY!
GET IN HERE AND KILL HER!
MISTER ROOKER, ARE YOU--
THERE!

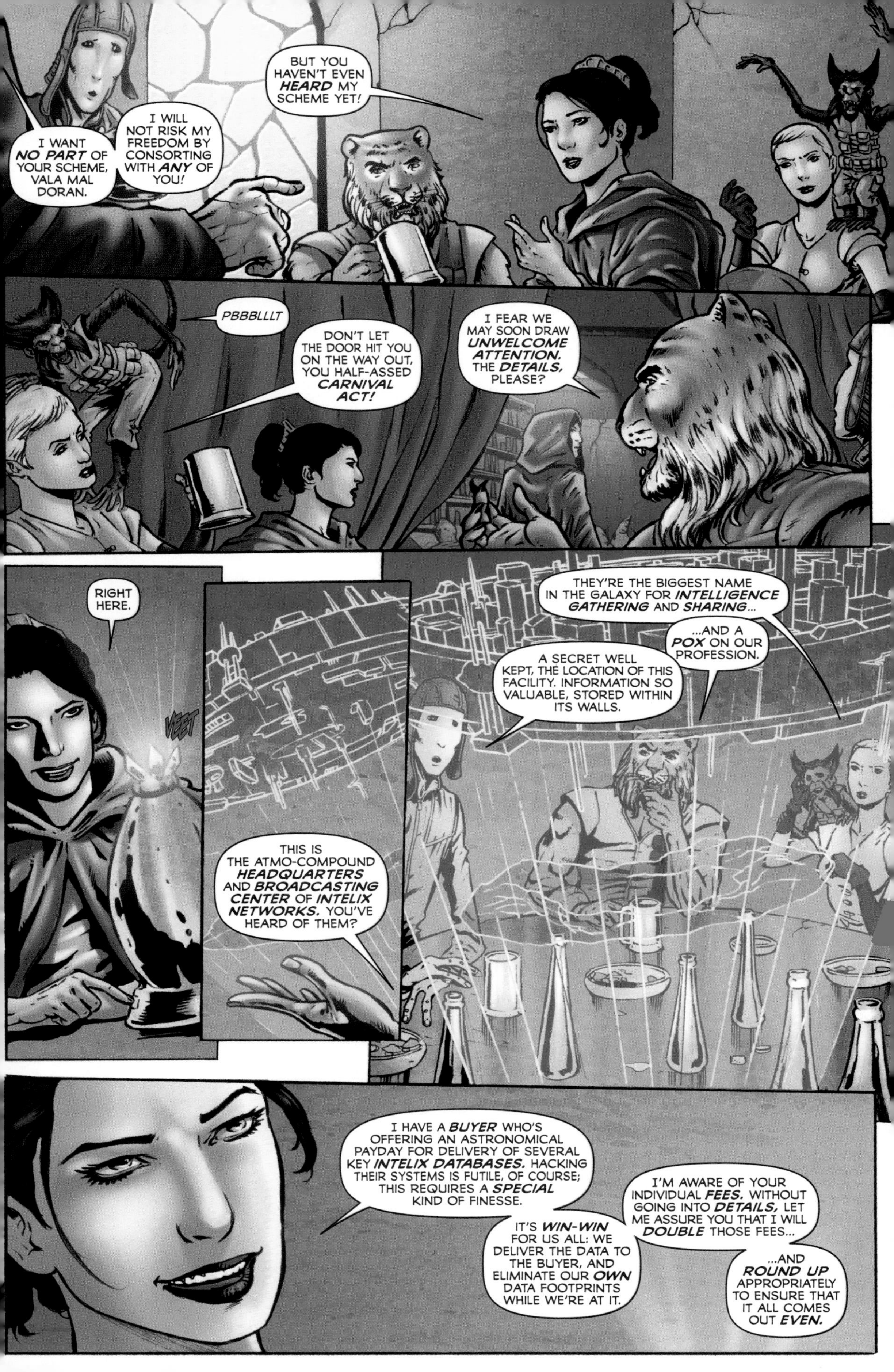

I WANT NO PART OF YOUR SCHEME, VALA MAL DORAN.
I WILL NOT RISK MY FREEDOM BY CONSORTING WITH ANY OF YOU!
BUT YOU HAVEN'T EVEN HEARD MY SCHEME YET!
PBBBLLLT
DON'T LET THE DOOR HIT YOU ON THE WAY OUT, YOU HALF-ASSED CARNIVAL ACT!
I FEAR WE MAY SOON DRAW UNWELCOME ATTENTION. THE DETAILS, PLEASE?
RIGHT HERE.
VEET
THIS IS THE ATMO-COMPOUND HEADQUARTERS AND BROADCASTING CENTER OF INTELIX NETWORKS. YOU'VE HEARD OF THEM?
THEY'RE THE BIGGEST NAME IN THE GALAXY FOR INTELLIGENCE GATHERING AND SHARING...
...AND A POX ON OUR PROFESSION.
A SECRET WELL KEPT, THE LOCATION OF THIS FACILITY. INFORMATION SO VALUABLE, STORED WITHIN ITS WALLS.
I HAVE A BUYER WHO'S OFFERING AN ASTRONOMICAL PAYDAY FOR DELIVERY OF SEVERAL KEY INTELIX DATABASES. HACKING THEIR SYSTEMS IS FUTILE, OF COURSE; THIS REQUIRES A SPECIAL KIND OF FINESSE.
IT'S WIN-WIN FOR US ALL: WE DELIVER THE DATA TO THE BUYER, AND ELIMINATE OUR OWN DATA FOOTPRINTS WHILE WE'RE AT IT.
I'M AWARE OF YOUR INDIVIDUAL FEES. WITHOUT GOING INTO DETAILS, LET ME ASSURE YOU THAT I WILL DOUBLE THOSE FEES...
...AND ROUND UP APPROPRIATELY TO ENSURE THAT IT ALL COMES OUT EVEN.

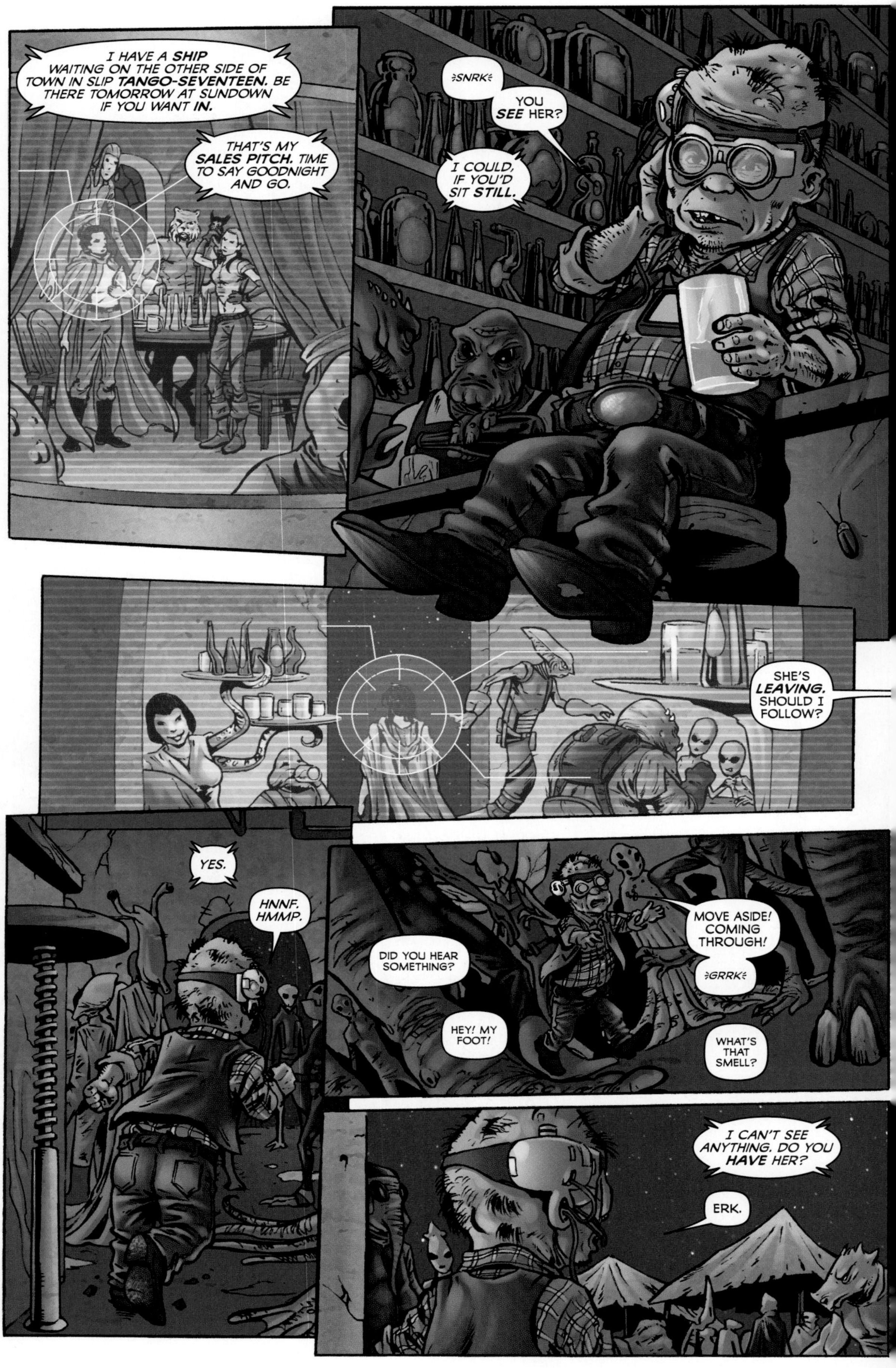

I HAVE A SHIP WAITING ON THE OTHER SIDE OF TOWN IN SLIP TANGO-SEVENTEEN. BE THERE TOMORROW AT SUNDOWN IF YOU WANT IN.
THAT'S MY SALES PITCH. TIME TO SAY GOODNIGHT AND GO.
SNRK
YOU SEE HER?
I COULD, IF YOU'D SIT STILL.
SHE'S LEAVING. SHOULD I FOLLOW?
YES.
HNNF. HMMP.
MOVE ASIDE! COMING THROUGH!
DID YOU HEAR SOMETHING?
GRRK
HEY! MY FOOT!
WHAT'S THAT SMELL?
I CAN'T SEE ANYTHING. DO YOU HAVE HER?
ERK.

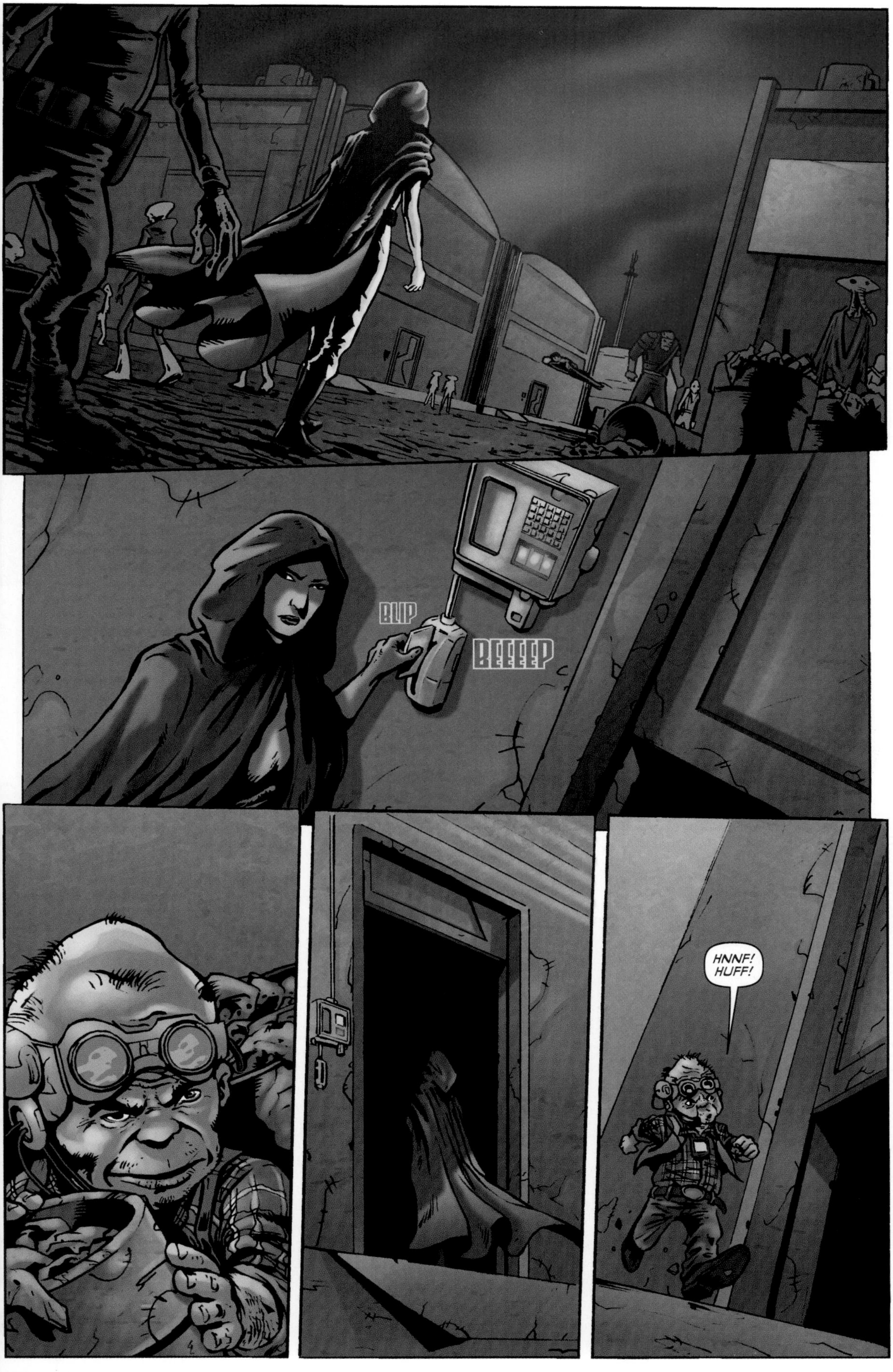
BLIP
BEEEEP
HNNF! HUFF!

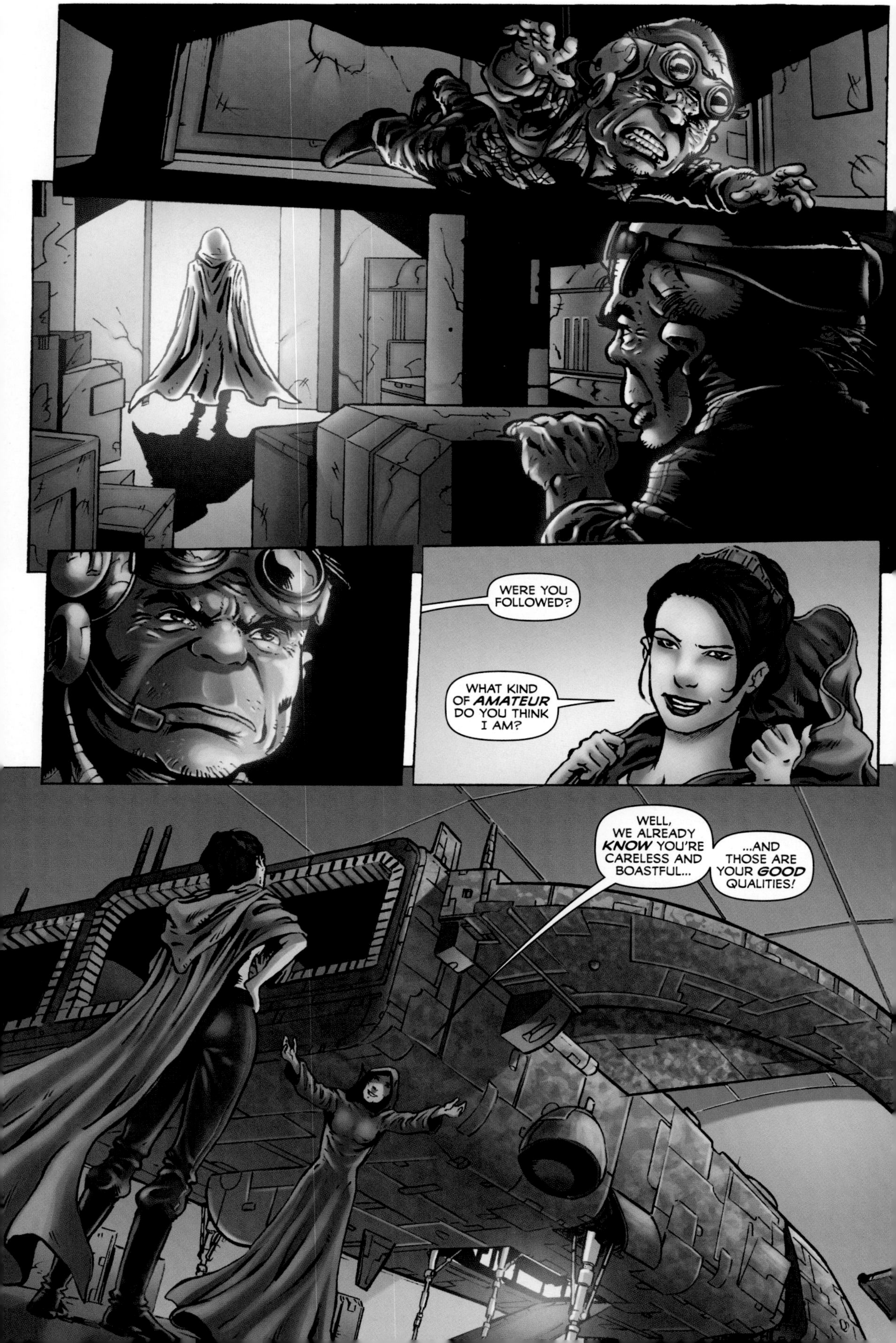

WERE YOU FOLLOWED?
WHAT KIND OF AMATEUR DO YOU THINK I AM?
WELL, WE ALREADY KNOW YOU'RE CARELESS AND BOASTFUL...
...AND THOSE ARE YOUR GOOD QUALITIES!

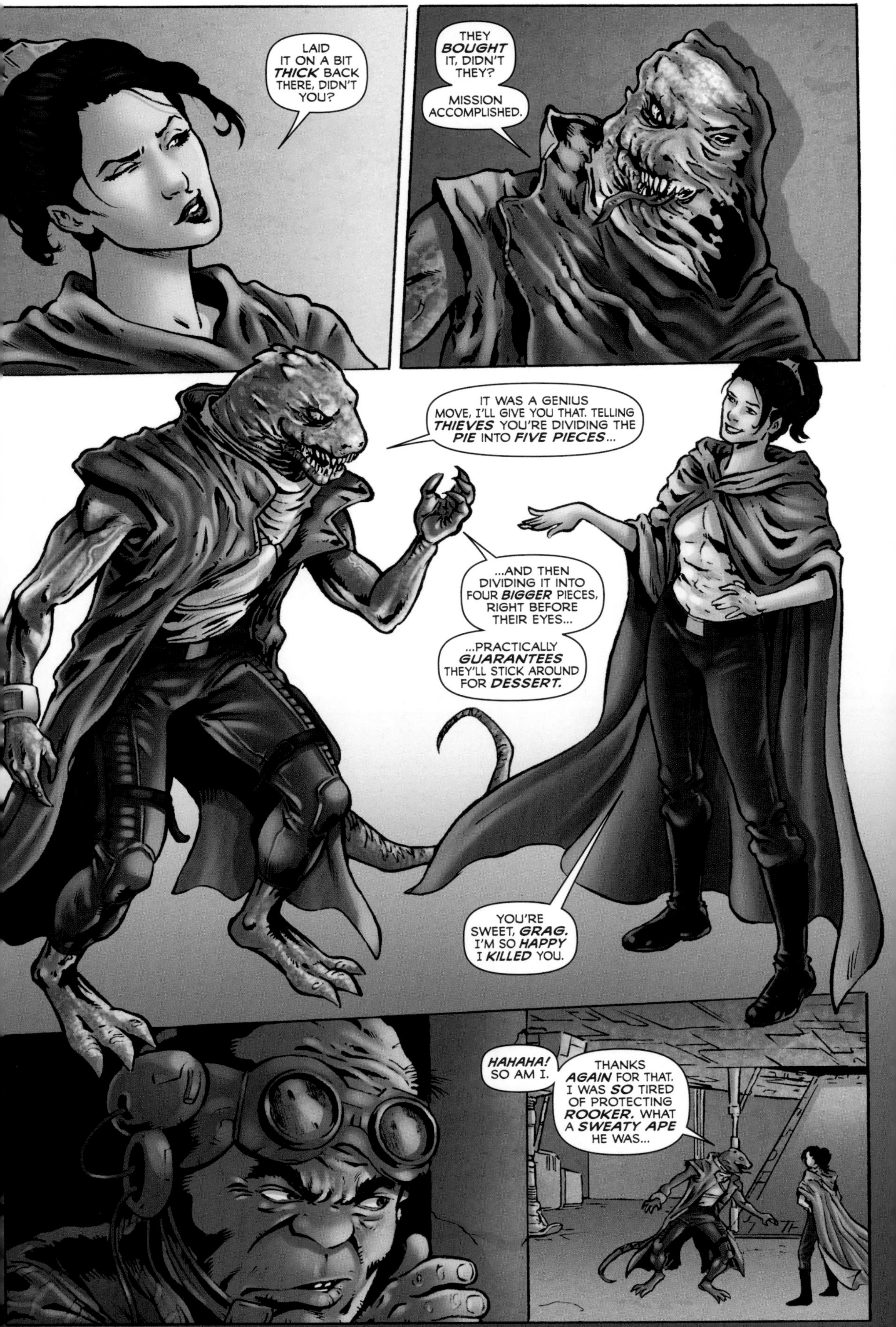
LAID IT ON A BIT THICK BACK THERE, DIDN'T YOU?
THEY BOUGHT IT, DIDN'T THEY?
MISSION ACCOMPLISHED.
IT WAS A GENIUS MOVE, I'LL GIVE YOU THAT. TELLING THIEVES YOU'RE DIVIDING THE PIE INTO FIVE PIECES...
...AND THEN DIVIDING IT INTO FOUR BIGGER PIECES, RIGHT BEFORE THEIR EYES...
...PRACTICALLY GUARANTEES THEY'LL STICK AROUND FOR DESSERT.
YOU'RE SWEET, GRAG. I'M SO HAPPY I KILLED YOU.
HAHAHA! SO AM I.
THANKS AGAIN FOR THAT. I WAS SO TIRED OF PROTECTING ROOKER. WHAT A SWEATY APE HE WAS...

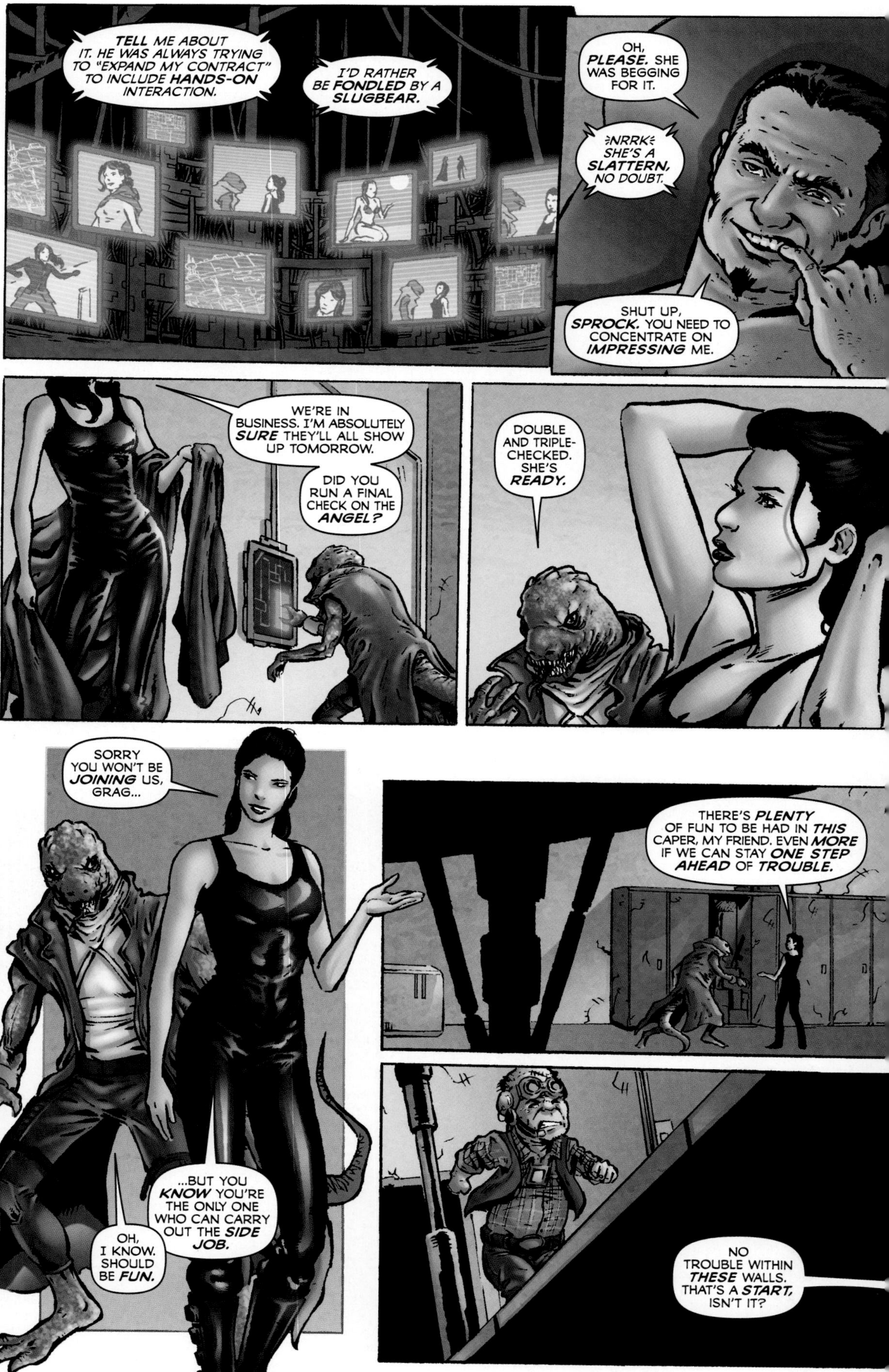
TELL ME ABOUT IT. HE WAS ALWAYS TRYING TO "EXPAND MY CONTRACT" TO INCLUDE HANDS-ON INTERACTION.
I'D RATHER BE FONDLED BY A SLUGBEAR.
OH, PLEASE. SHE WAS BEGGING FOR IT.
NRRK SHE'S A SLATTERN, NO DOUBT.
SHUT UP, SPROCK. YOU NEED TO CONCENTRATE ON IMPRESSING ME.
WE'RE IN BUSINESS. I'M ABSOLUTELY SURE THEY'LL ALL SHOW UP TOMORROW.
DID YOU RUN A FINAL CHECK ON THE ANGEL?
DOUBLE AND TRIPLE-CHECKED. SHE'S READY.
SORRY YOU WON'T BE JOINING US, GRAG...
...BUT YOU KNOW YOU'RE THE ONLY ONE WHO CAN CARRY OUT THE SIDE JOB.
OH, I KNOW. SHOULD BE FUN.
THERE'S PLENTY OF FUN TO BE HAD IN THIS CAPER, MY FRIEND. EVEN MORE IF WE CAN STAY ONE STEP AHEAD OF TROUBLE.
NO TROUBLE WITHIN THESE WALLS. THAT'S A START, ISN'T IT?

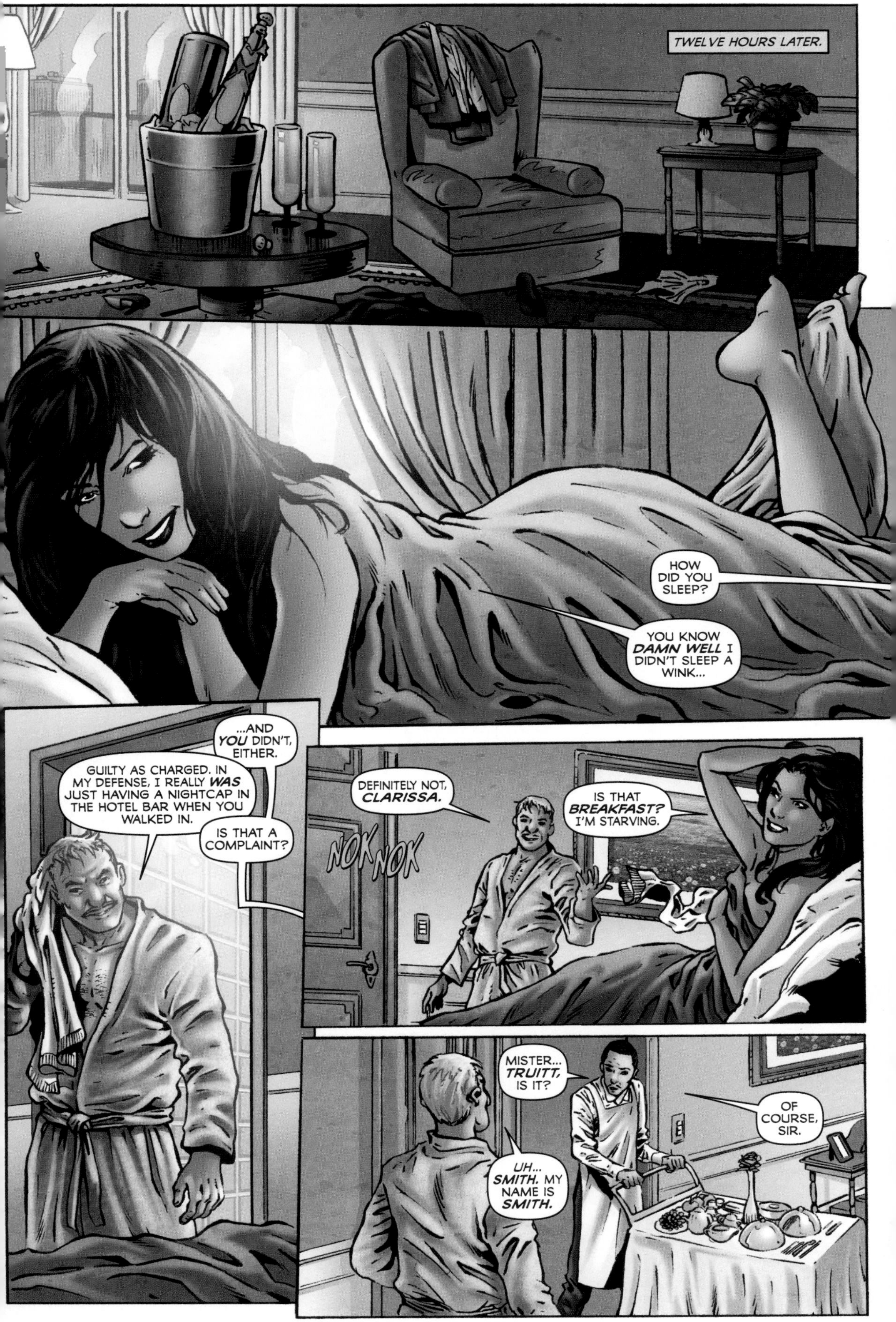
TWELVE HOURS LATER.
HOW DID YOU SLEEP?
YOU KNOW DAMN WELL I DIDN'T SLEEP A WINK...
...AND YOU DIDN'T, EITHER.
GUILTY AS CHARGED. IN MY DEFENSE, I REALLY WAS JUST HAVING A NIGHTCAP IN THE HOTEL BAR WHEN YOU WALKED IN.
IS THAT A COMPLAINT?
DEFINITELY NOT, CLARISSA.
IS THAT BREAKFAST? I'M STARVING.
NOK NOK
MISTER... TRUITT, IS IT?
UH... SMITH. MY NAME IS SMITH.
OF COURSE, SIR.

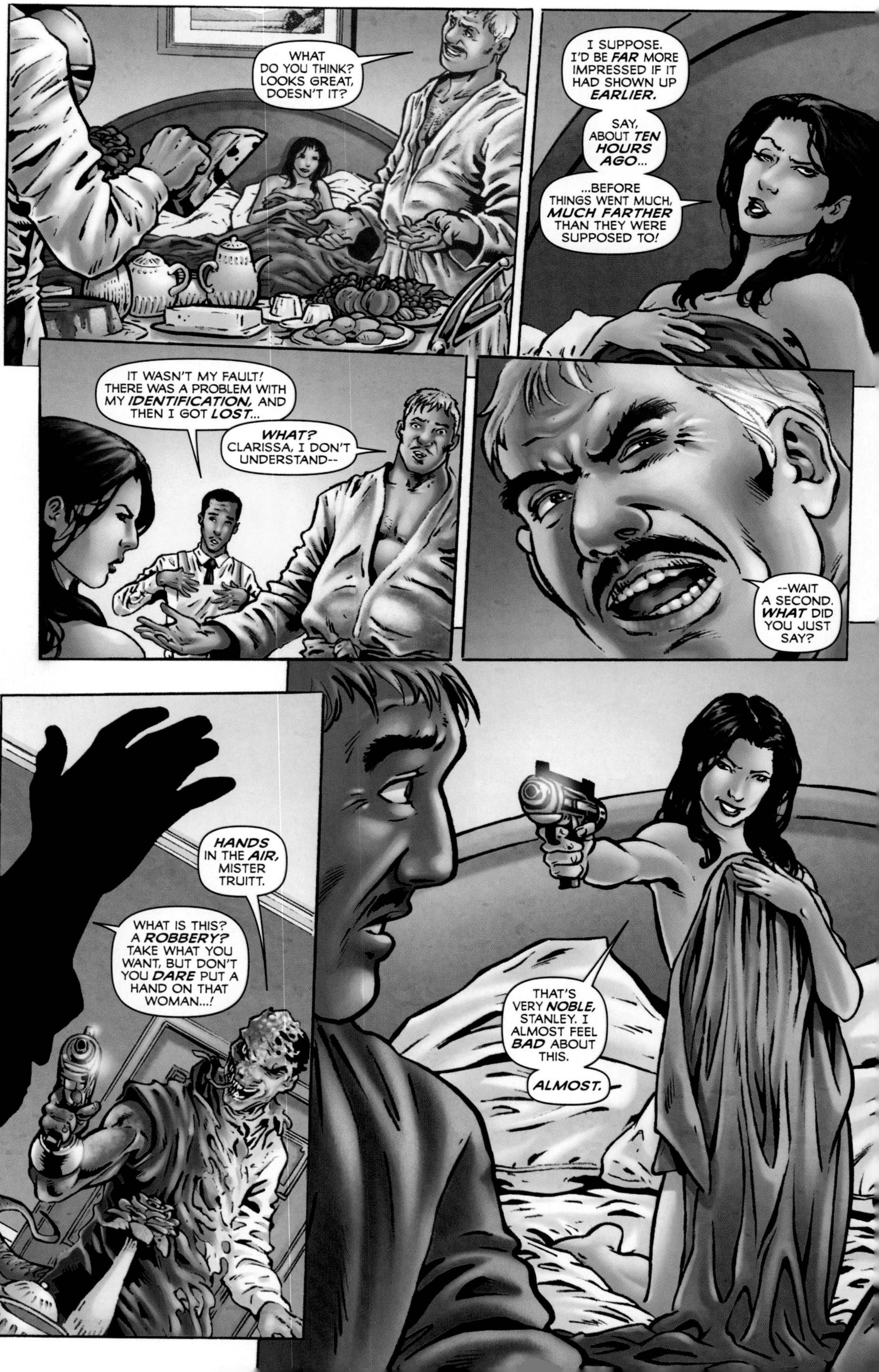
WHAT DO YOU THINK? LOOKS GREAT, DOESN'T IT?
I SUPPOSE. I'D BE FAR MORE IMPRESSED IF IT HAD SHOWN UP EARLIER.
SAY, ABOUT TEN HOURS AGO...
...BEFORE THINGS WENT MUCH, MUCH FARTHER THAN THEY WERE SUPPOSED TO!
IT WASN'T MY FAULT! THERE WAS A PROBLEM WITH MY IDENTIFICATION, AND THEN I GOT LOST...
WHAT? CLARISSA, I DON'T UNDERSTAND--
--WAIT A SECOND. WHAT DID YOU JUST SAY?
HANDS IN THE AIR, MISTER TRUITT.
WHAT IS THIS? A ROBBERY? TAKE WHAT YOU WANT, BUT DON'T YOU DARE PUT A HAND ON THAT WOMAN...!
THAT'S VERY NOBLE, STANLEY. I ALMOST FEEL BAD ABOUT THIS.
ALMOST.

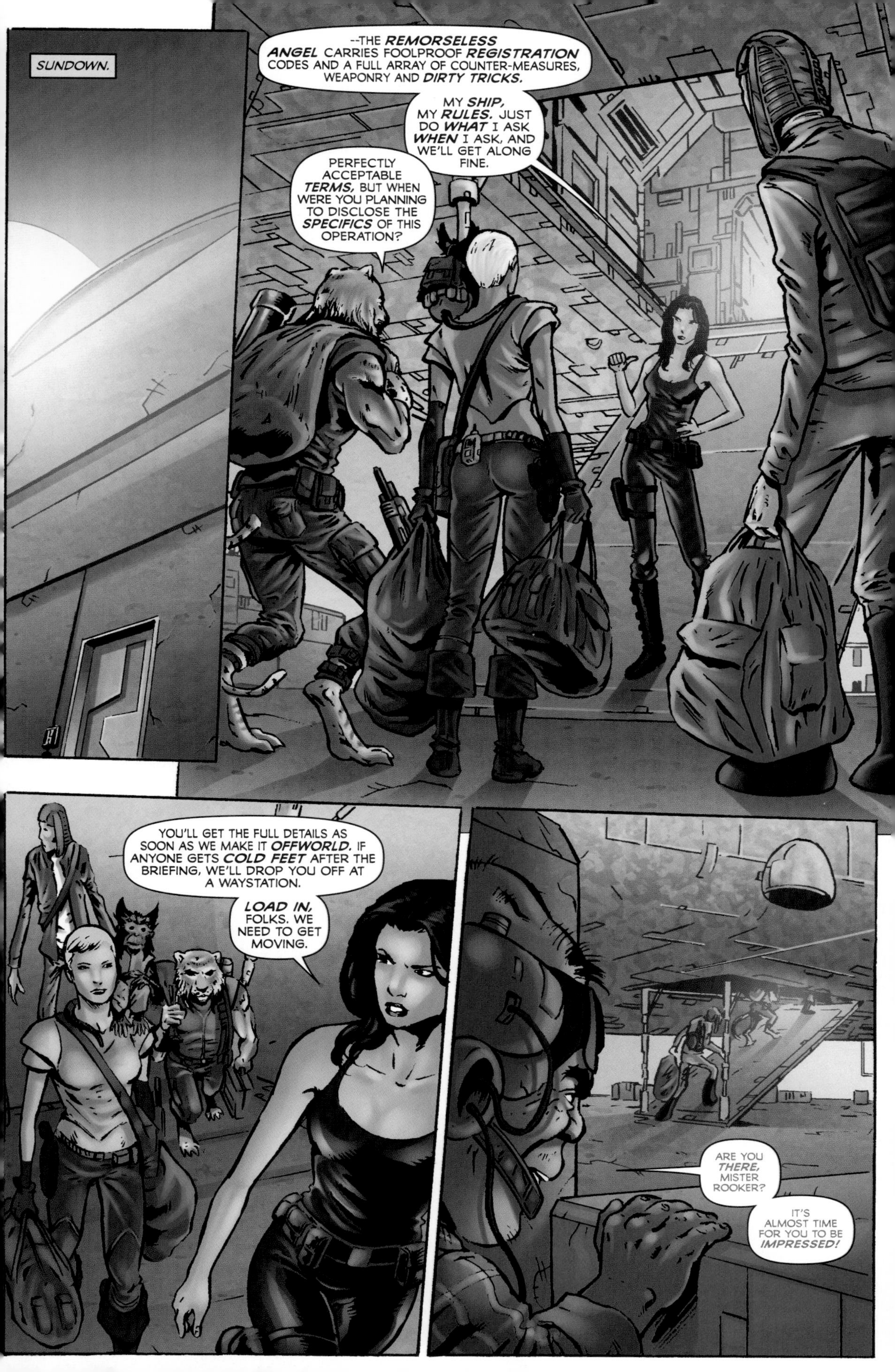
SUNDOWN.
--THE REMORSELESS ANGEL CARRIES FOOLPROOF REGISTRATION CODES AND A FULL ARRAY OF COUNTER-MEASURES, WEAPONRY AND DIRTY TRICKS.
MY SHIP, MY RULES. JUST DO WHAT I ASK WHEN I ASK, AND WE'LL GET ALONG FINE.
PERFECTLY ACCEPTABLE TERMS, BUT WHEN WERE YOU PLANNING TO DISCLOSE THE SPECIFICS OF THIS OPERATION?
YOU'LL GET THE FULL DETAILS AS SOON AS WE MAKE IT OFFWORLD. IF ANYONE GETS COLD FEET AFTER THE BRIEFING, WE'LL DROP YOU OFF AT A WAYSTATION.
LOAD IN, FOLKS. WE NEED TO GET MOVING.
ARE YOU THERE, MISTER ROOKER?
IT'S ALMOST TIME FOR YOU TO BE IMPRESSED!

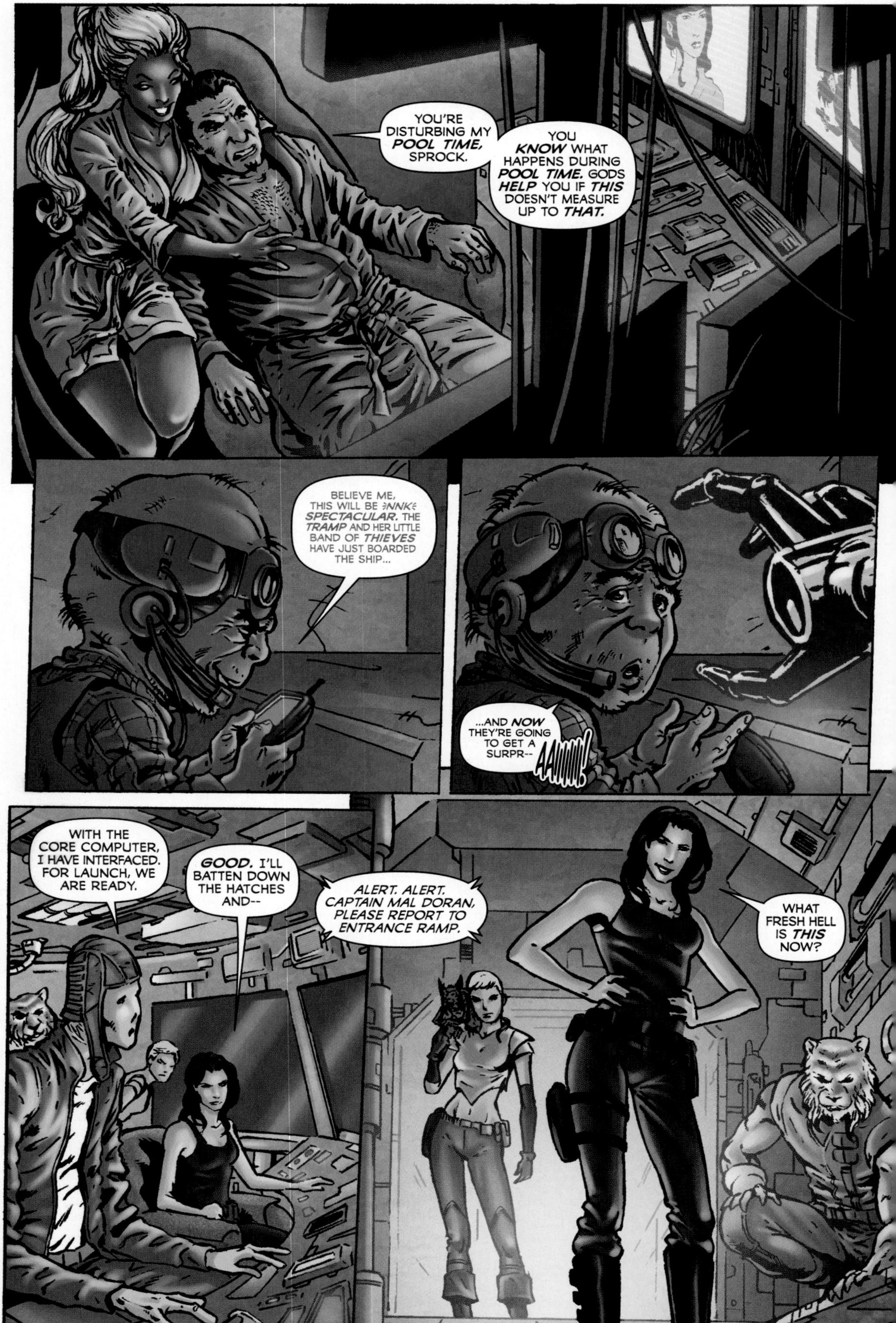
YOU'RE DISTURBING MY POOL TIME, SPROCK.
YOU KNOW WHAT HAPPENS DURING POOL TIME. GODS HELP YOU IF THIS DOESN'T MEASURE UP TO THAT.
BELIEVE ME, THIS WILL BE NNK SPECTACULAR. THE TRAMP AND HER LITTLE BAND OF THIEVES HAVE JUST BOARDED THE SHIP...
...AND NOW THEY'RE GOING TO GET A SURPR--
AAIIIIIII!
WITH THE CORE COMPUTER, I HAVE INTERFACED. FOR LAUNCH, WE ARE READY.
GOOD. I'LL BATTEN DOWN THE HATCHES AND--
ALERT. ALERT. CAPTAIN MAL DORAN, PLEASE REPORT TO ENTRANCE RAMP.
WHAT FRESH HELL IS THIS NOW?

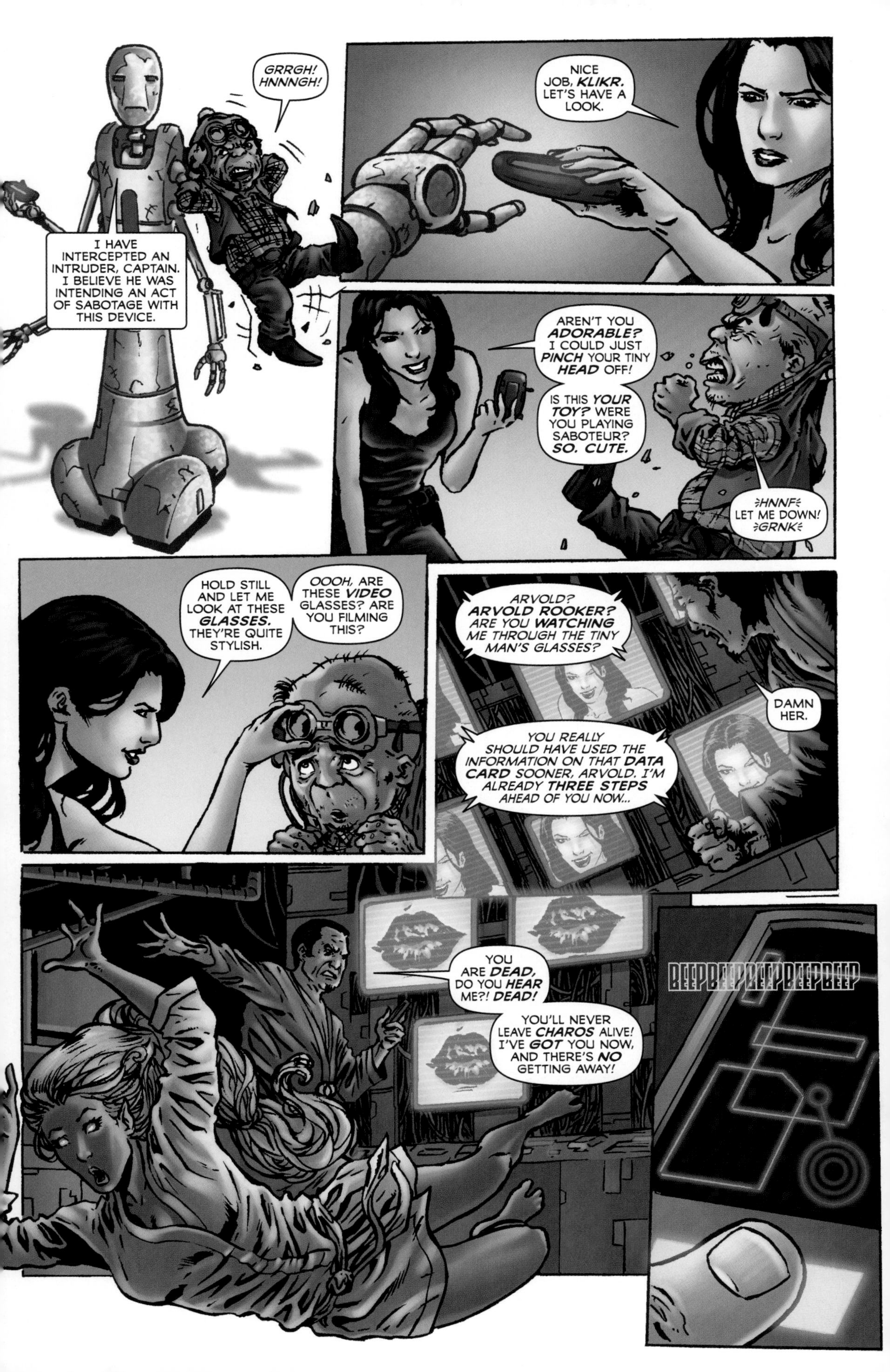
GRRGH! HNNNGH!
I HAVE INTERCEPTED AN INTRUDER, CAPTAIN. I BELIEVE HE WAS INTENDING AN ACT OF SABOTAGE WITH THIS DEVICE.
NICE JOB, KLIKR. LET'S HAVE A LOOK.
AREN'T YOU ADORABLE? I COULD JUST PINCH YOUR TINY HEAD OFF!
IS THIS YOUR TOY? WERE YOU PLAYING SABOTEUR? SO. CUTE.
HNNF LET ME DOWN! GRNK
HOLD STILL AND LET ME LOOK AT THESE GLASSES. THEY'RE QUITE STYLISH.
OOOH, ARE THESE VIDEO GLASSES? ARE YOU FILMING THIS?
ARVOLD? ARVOLD ROOKER? ARE YOU WATCHING ME THROUGH THE TINY MAN'S GLASSES?
DAMN HER.
YOU REALLY SHOULD HAVE USED THE INFORMATION ON THAT DATA CARD SOONER, ARVOLD. I'M ALREADY THREE STEPS AHEAD OF YOU NOW...
YOU ARE DEAD, DO YOU HEAR ME?! DEAD!
YOU'LL NEVER LEAVE CHAROS ALIVE! I'VE GOT YOU NOW, AND THERE'S NO GETTING AWAY!
BEEPBEEPBEEPBEEPBEEP

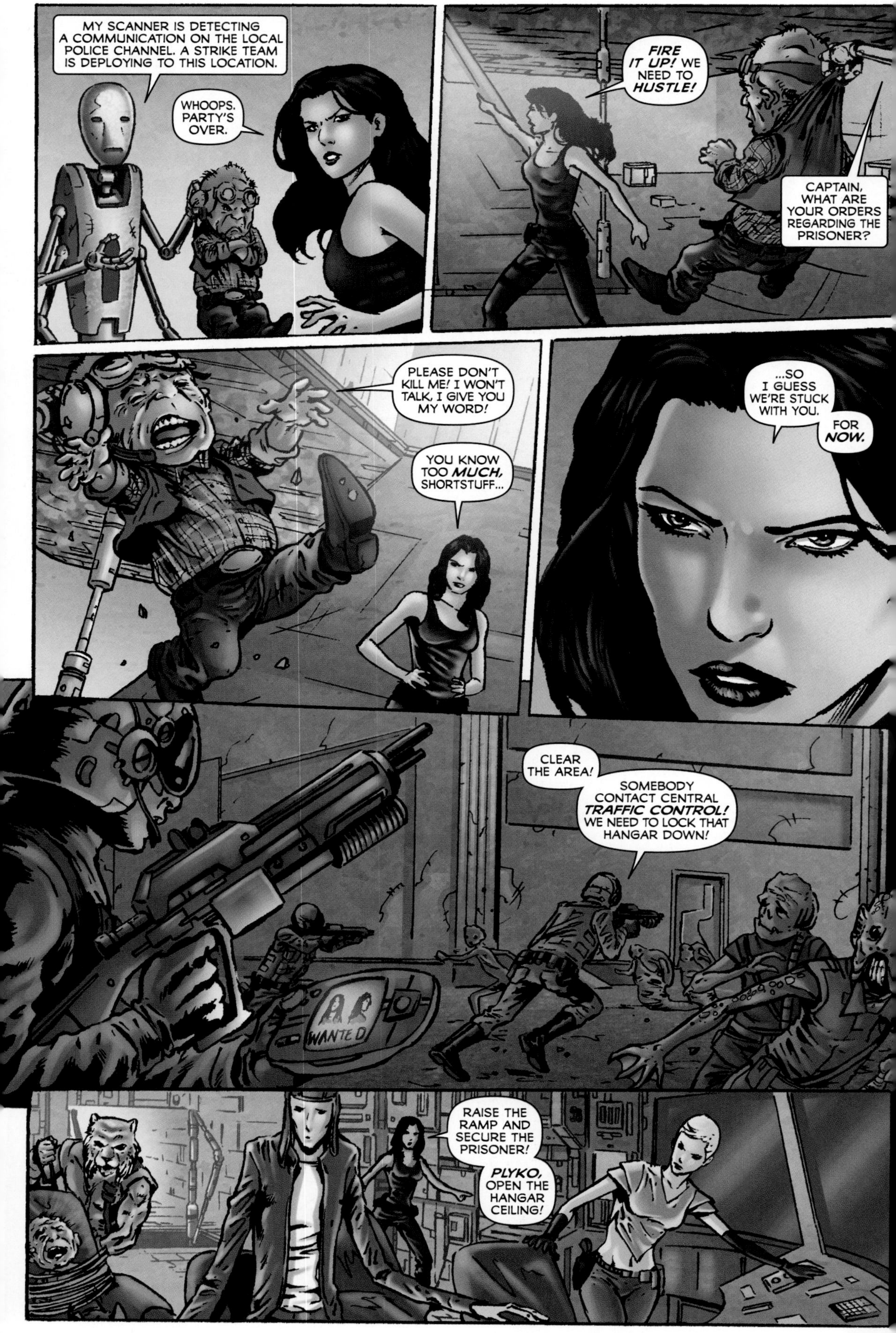
MY SCANNER IS DETECTING A COMMUNICATION ON THE LOCAL POLICE CHANNEL. A STRIKE TEAM IS DEPLOYING TO THIS LOCATION.
WHOOPS. PARTY'S OVER.
FIRE IT UP! WE NEED TO HUSTLE!
CAPTAIN, WHAT ARE YOUR ORDERS REGARDING THE PRISONER?
PLEASE DON'T KILL ME! I WON'T TALK, I GIVE YOU MY WORD!
YOU KNOW TOO MUCH, SHORTSTUFF...
...SO I GUESS WE'RE STUCK WITH YOU.
FOR NOW.
CLEAR THE AREA!
SOMEBODY CONTACT CENTRAL TRAFFIC CONTROL! WE NEED TO LOCK THAT HANGAR DOWN!
WANTED
RAISE THE RAMP AND SECURE THE PRISONER!
PLYKO, OPEN THE HANGAR CEILING!

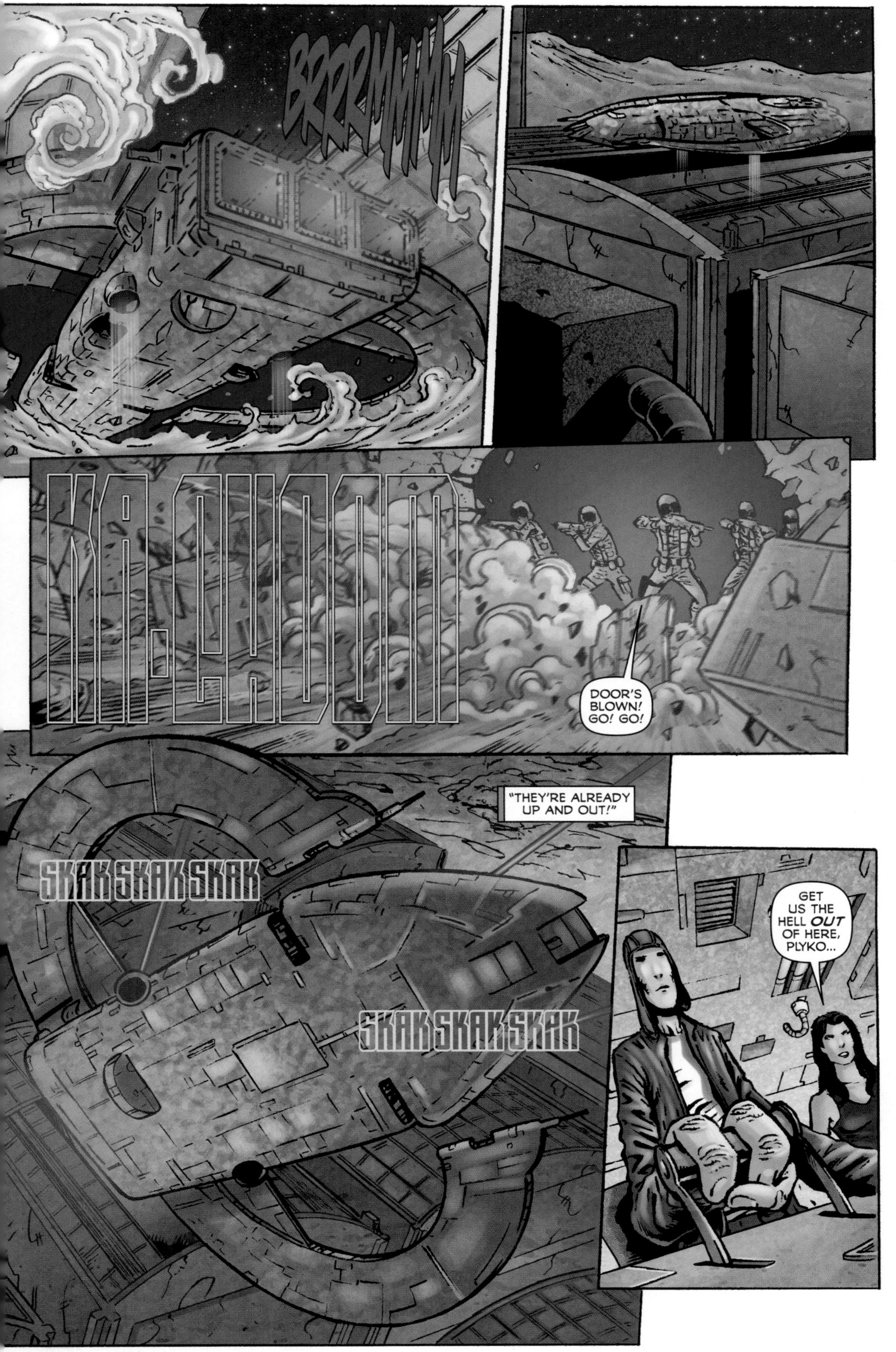
BRRRMMMM
KA-CHOOM
DOOR'S BLOWN! GO! GO!
"THEY'RE ALREADY UP AND OUT!"
SKAK SKAK SKAK
SKAK SKAK SKAK
GET US THE HELL *OUT* OF HERE, PLYKO...

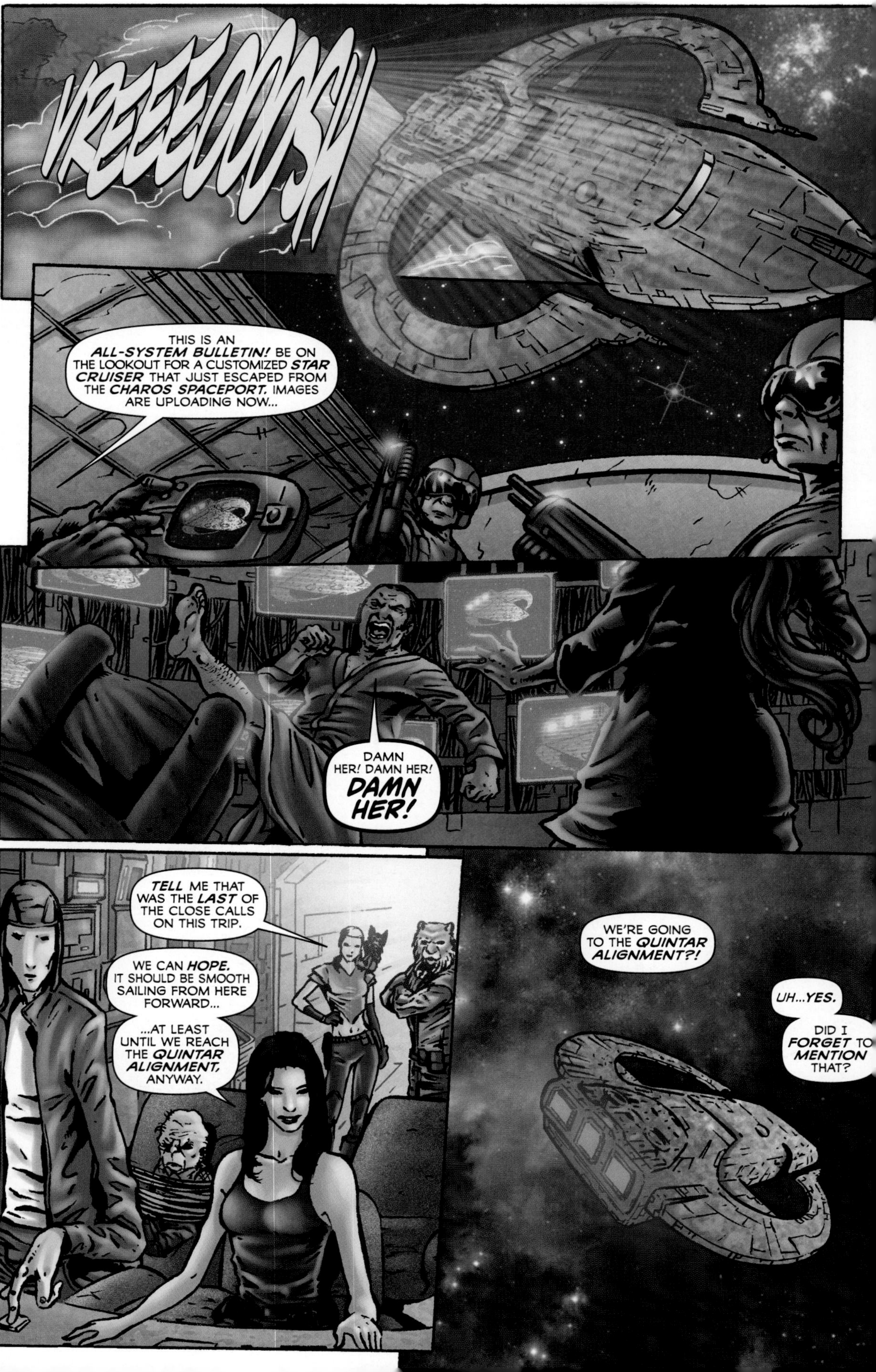
VREEEOOOSH
THIS IS AN ALL-SYSTEM BULLETIN! BE ON THE LOOKOUT FOR A CUSTOMIZED STAR CRUISER THAT JUST ESCAPED FROM THE CHAROS SPACEPORT. IMAGES ARE UPLOADING NOW...
DAMN HER! DAMN HER! DAMN HER!
TELL ME THAT WAS THE LAST OF THE CLOSE CALLS ON THIS TRIP.
WE CAN HOPE. IT SHOULD BE SMOOTH SAILING FROM HERE FORWARD...
...AT LEAST UNTIL WE REACH THE QUINTAR ALIGNMENT, ANYWAY.
WE'RE GOING TO THE QUINTAR ALIGNMENT?!
UH...YES.
DID I FORGET TO MENTION THAT?

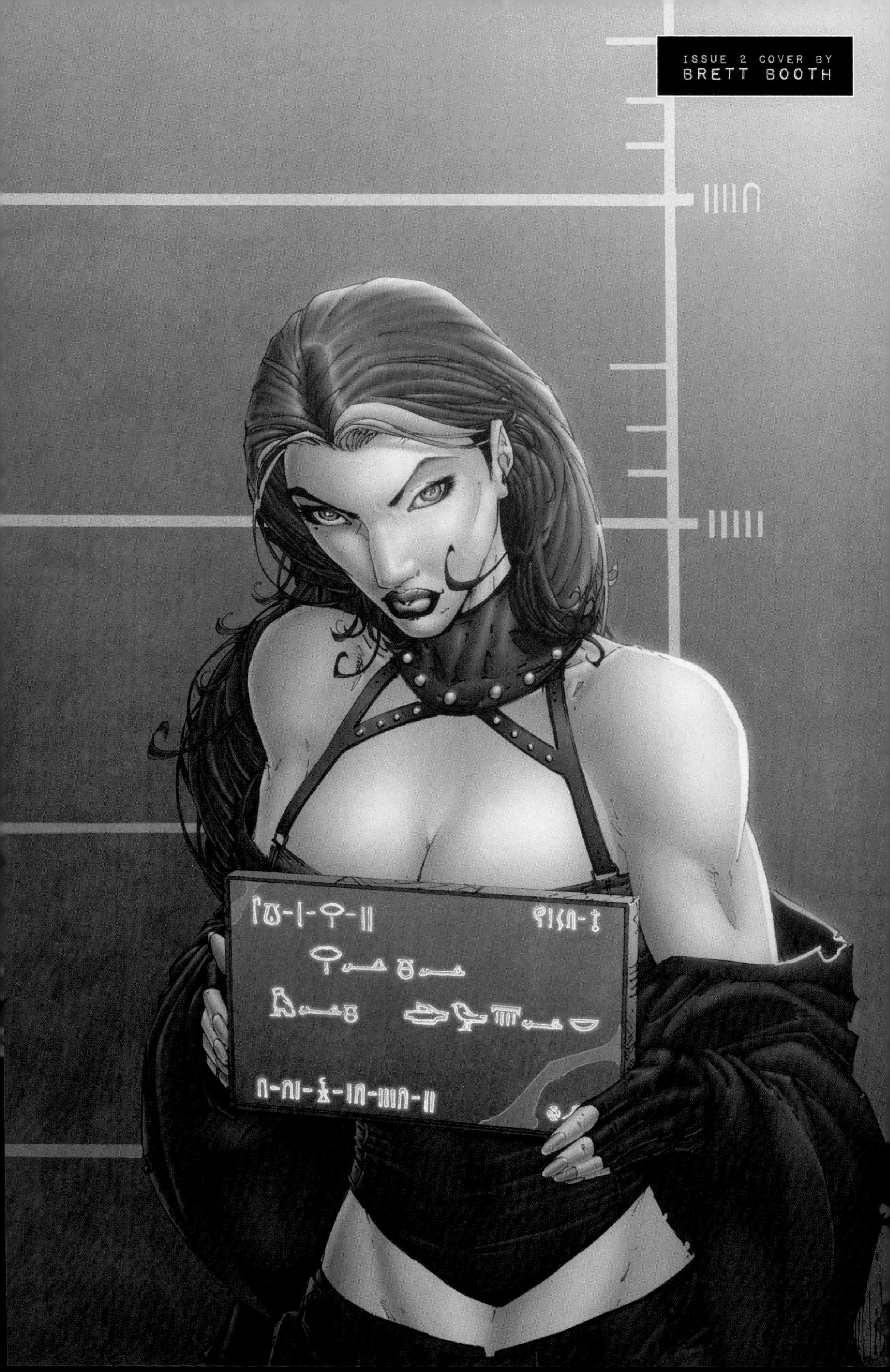
ISSUE 2 COVER BY
BRETT BOOTH

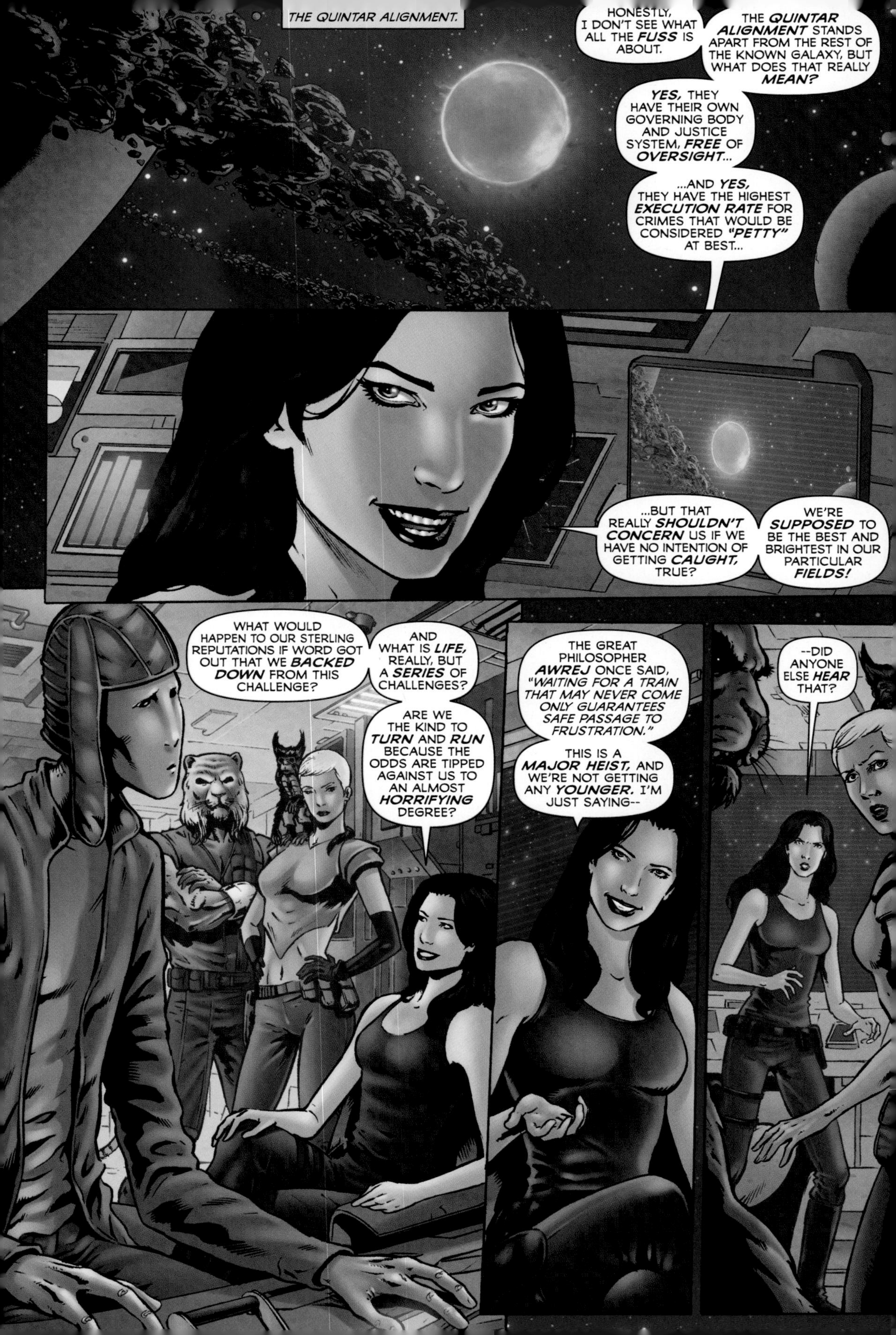
THE QUINTAR ALIGNMENT.
HONESTLY, I DON'T SEE WHAT ALL THE FUSS IS ABOUT.
THE QUINTAR ALIGNMENT STANDS APART FROM THE REST OF THE KNOWN GALAXY, BUT WHAT DOES THAT REALLY MEAN?
YES, THEY HAVE THEIR OWN GOVERNING BODY AND JUSTICE SYSTEM, FREE OF OVERSIGHT...
...AND YES, THEY HAVE THE HIGHEST EXECUTION RATE FOR CRIMES THAT WOULD BE CONSIDERED "PETTY" AT BEST...
...BUT THAT REALLY SHOULDN'T CONCERN US IF WE HAVE NO INTENTION OF GETTING CAUGHT, TRUE?
WE'RE SUPPOSED TO BE THE BEST AND BRIGHTEST IN OUR PARTICULAR FIELDS!
WHAT WOULD HAPPEN TO OUR STERLING REPUTATIONS IF WORD GOT OUT THAT WE BACKED DOWN FROM THIS CHALLENGE?
AND WHAT IS LIFE, REALLY, BUT A SERIES OF CHALLENGES?
ARE WE THE KIND TO TURN AND RUN BECAUSE THE ODDS ARE TIPPED AGAINST US TO AN ALMOST HORRIFYING DEGREE?
THE GREAT PHILOSOPHER AWREJ ONCE SAID, "WAITING FOR A TRAIN THAT MAY NEVER COME ONLY GUARANTEES SAFE PASSAGE TO FRUSTRATION."
THIS IS A MAJOR HEIST, AND WE'RE NOT GETTING ANY YOUNGER. I'M JUST SAYING--
--DID ANYONE ELSE HEAR THAT?

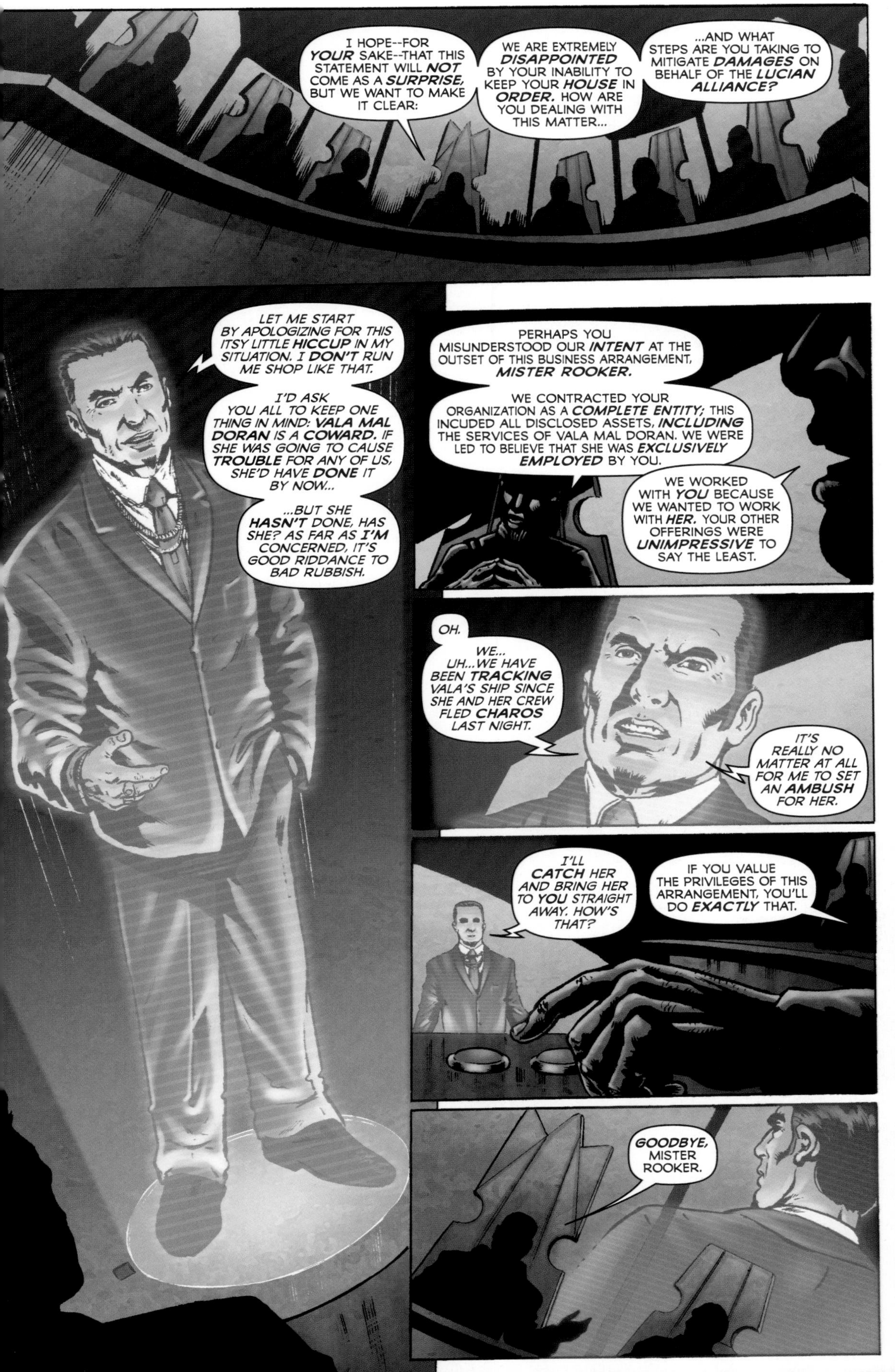
I HOPE--FOR YOUR SAKE--THAT THIS STATEMENT WILL NOT COME AS A SURPRISE, BUT WE WANT TO MAKE IT CLEAR:
WE ARE EXTREMELY DISAPPOINTED BY YOUR INABILITY TO KEEP YOUR HOUSE IN ORDER. HOW ARE YOU DEALING WITH THIS MATTER...
...AND WHAT STEPS ARE YOU TAKING TO MITIGATE DAMAGES ON BEHALF OF THE LUCIAN ALLIANCE?
LET ME START BY APOLOGIZING FOR THIS ITSY LITTLE HICCUP IN MY SITUATION. I DON'T RUN ME SHOP LIKE THAT.
I'D ASK YOU ALL TO KEEP ONE THING IN MIND: VALA MAL DORAN IS A COWARD. IF SHE WAS GOING TO CAUSE TROUBLE FOR ANY OF US, SHE'D HAVE DONE IT BY NOW...
...BUT SHE HASN'T DONE, HAS SHE? AS FAR AS I'M CONCERNED, IT'S GOOD RIDDANCE TO BAD RUBBISH.
PERHAPS YOU MISUNDERSTOOD OUR INTENT AT THE OUTSET OF THIS BUSINESS ARRANGEMENT, MISTER ROOKER.
WE CONTRACTED YOUR ORGANIZATION AS A COMPLETE ENTITY; THIS INCUDED ALL DISCLOSED ASSETS, INCLUDING THE SERVICES OF VALA MAL DORAN. WE WERE LED TO BELIEVE THAT SHE WAS EXCLUSIVELY EMPLOYED BY YOU.
WE WORKED WITH YOU BECAUSE WE WANTED TO WORK WITH HER. YOUR OTHER OFFERINGS WERE UNIMPRESSIVE TO SAY THE LEAST.
OH.
WE... UH...WE HAVE BEEN TRACKING VALA'S SHIP SINCE SHE AND HER CREW FLED CHAROS LAST NIGHT.
IT'S REALLY NO MATTER AT ALL FOR ME TO SET AN AMBUSH FOR HER.
I'LL CATCH HER AND BRING HER TO YOU STRAIGHT AWAY. HOW'S THAT?
IF YOU VALUE THE PRIVILEGES OF THIS ARRANGEMENT, YOU'LL DO EXACTLY THAT.
GOODBYE, MISTER ROOKER.

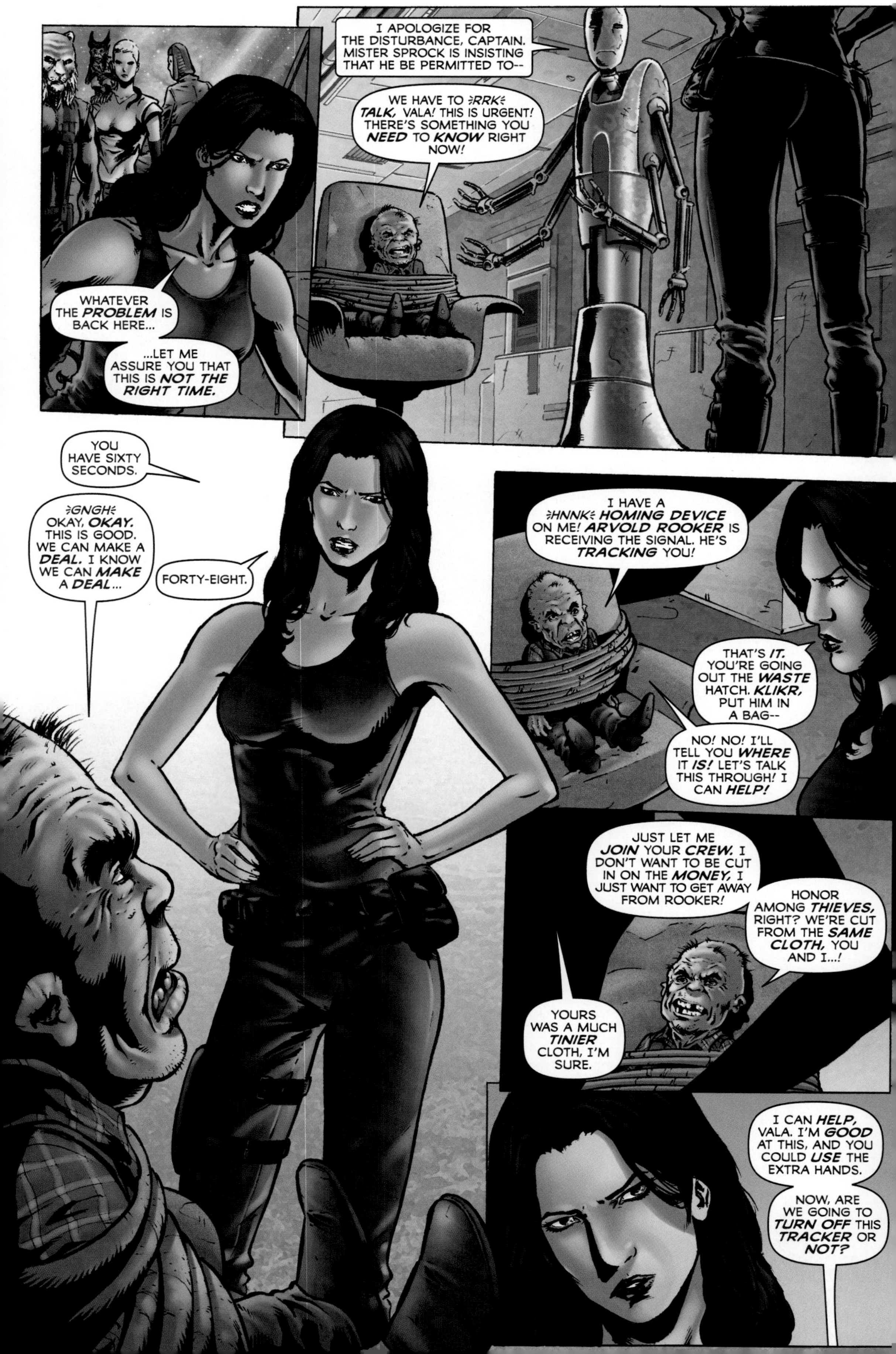

I APOLOGIZE FOR THE DISTURBANCE, CAPTAIN. MISTER SPROCK IS INSISTING THAT HE BE PERMITTED TO--
WE HAVE TO *RRK* TALK, VALA! THIS IS URGENT! THERE'S SOMETHING YOU NEED TO KNOW RIGHT NOW!
WHATEVER THE PROBLEM IS BACK HERE...
...LET ME ASSURE YOU THAT THIS IS NOT THE RIGHT TIME.
YOU HAVE SIXTY SECONDS.
GNGH OKAY, OKAY. THIS IS GOOD. WE CAN MAKE A DEAL. I KNOW WE CAN MAKE A DEAL...
FORTY-EIGHT.
I HAVE A *HNNK* HOMING DEVICE ON ME! ARVOLD ROOKER IS RECEIVING THE SIGNAL. HE'S TRACKING YOU!
THAT'S IT. YOU'RE GOING OUT THE WASTE HATCH. KLIKR, PUT HIM IN A BAG--
NO! NO! I'LL TELL YOU WHERE IT IS! LET'S TALK THIS THROUGH! I CAN HELP!
JUST LET ME JOIN YOUR CREW. I DON'T WANT TO BE CUT IN ON THE MONEY, I JUST WANT TO GET AWAY FROM ROOKER!
HONOR AMONG THIEVES, RIGHT? WE'RE CUT FROM THE SAME CLOTH, YOU AND I...!
YOURS WAS A MUCH TINIER CLOTH, I'M SURE.
I CAN HELP, VALA. I'M GOOD AT THIS, AND YOU COULD USE THE EXTRA HANDS.
NOW, ARE WE GOING TO TURN OFF THIS TRACKER OR NOT?

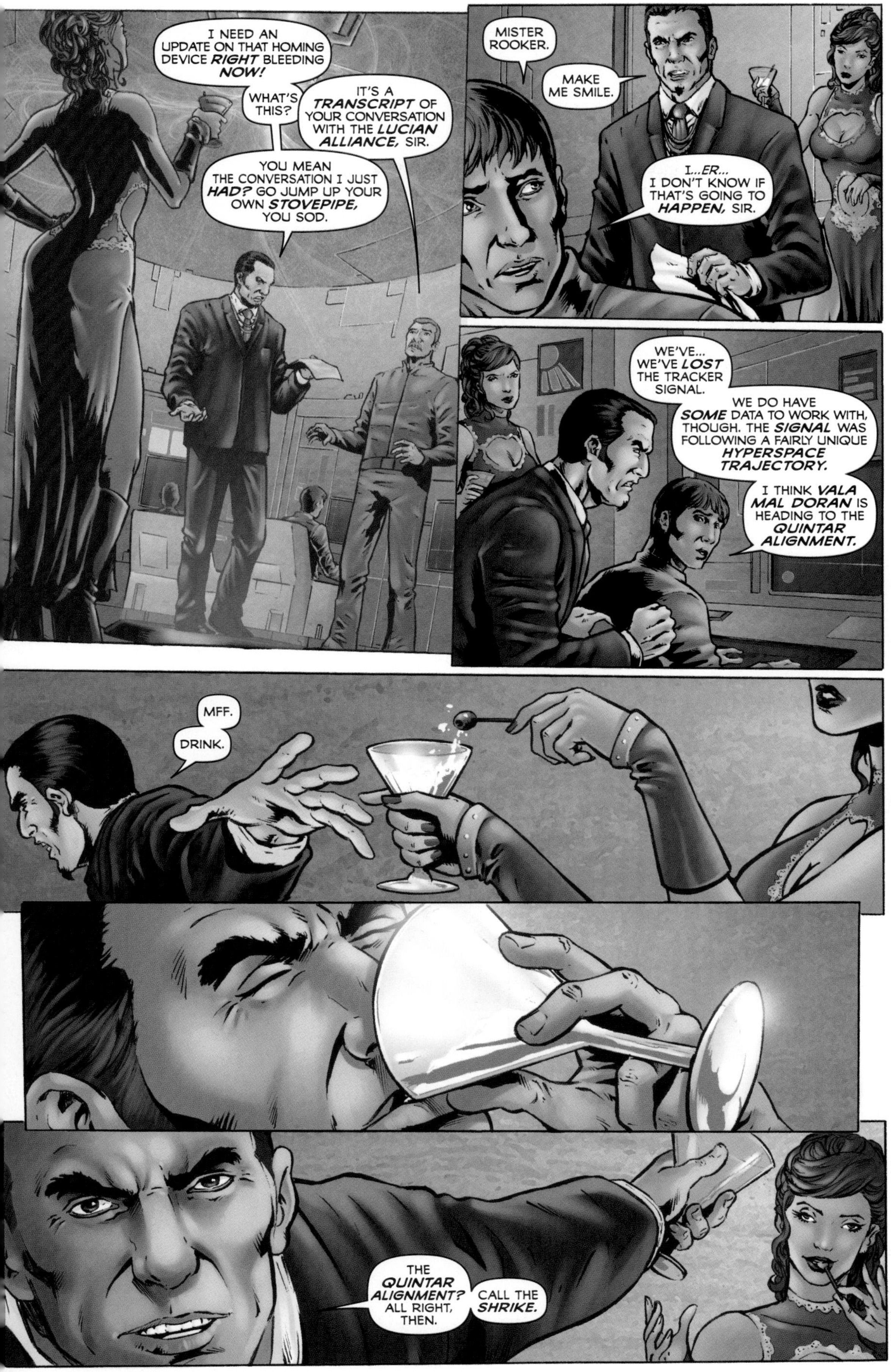
I NEED AN UPDATE ON THAT HOMING DEVICE *RIGHT* BLEEDING *NOW!*
WHAT'S THIS?
IT'S A *TRANSCRIPT* OF YOUR CONVERSATION WITH THE *LUCIAN ALLIANCE,* SIR.
YOU MEAN THE CONVERSATION I JUST *HAD?* GO JUMP UP YOUR OWN *STOVEPIPE,* YOU SOD.
MISTER ROOKER.
MAKE ME SMILE.
I...*ER*... I DON'T KNOW IF THAT'S GOING TO *HAPPEN,* SIR.
WE'VE... WE'VE *LOST* THE TRACKER SIGNAL.
WE DO HAVE *SOME* DATA TO WORK WITH, THOUGH. THE *SIGNAL* WAS FOLLOWING A FAIRLY UNIQUE *HYPERSPACE TRAJECTORY.*
I THINK *VALA MAL DORAN* IS HEADING TO THE *QUINTAR ALIGNMENT.*
MFF.
DRINK.
THE *QUINTAR ALIGNMENT?* ALL RIGHT, THEN.
CALL THE *SHRIKE.*

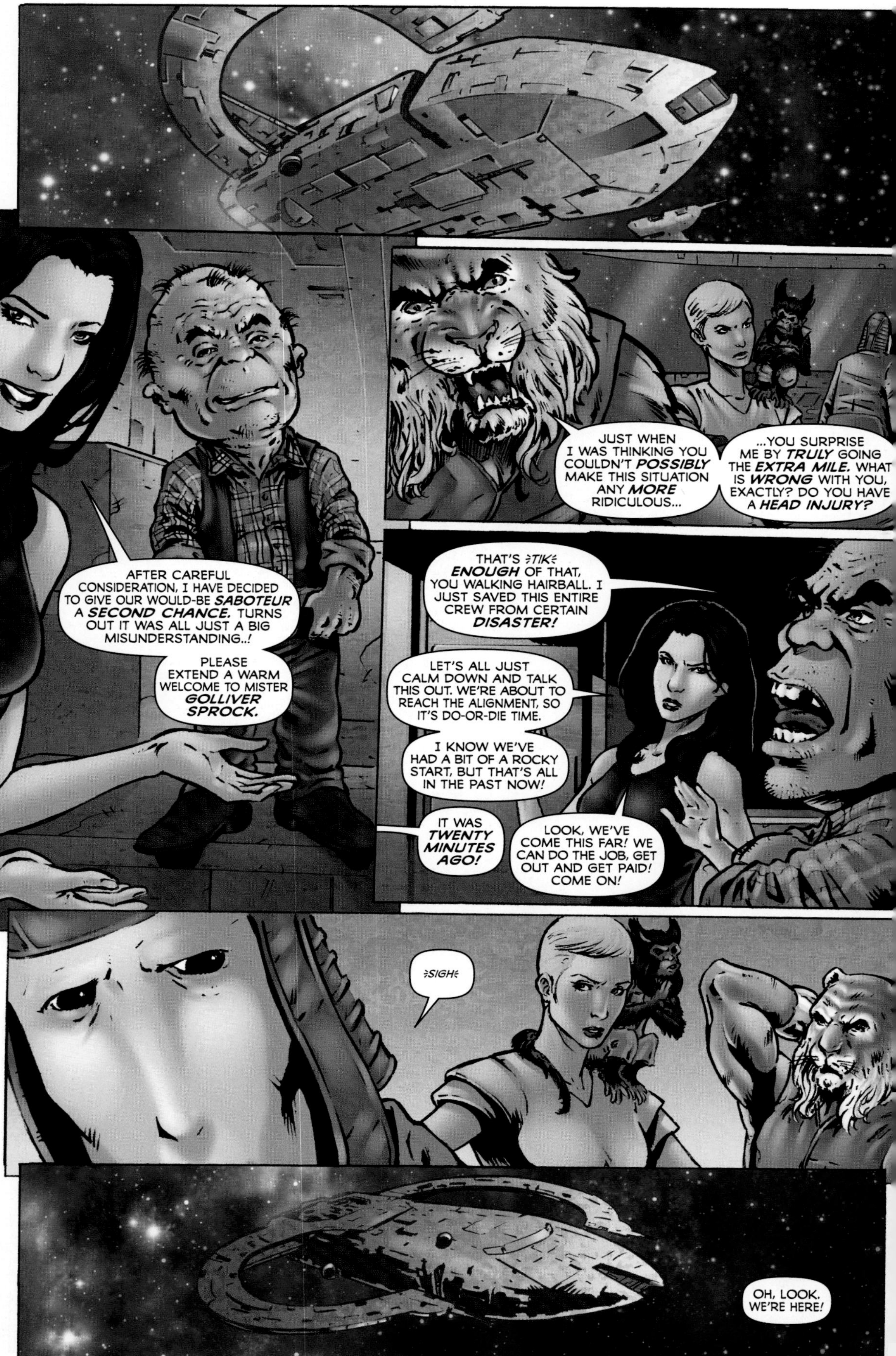
AFTER CAREFUL CONSIDERATION, I HAVE DECIDED TO GIVE OUR WOULD-BE *SABOTEUR* A *SECOND CHANCE.* TURNS OUT IT WAS ALL JUST A BIG MISUNDERSTANDING..!
PLEASE EXTEND A WARM WELCOME TO MISTER *GOLLIVER SPROCK.*
JUST WHEN I WAS THINKING YOU COULDN'T *POSSIBLY* MAKE THIS SITUATION ANY *MORE* RIDICULOUS...
...YOU SURPRISE ME BY *TRULY* GOING THE *EXTRA MILE.* WHAT IS *WRONG* WITH YOU, EXACTLY? DO YOU HAVE A *HEAD INJURY?*
THAT'S *TIK* *ENOUGH* OF THAT, YOU WALKING HAIRBALL. I JUST SAVED THIS ENTIRE CREW FROM CERTAIN *DISASTER!*
LET'S ALL JUST CALM DOWN AND TALK THIS OUT. WE'RE ABOUT TO REACH THE ALIGNMENT, SO IT'S DO-OR-DIE TIME.
I KNOW WE'VE HAD A BIT OF A ROCKY START, BUT THAT'S ALL IN THE PAST NOW!
IT WAS *TWENTY MINUTES AGO!*
LOOK, WE'VE COME THIS FAR! WE CAN DO THE JOB, GET OUT AND GET PAID! COME ON!
SIGH
OH, LOOK. WE'RE HERE!

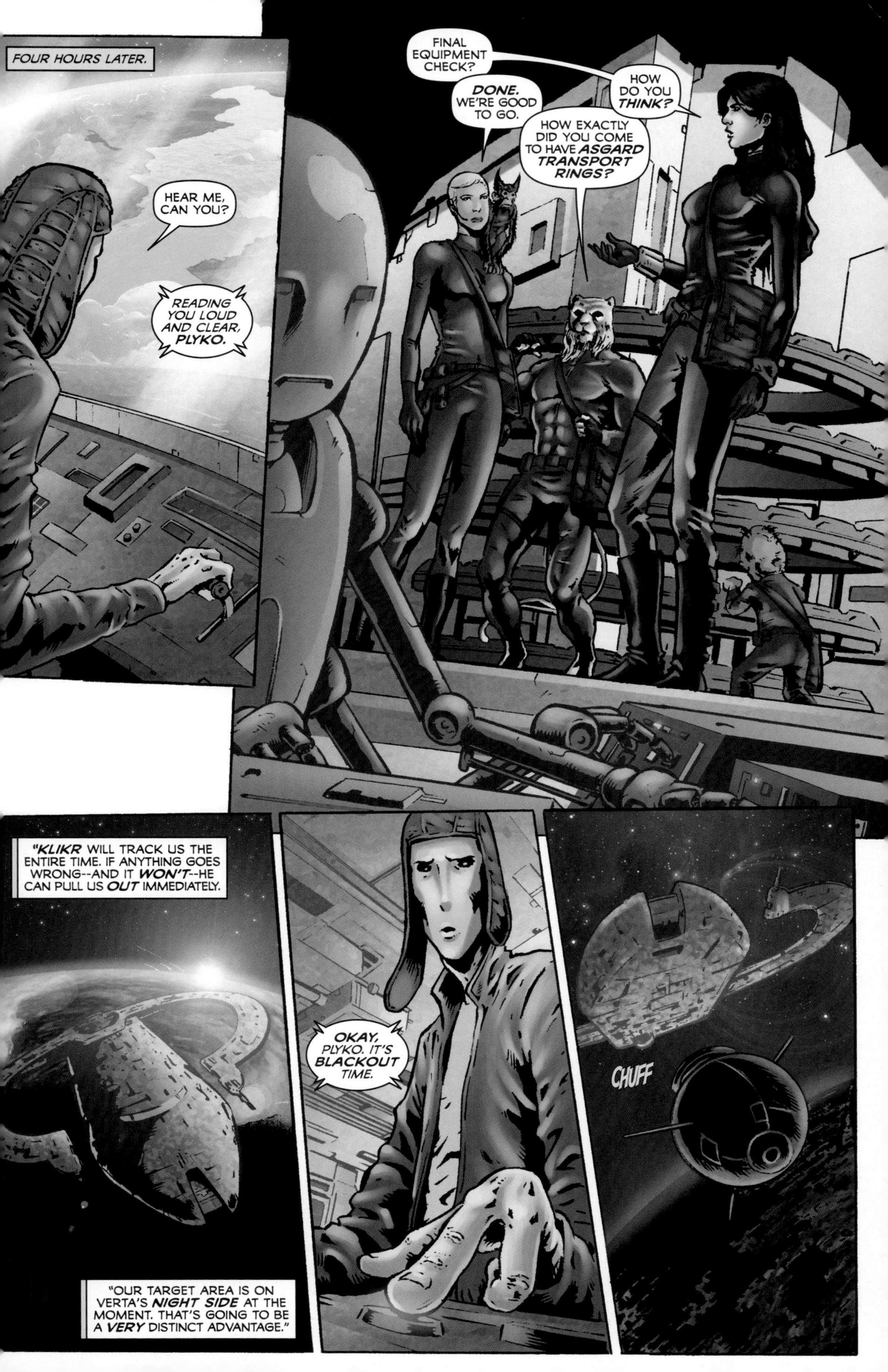
FOUR HOURS LATER.
HEAR ME, CAN YOU?
READING YOU LOUD AND CLEAR, PLYKO.
FINAL EQUIPMENT CHECK?
DONE. WE'RE GOOD TO GO.
HOW DO YOU THINK?
HOW EXACTLY DID YOU COME TO HAVE ASGARD TRANSPORT RINGS?
"KLIKR WILL TRACK US THE ENTIRE TIME. IF ANYTHING GOES WRONG--AND IT WON'T--HE CAN PULL US OUT IMMEDIATELY.
"OUR TARGET AREA IS ON VERTA'S NIGHT SIDE AT THE MOMENT. THAT'S GOING TO BE A VERY DISTINCT ADVANTAGE."
OKAY, PLYKO. IT'S BLACKOUT TIME.
CHUFF

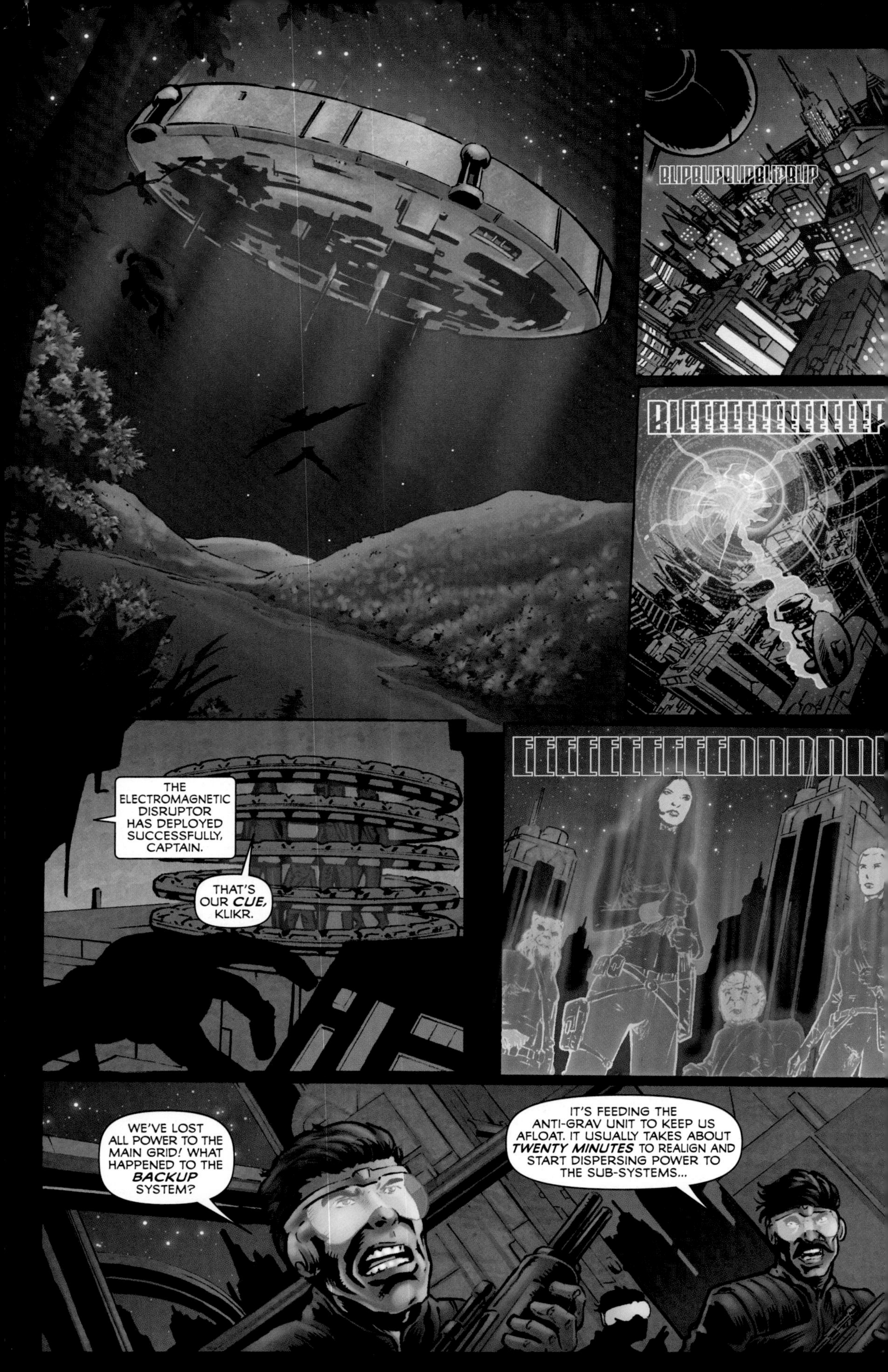
BLIPBLIPBLIPBLIPBLIP
BLEEEEEEEEEEEEEEP
THE ELECTROMAGNETIC DISRUPTOR HAS DEPLOYED SUCCESSFULLY, CAPTAIN.
THAT'S OUR CUE, KLIKR.
EEEEEEEEEEENNNNNN
WE'VE LOST ALL POWER TO THE MAIN GRID! WHAT HAPPENED TO THE BACKUP SYSTEM?
IT'S FEEDING THE ANTI-GRAV UNIT TO KEEP US AFLOAT. IT USUALLY TAKES ABOUT TWENTY MINUTES TO REALIGN AND START DISPERSING POWER TO THE SUB-SYSTEMS...

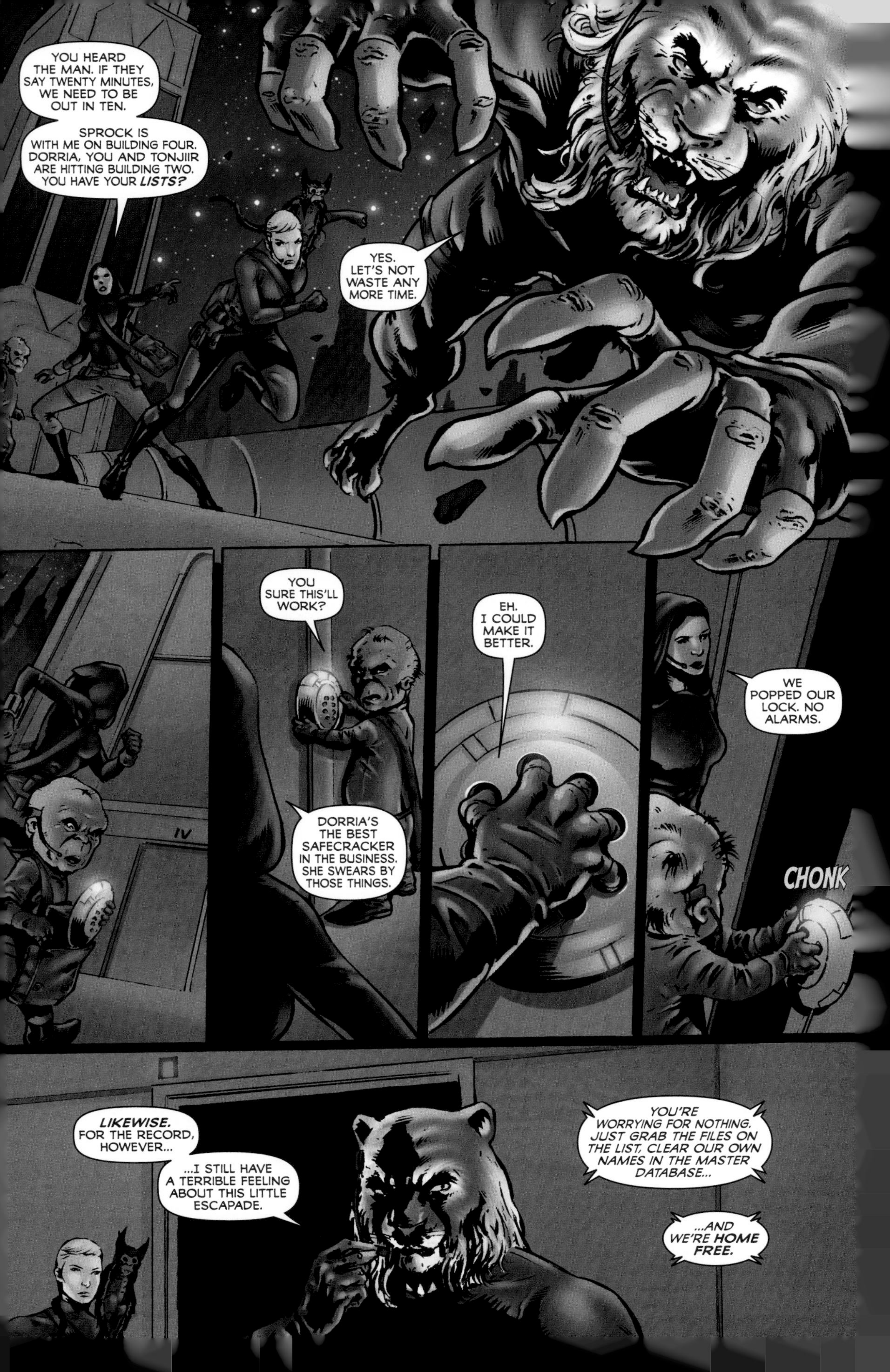
YOU HEARD THE MAN. IF THEY SAY TWENTY MINUTES, WE NEED TO BE OUT IN TEN.
SPROCK IS WITH ME ON BUILDING FOUR. DORRIA, YOU AND TONJIIR ARE HITTING BUILDING TWO. YOU HAVE YOUR *LISTS?*
YES. LET'S NOT WASTE ANY MORE TIME.
IV
YOU SURE THIS'LL WORK?
DORRIA'S THE BEST SAFECRACKER IN THE BUSINESS. SHE SWEARS BY THOSE THINGS.
EH. I COULD MAKE IT BETTER.
WE POPPED OUR LOCK. NO ALARMS.
CHONK
LIKEWISE. FOR THE RECORD, HOWEVER...
...I STILL HAVE A TERRIBLE FEELING ABOUT THIS LITTLE ESCAPADE.
YOU'RE WORRYING FOR NOTHING. JUST GRAB THE FILES ON THE LIST, CLEAR OUR OWN NAMES IN THE MASTER DATABASE...
*...AND WE'RE **HOME FREE.***

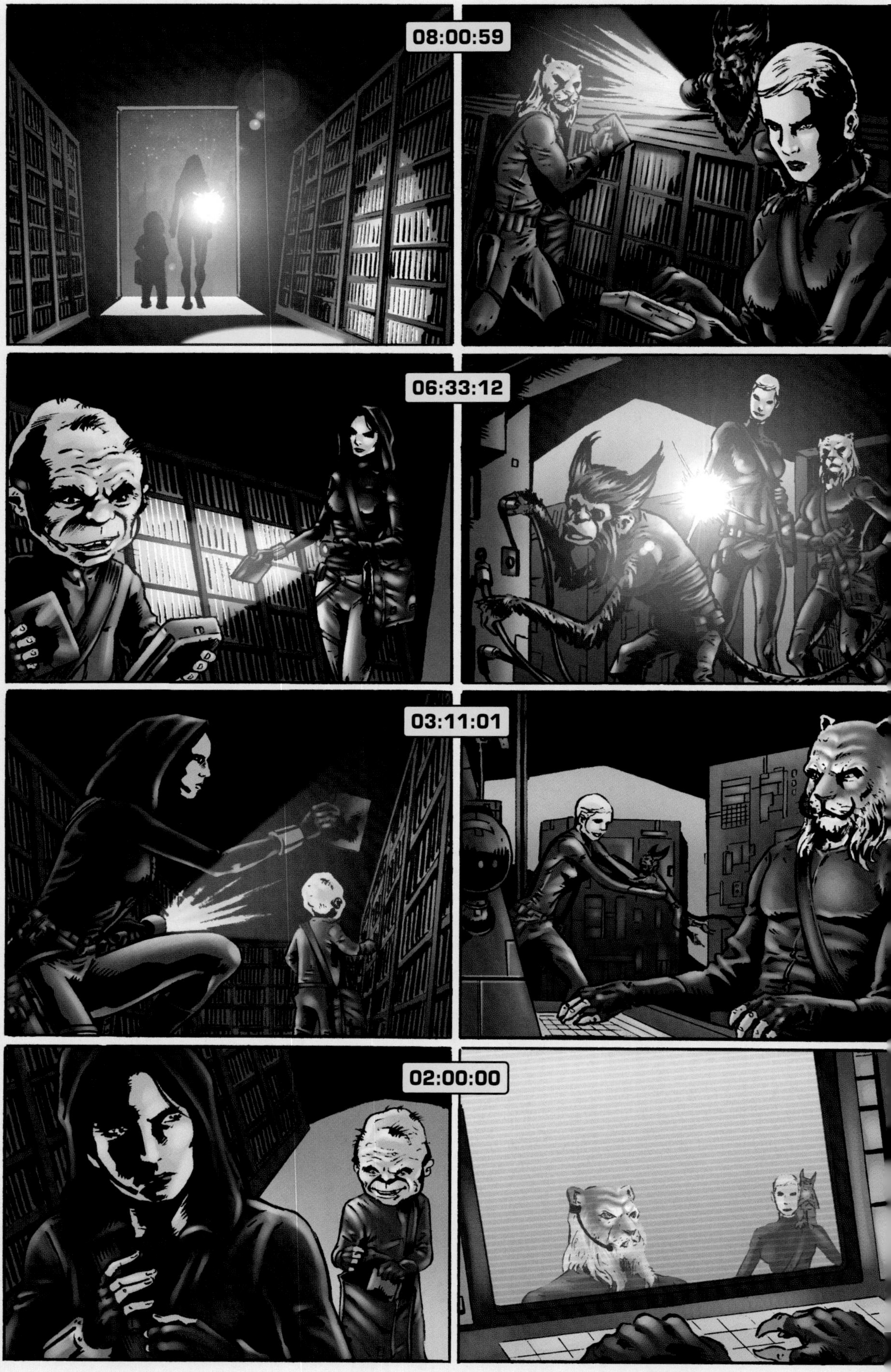
08:00:59
06:33:12
03:11:01
02:00:00

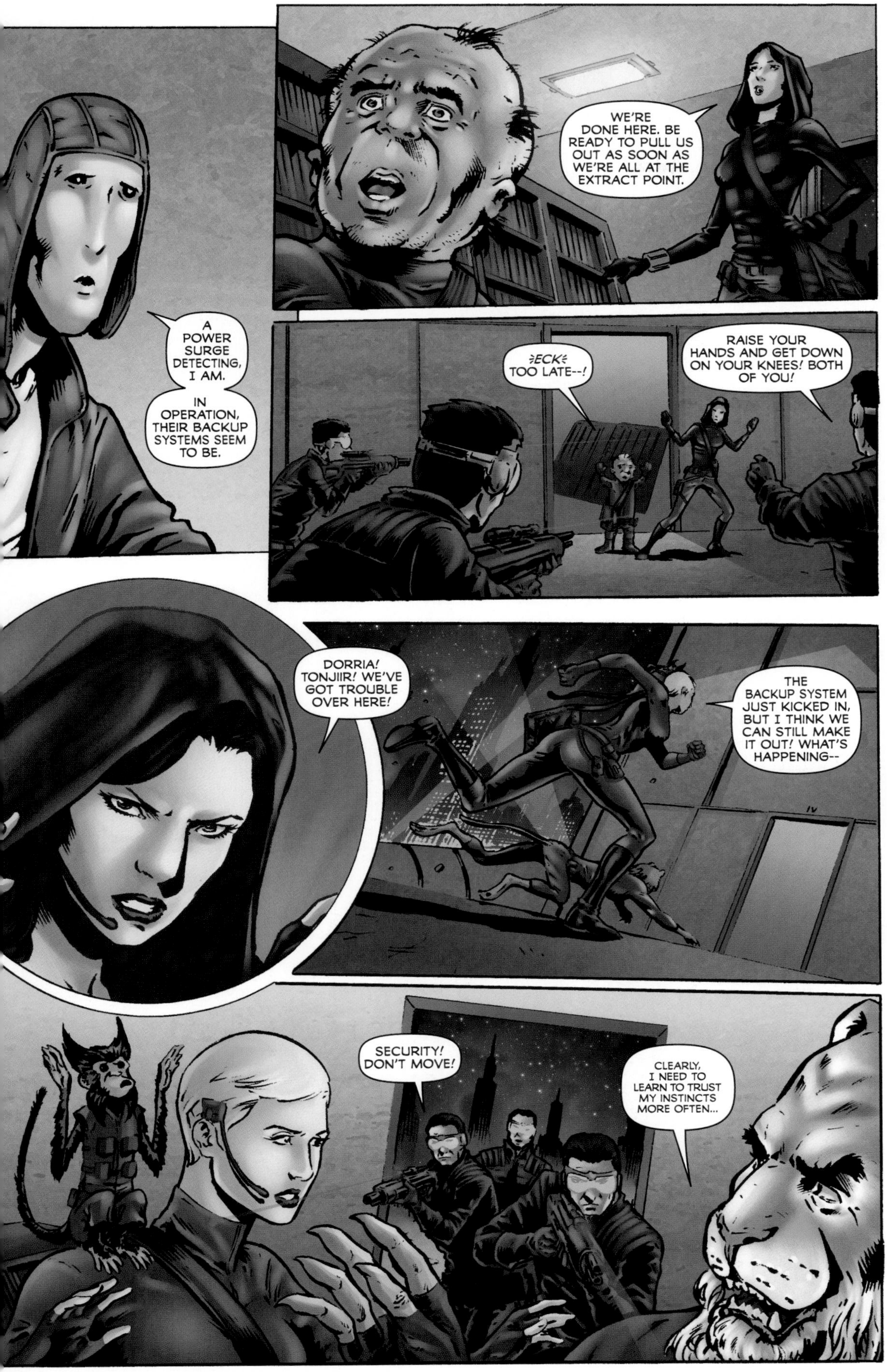
WE'RE DONE HERE. BE READY TO PULL US OUT AS SOON AS WE'RE ALL AT THE EXTRACT POINT.
A POWER SURGE DETECTING, I AM.
IN OPERATION, THEIR BACKUP SYSTEMS SEEM TO BE.
ECK TOO LATE--!
RAISE YOUR HANDS AND GET DOWN ON YOUR KNEES! BOTH OF YOU!
DORRIA! TONJIIR! WE'VE GOT TROUBLE OVER HERE!
THE BACKUP SYSTEM JUST KICKED IN, BUT I THINK WE CAN STILL MAKE IT OUT! WHAT'S HAPPENING--
SECURITY! DON'T MOVE!
CLEARLY, I NEED TO LEARN TO TRUST MY INSTINCTS MORE OFTEN...

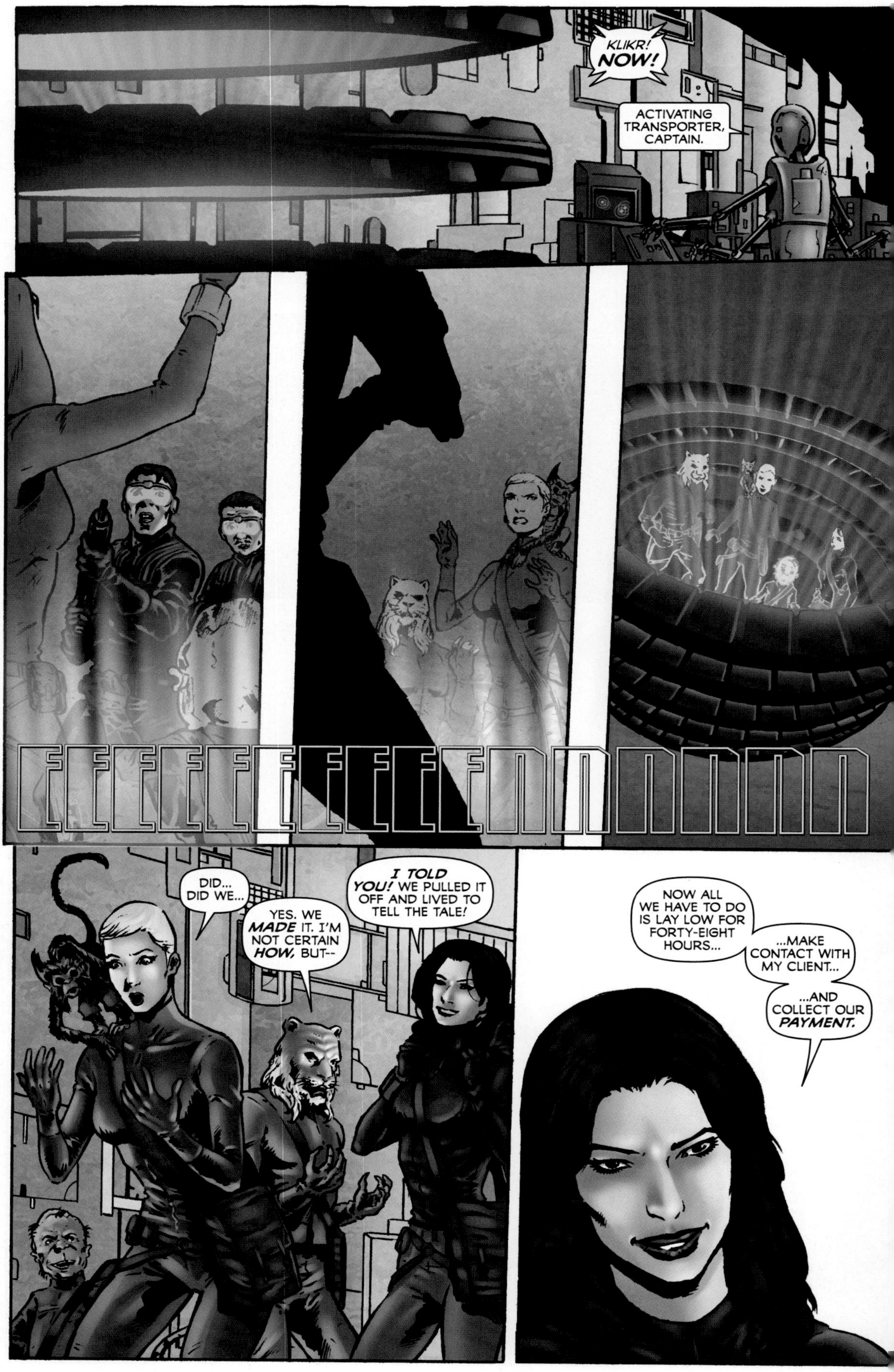
KLIKR! NOW!
ACTIVATING TRANSPORTER, CAPTAIN.
EEEEEEEEEENNNNNN
DID... DID WE...
YES. WE MADE IT. I'M NOT CERTAIN HOW, BUT--
I TOLD YOU! WE PULLED IT OFF AND LIVED TO TELL THE TALE!
NOW ALL WE HAVE TO DO IS LAY LOW FOR FORTY-EIGHT HOURS...
...MAKE CONTACT WITH MY CLIENT...
...AND COLLECT OUR PAYMENT.

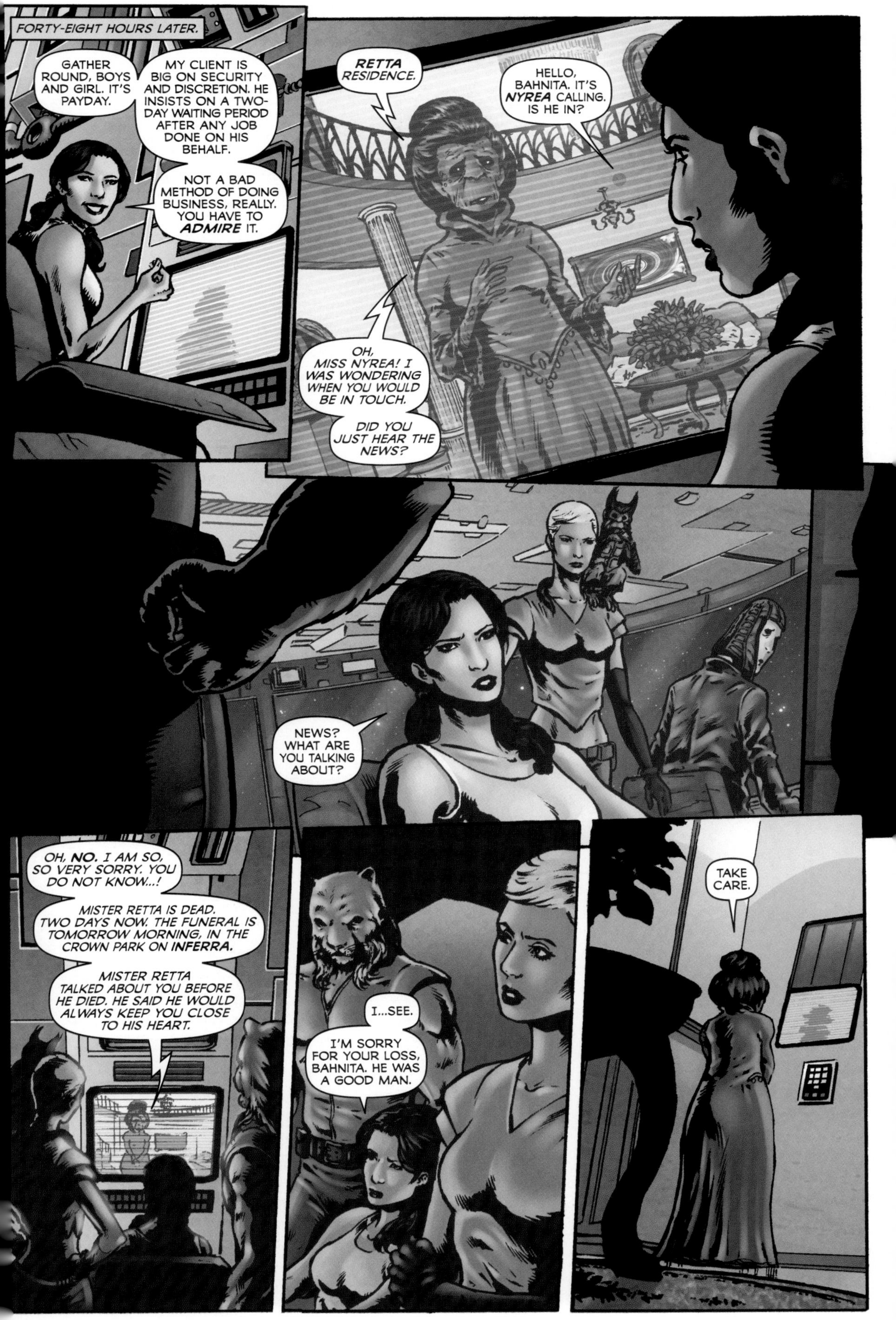
FORTY-EIGHT HOURS LATER.
GATHER ROUND, BOYS AND GIRL. IT'S PAYDAY.
MY CLIENT IS BIG ON SECURITY AND DISCRETION. HE INSISTS ON A TWO-DAY WAITING PERIOD AFTER ANY JOB DONE ON HIS BEHALF.
NOT A BAD METHOD OF DOING BUSINESS, REALLY. YOU HAVE TO ADMIRE IT.
RETTA RESIDENCE.
HELLO, BAHNITA. IT'S NYREA CALLING. IS HE IN?
OH, MISS NYREA! I WAS WONDERING WHEN YOU WOULD BE IN TOUCH.
DID YOU JUST HEAR THE NEWS?
NEWS? WHAT ARE YOU TALKING ABOUT?
OH, NO. I AM SO, SO VERY SORRY. YOU DO NOT KNOW...!
MISTER RETTA IS DEAD. TWO DAYS NOW. THE FUNERAL IS TOMORROW MORNING, IN THE CROWN PARK ON INFERRA.
MISTER RETTA TALKED ABOUT YOU BEFORE HE DIED. HE SAID HE WOULD ALWAYS KEEP YOU CLOSE TO HIS HEART.
I...SEE.
I'M SORRY FOR YOUR LOSS, BAHNITA. HE WAS A GOOD MAN.
TAKE CARE.

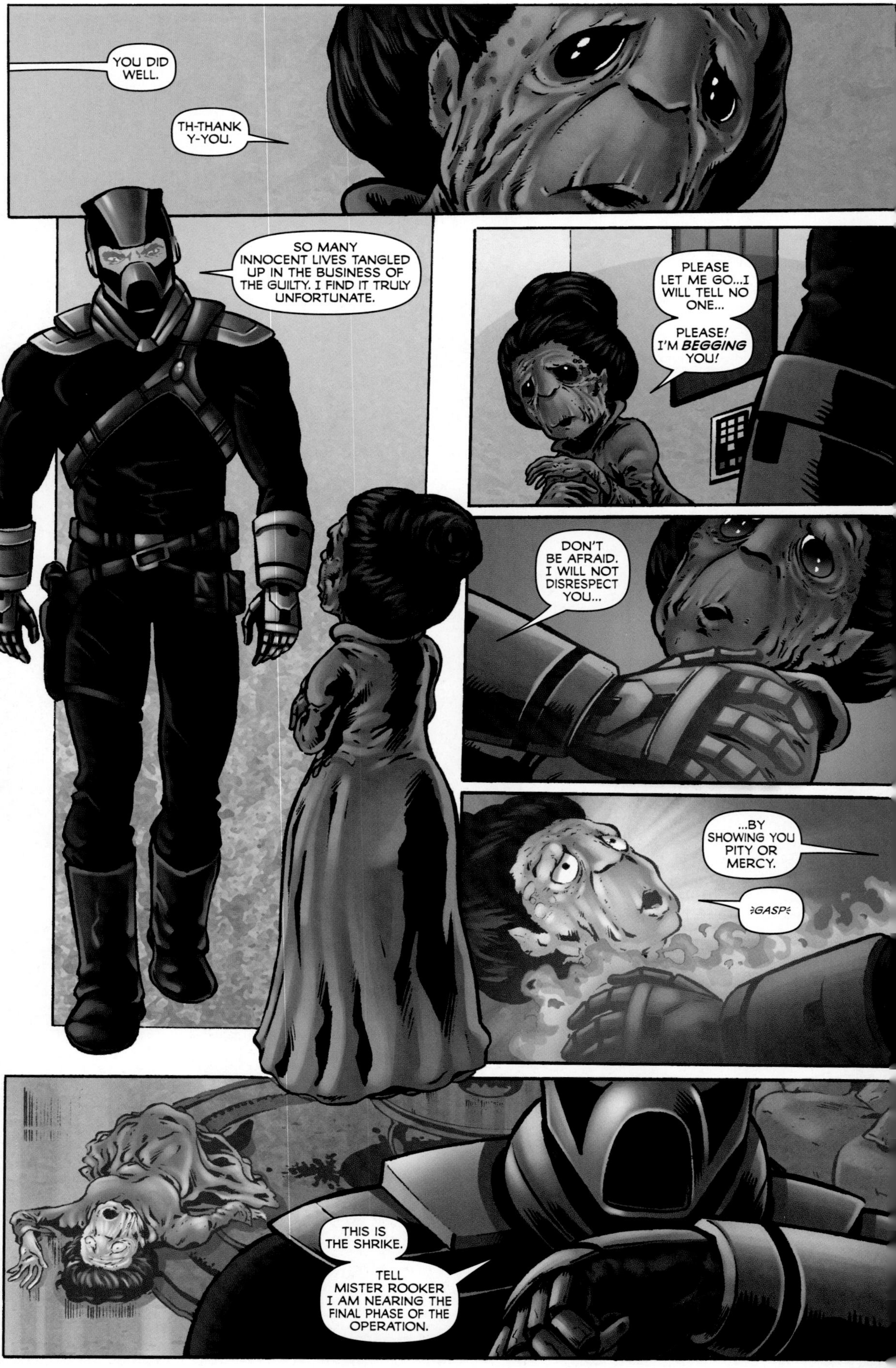
YOU DID WELL.
TH-THANK Y-YOU.
SO MANY INNOCENT LIVES TANGLED UP IN THE BUSINESS OF THE GUILTY. I FIND IT TRULY UNFORTUNATE.
PLEASE LET ME GO...I WILL TELL NO ONE...
PLEASE! I'M **BEGGING** YOU!
DON'T BE AFRAID. I WILL NOT DISRESPECT YOU...
...BY SHOWING YOU PITY OR MERCY.
GASP
THIS IS THE SHRIKE.
TELL MISTER ROOKER I AM NEARING THE FINAL PHASE OF THE OPERATION.

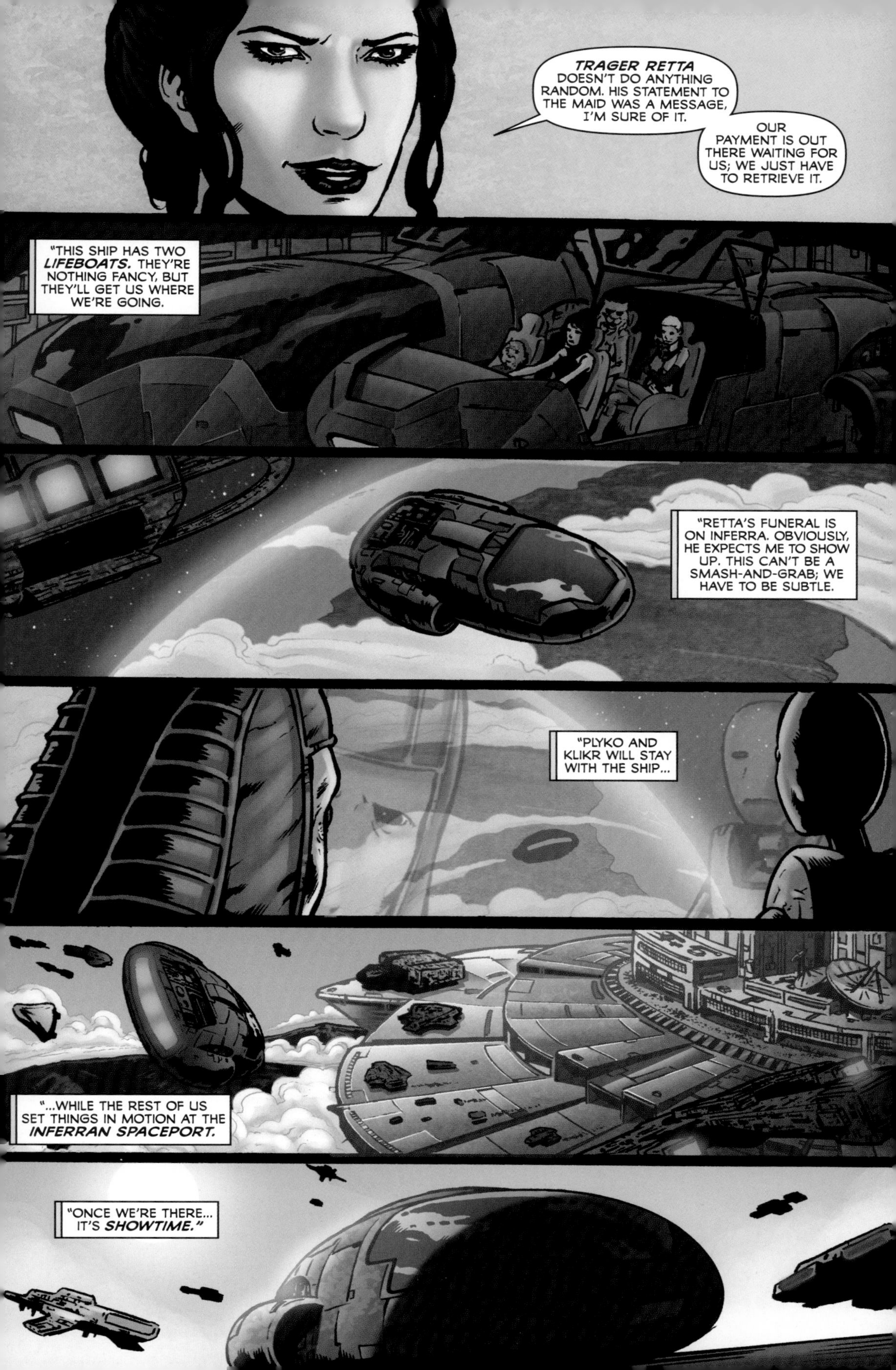

TRAGER RETTA DOESN'T DO ANYTHING RANDOM. HIS STATEMENT TO THE MAID WAS A MESSAGE, I'M SURE OF IT.
OUR PAYMENT IS OUT THERE WAITING FOR US; WE JUST HAVE TO RETRIEVE IT.
"THIS SHIP HAS TWO *LIFEBOATS.* THEY'RE NOTHING FANCY, BUT THEY'LL GET US WHERE WE'RE GOING.
"RETTA'S FUNERAL IS ON INFERRA. OBVIOUSLY, HE EXPECTS ME TO SHOW UP. THIS CAN'T BE A SMASH-AND-GRAB; WE HAVE TO BE SUBTLE.
"PLYKO AND KLIKR WILL STAY WITH THE SHIP...
"...WHILE THE REST OF US SET THINGS IN MOTION AT THE *INFERRAN SPACEPORT.*
"ONCE WE'RE THERE... IT'S *SHOWTIME."*

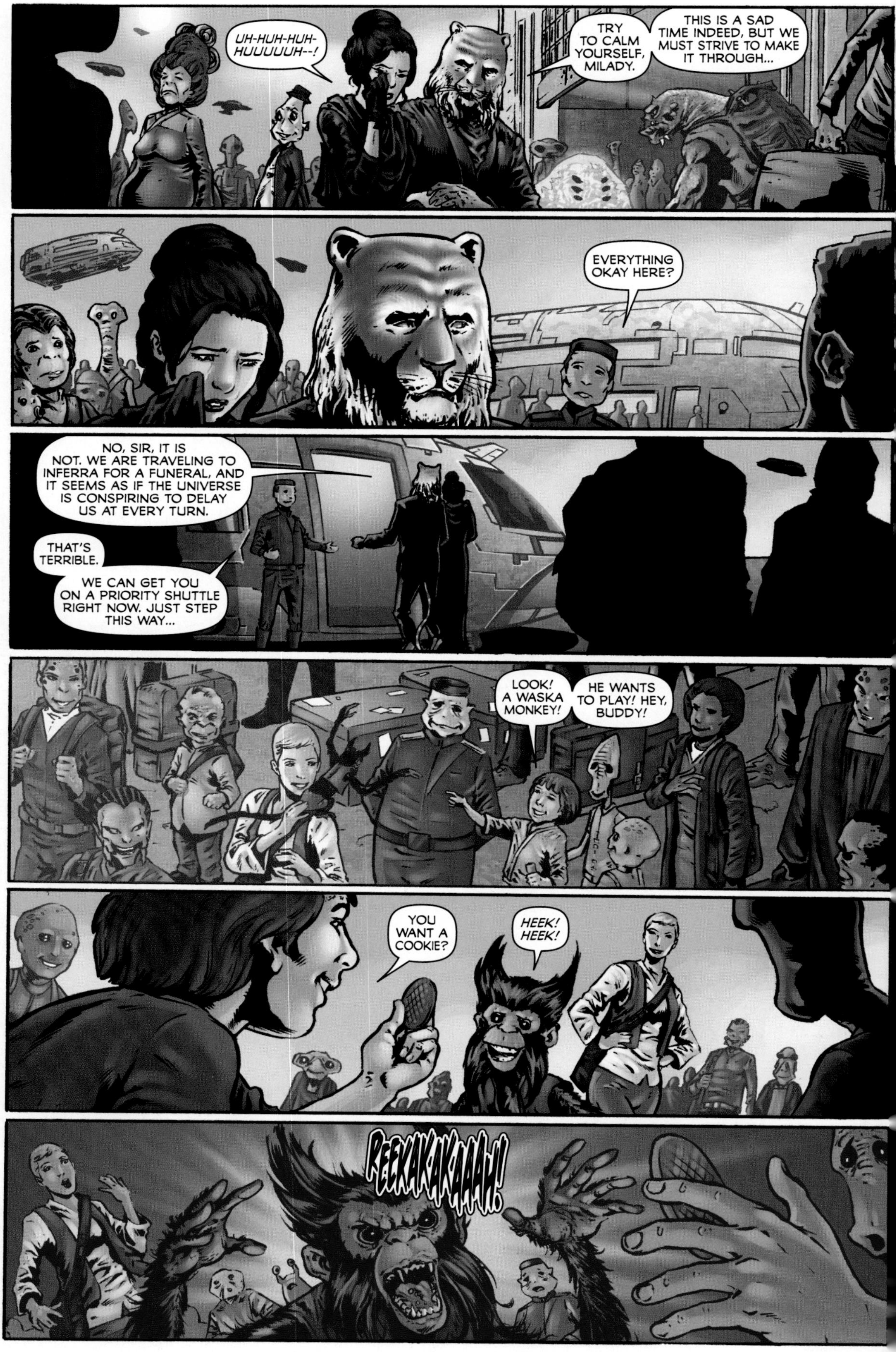
UH-HUH-HUH-HUUUUUH--!
TRY TO CALM YOURSELF, MILADY.
THIS IS A SAD TIME INDEED, BUT WE MUST STRIVE TO MAKE IT THROUGH...
EVERYTHING OKAY HERE?
NO, SIR, IT IS NOT. WE ARE TRAVELING TO INFERRA FOR A FUNERAL, AND IT SEEMS AS IF THE UNIVERSE IS CONSPIRING TO DELAY US AT EVERY TURN.
THAT'S TERRIBLE.
WE CAN GET YOU ON A PRIORITY SHUTTLE RIGHT NOW. JUST STEP THIS WAY...
LOOK! A WASKA MONKEY!
HE WANTS TO PLAY! HEY, BUDDY!
YOU WANT A COOKIE?
HEEK! HEEK!
REEKAKAKAAAH!

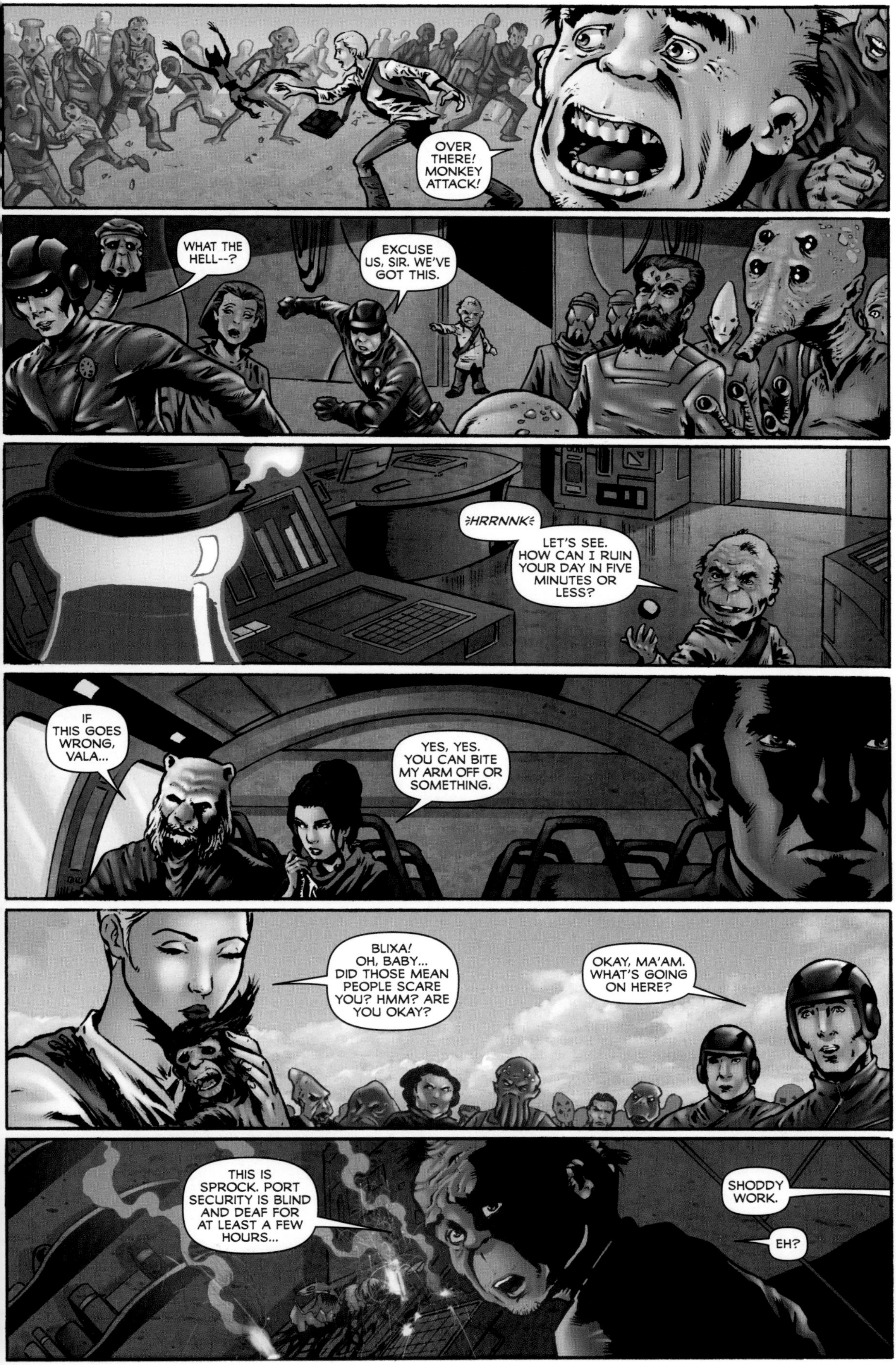
OVER THERE! MONKEY ATTACK!
WHAT THE HELL--?
EXCUSE US, SIR. WE'VE GOT THIS.
HRRNNK
LET'S SEE. HOW CAN I RUIN YOUR DAY IN FIVE MINUTES OR LESS?
IF THIS GOES WRONG, VALA...
YES, YES. YOU CAN BITE MY ARM OFF OR SOMETHING.
BLIXA! OH, BABY... DID THOSE MEAN PEOPLE SCARE YOU? HMM? ARE YOU OKAY?
OKAY, MA'AM. WHAT'S GOING ON HERE?
THIS IS SPROCK. PORT SECURITY IS BLIND AND DEAF FOR AT LEAST A FEW HOURS...
SHODDY WORK.
EH?

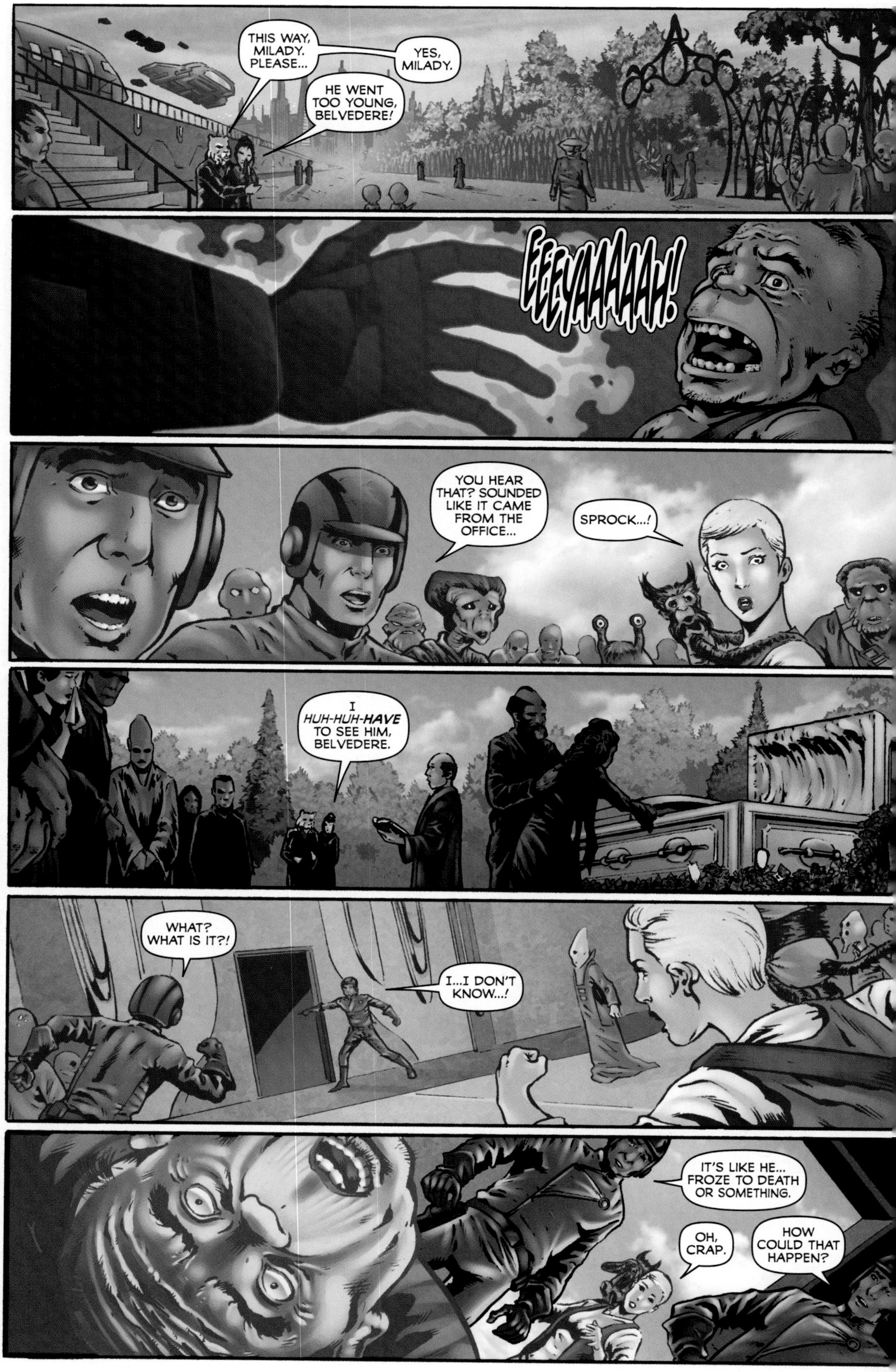
THIS WAY, MILADY. PLEASE...
YES, MILADY.
HE WENT TOO YOUNG, BELVEDERE!
EEEYAAAAAH!
YOU HEAR THAT? SOUNDED LIKE IT CAME FROM THE OFFICE...
SPROCK...!
I *HUH-HUH-**HAVE*** TO SEE HIM, BELVEDERE.
WHAT? WHAT IS IT?!
I...I DON'T KNOW...!
IT'S LIKE HE... FROZE TO DEATH OR SOMETHING.
OH, CRAP.
HOW COULD THAT HAPPEN?

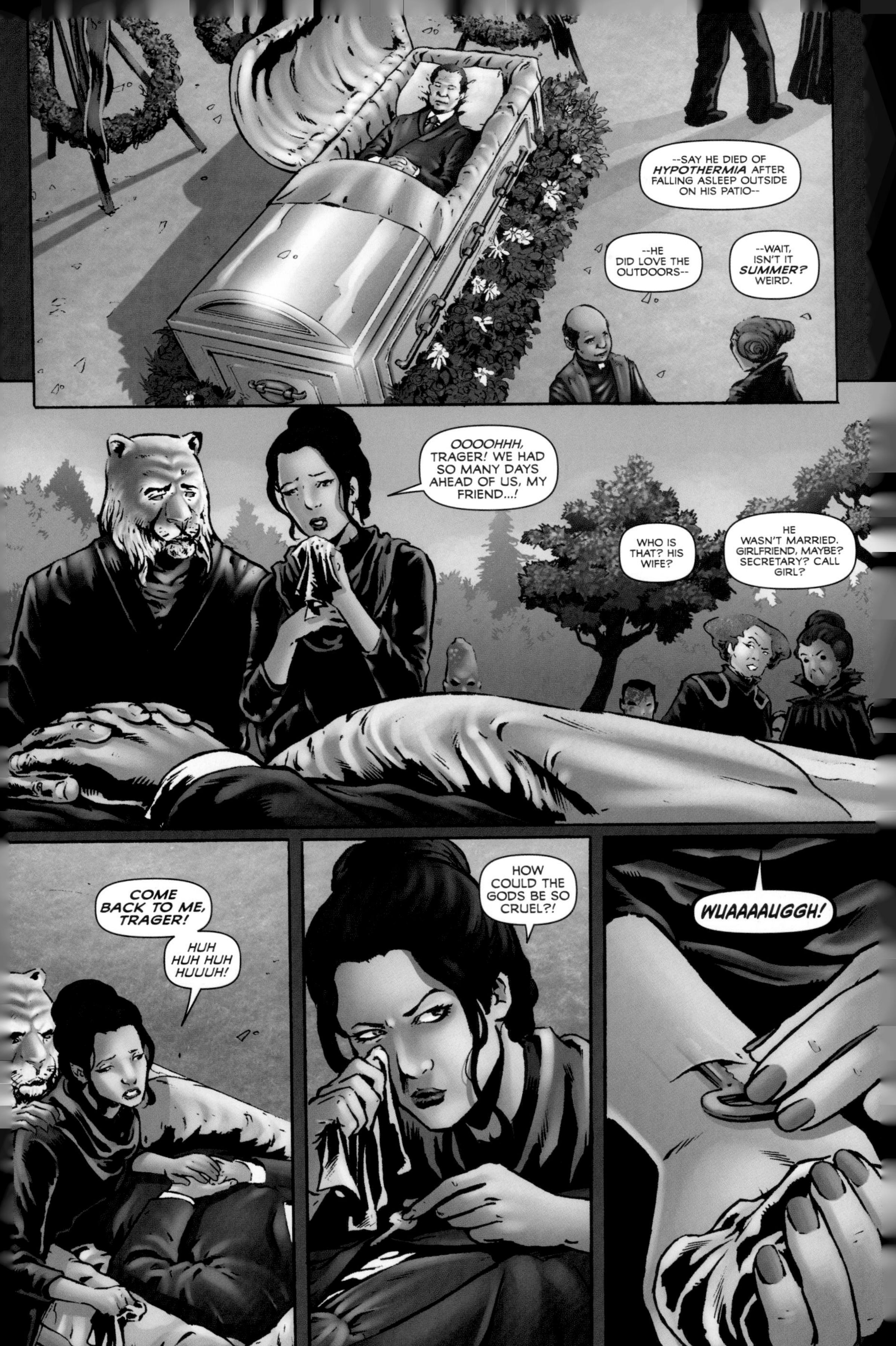
--SAY HE DIED OF HYPOTHERMIA AFTER FALLING ASLEEP OUTSIDE ON HIS PATIO--
--HE DID LOVE THE OUTDOORS--
--WAIT, ISN'T IT SUMMER? WEIRD.
OOOOHHH, TRAGER! WE HAD SO MANY DAYS AHEAD OF US, MY FRIEND...!
WHO IS THAT? HIS WIFE?
HE WASN'T MARRIED. GIRLFRIEND, MAYBE? SECRETARY? CALL GIRL?
COME BACK TO ME, TRAGER!
HUH HUH HUH HUUUH!
HOW COULD THE GODS BE SO CRUEL?!
WUAAAAUGGH!

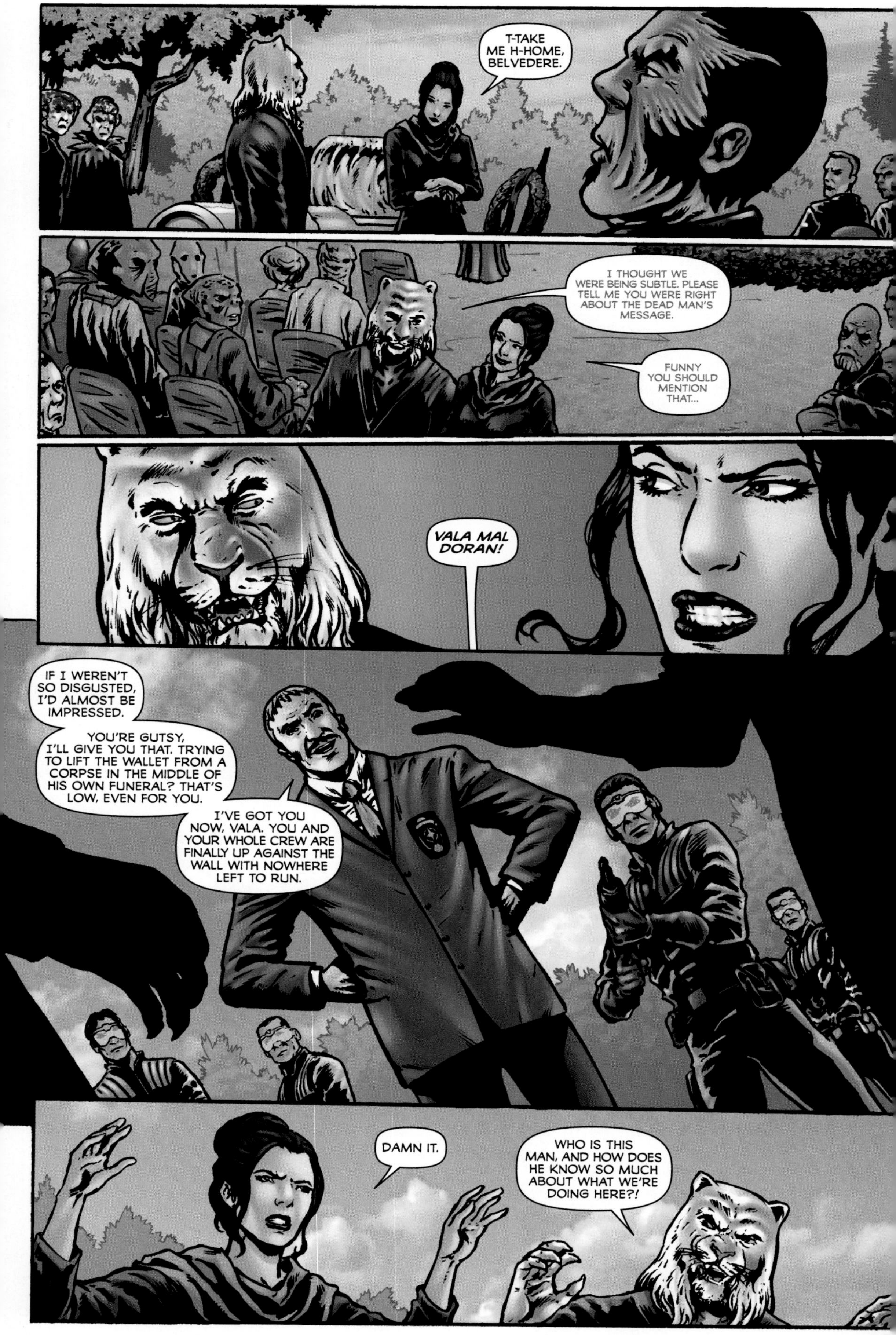
T-TAKE ME H-HOME, BELVEDERE.
I THOUGHT WE WERE BEING SUBTLE. PLEASE TELL ME YOU WERE RIGHT ABOUT THE DEAD MAN'S MESSAGE.
FUNNY YOU SHOULD MENTION THAT...
VALA MAL DORAN!
IF I WEREN'T SO DISGUSTED, I'D ALMOST BE IMPRESSED.
YOU'RE GUTSY, I'LL GIVE YOU THAT. TRYING TO LIFT THE WALLET FROM A CORPSE IN THE MIDDLE OF HIS OWN FUNERAL? THAT'S LOW, EVEN FOR YOU.
I'VE GOT YOU NOW, VALA. YOU AND YOUR WHOLE CREW ARE FINALLY UP AGAINST THE WALL WITH NOWHERE LEFT TO RUN.
DAMN IT.
WHO IS THIS MAN, AND HOW DOES HE KNOW SO MUCH ABOUT WHAT WE'RE DOING HERE?!

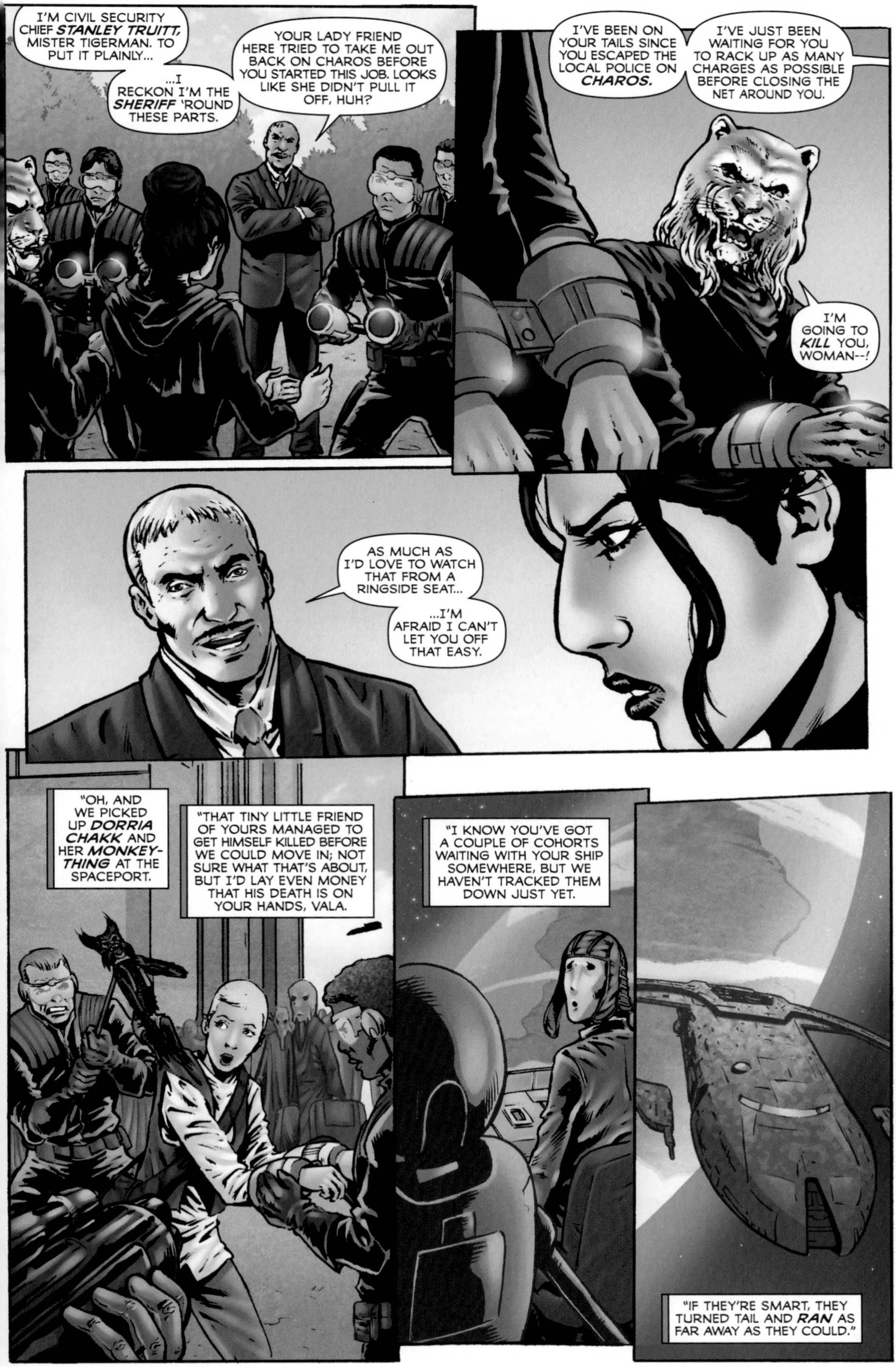
I'M CIVIL SECURITY CHIEF STANLEY TRUITT, MISTER TIGERMAN. TO PUT IT PLAINLY...
...I RECKON I'M THE SHERIFF 'ROUND THESE PARTS.
YOUR LADY FRIEND HERE TRIED TO TAKE ME OUT BACK ON CHAROS BEFORE YOU STARTED THIS JOB. LOOKS LIKE SHE DIDN'T PULL IT OFF, HUH?
I'VE BEEN ON YOUR TAILS SINCE YOU ESCAPED THE LOCAL POLICE ON CHAROS.
I'VE JUST BEEN WAITING FOR YOU TO RACK UP AS MANY CHARGES AS POSSIBLE BEFORE CLOSING THE NET AROUND YOU.
I'M GOING TO KILL YOU, WOMAN--!
AS MUCH AS I'D LOVE TO WATCH THAT FROM A RINGSIDE SEAT...
...I'M AFRAID I CAN'T LET YOU OFF THAT EASY.
"OH, AND WE PICKED UP DORRIA CHAKK AND HER MONKEY-THING AT THE SPACEPORT.
"THAT TINY LITTLE FRIEND OF YOURS MANAGED TO GET HIMSELF KILLED BEFORE WE COULD MOVE IN; NOT SURE WHAT THAT'S ABOUT, BUT I'D LAY EVEN MONEY THAT HIS DEATH IS ON YOUR HANDS, VALA.
"I KNOW YOU'VE GOT A COUPLE OF COHORTS WAITING WITH YOUR SHIP SOMEWHERE, BUT WE HAVEN'T TRACKED THEM DOWN JUST YET.
"IF THEY'RE SMART, THEY TURNED TAIL AND RAN AS FAR AWAY AS THEY COULD."

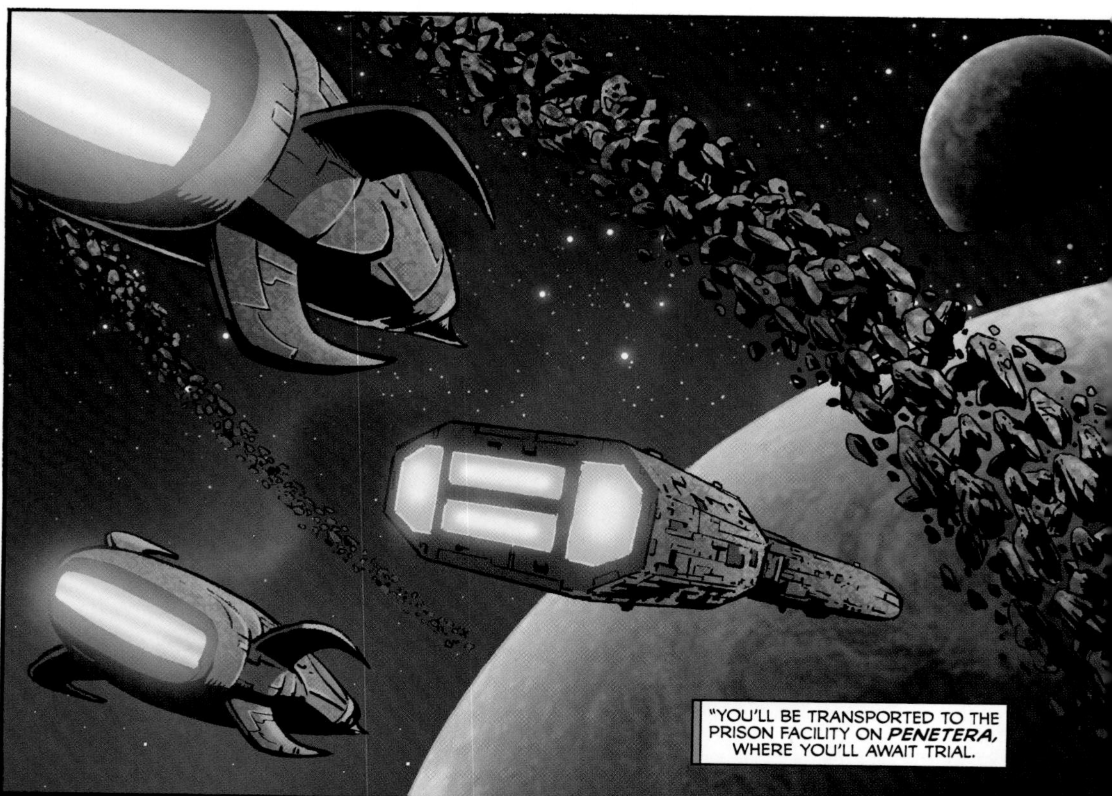
"YOU'LL BE TRANSPORTED TO THE PRISON FACILITY ON *PENETERA,* WHERE YOU'LL AWAIT TRIAL.

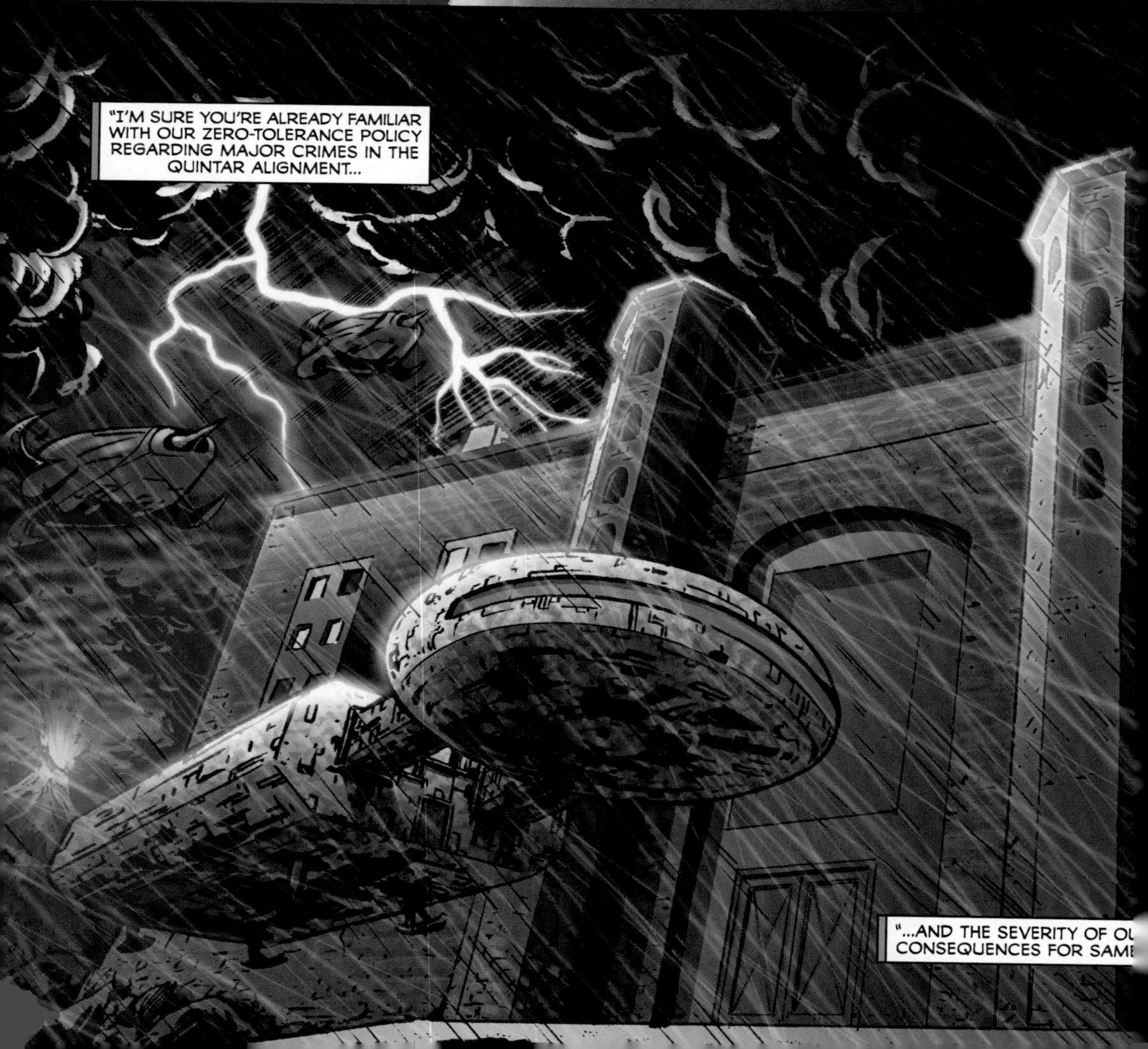
"I'M SURE YOU'RE ALREADY FAMILIAR WITH OUR ZERO-TOLERANCE POLICY REGARDING MAJOR CRIMES IN THE QUINTAR ALIGNMENT...
"...AND THE SEVERITY OF OU
CONSEQUENCES FOR SAME

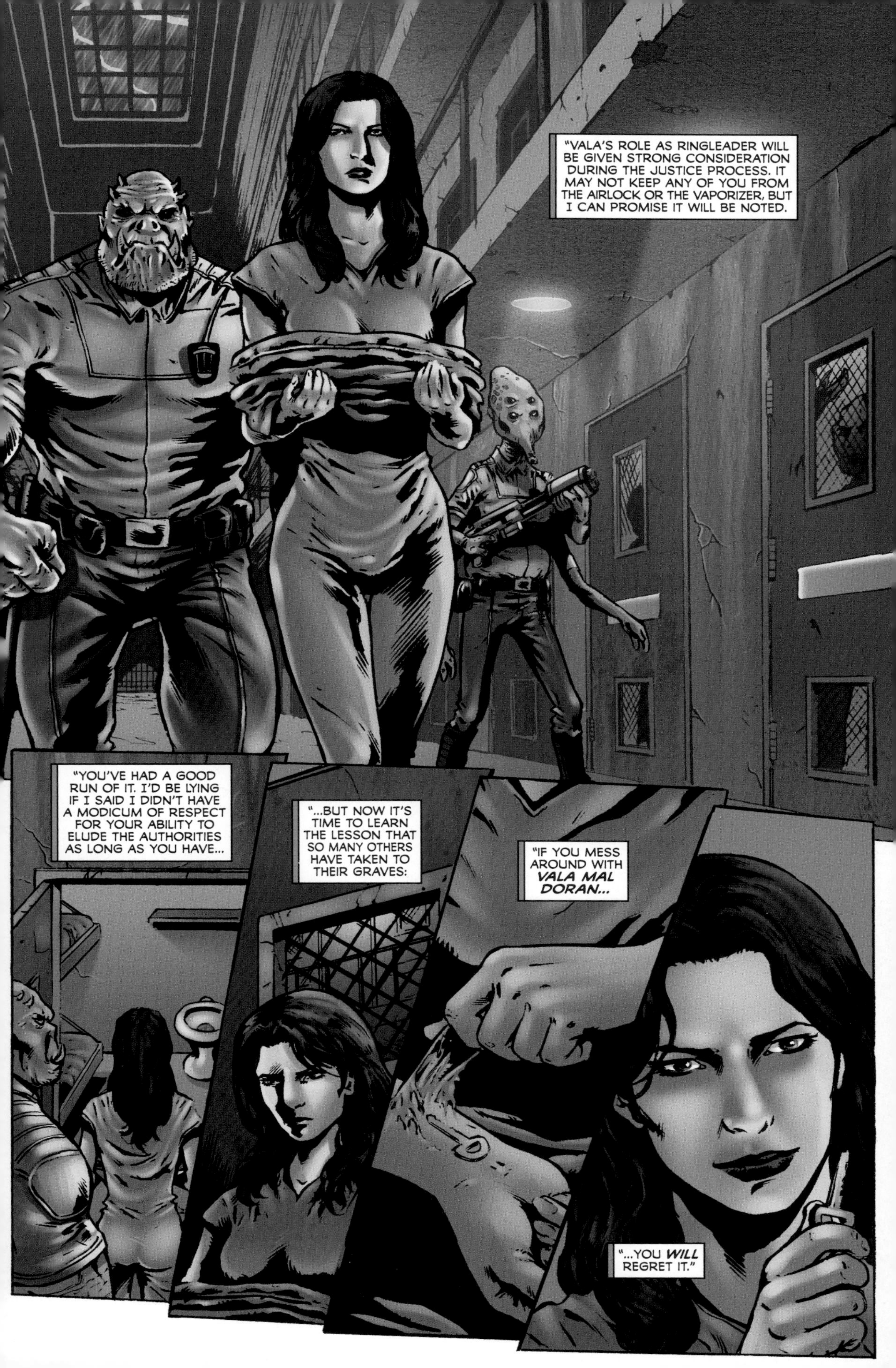
"VALA'S ROLE AS RINGLEADER WILL BE GIVEN STRONG CONSIDERATION DURING THE JUSTICE PROCESS. IT MAY NOT KEEP ANY OF YOU FROM THE AIRLOCK OR THE VAPORIZER, BUT I CAN PROMISE IT WILL BE NOTED.
"YOU'VE HAD A GOOD RUN OF IT. I'D BE LYING IF I SAID I DIDN'T HAVE A MODICUM OF RESPECT FOR YOUR ABILITY TO ELUDE THE AUTHORITIES AS LONG AS YOU HAVE...
"...BUT NOW IT'S TIME TO LEARN THE LESSON THAT SO MANY OTHERS HAVE TAKEN TO THEIR GRAVES:
"IF YOU MESS AROUND WITH *VALA MAL DORAN...*
"...YOU *WILL* REGRET IT."

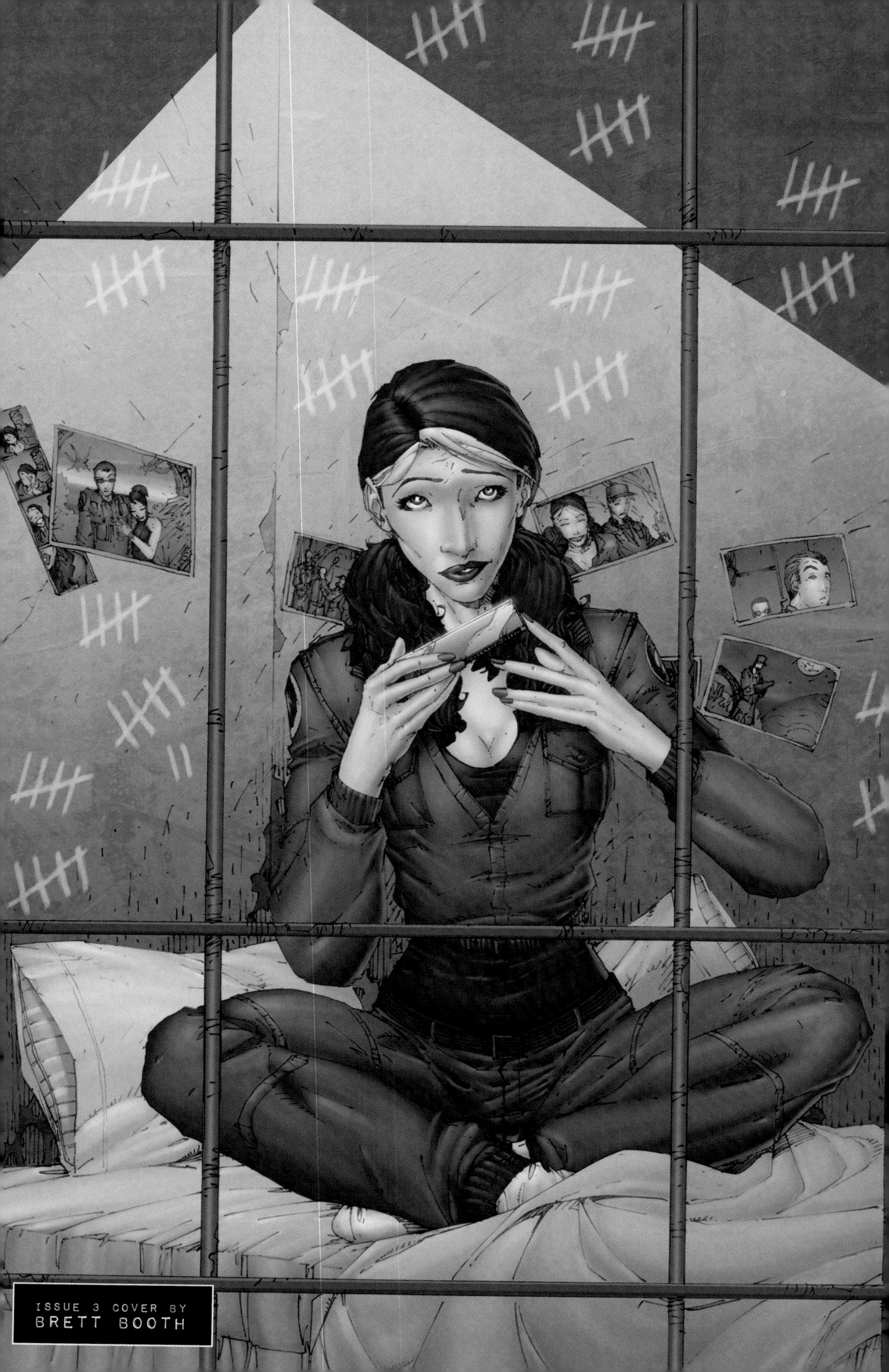

ISSUE 3 COVER BY
BRETT BOOTH

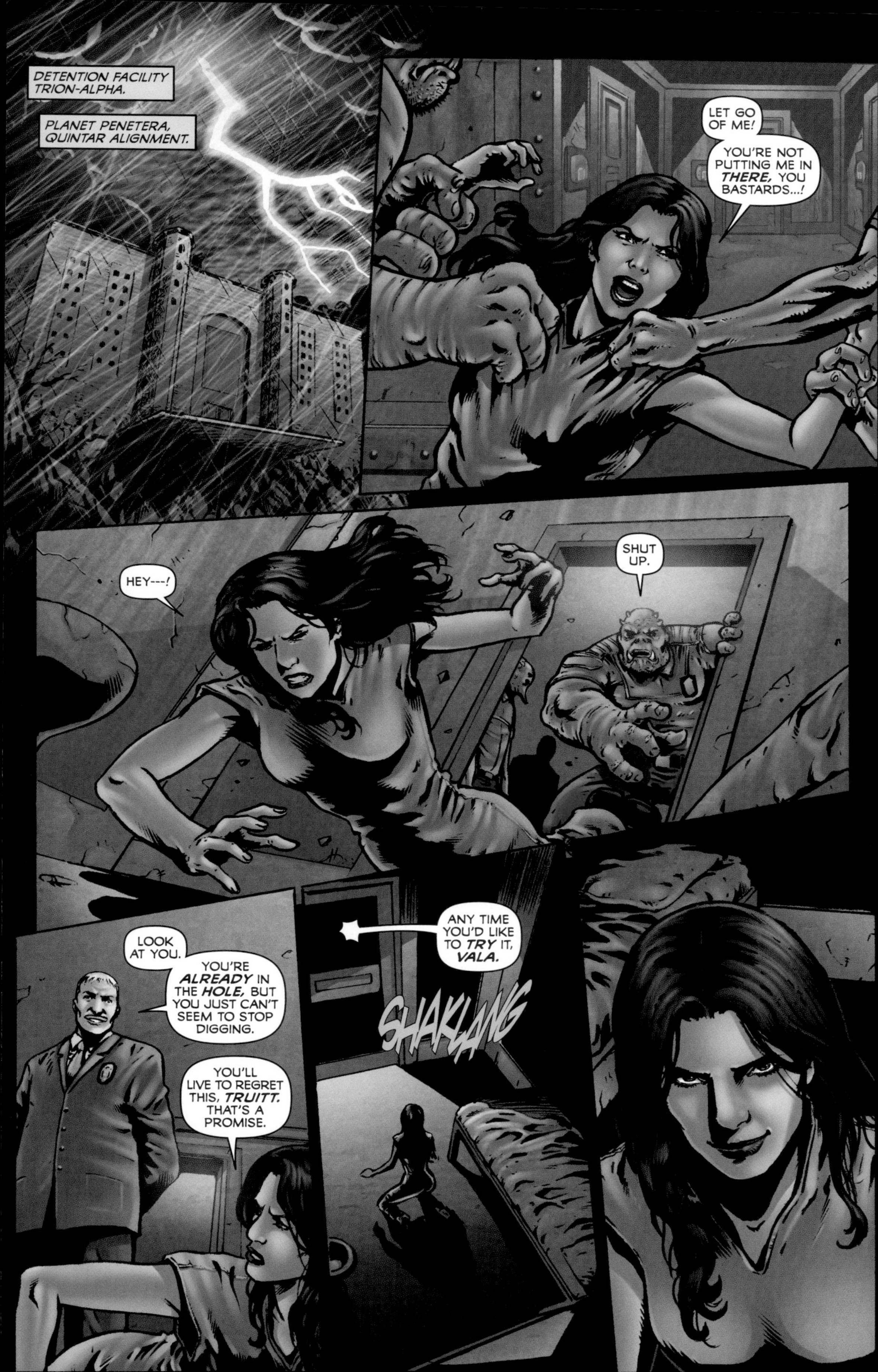

DETENTION FACILITY TRION-ALPHA.
PLANET PENETERA, QUINTAR ALIGNMENT.
LET GO OF ME!
YOU'RE NOT PUTTING ME IN THERE, YOU BASTARDS...!
HEY---!
SHUT UP.
LOOK AT YOU.
YOU'RE ALREADY IN THE HOLE, BUT YOU JUST CAN'T SEEM TO STOP DIGGING.
YOU'LL LIVE TO REGRET THIS, TRUITT. THAT'S A PROMISE.
ANY TIME YOU'D LIKE TO TRY IT, VALA.
SHAKLANG

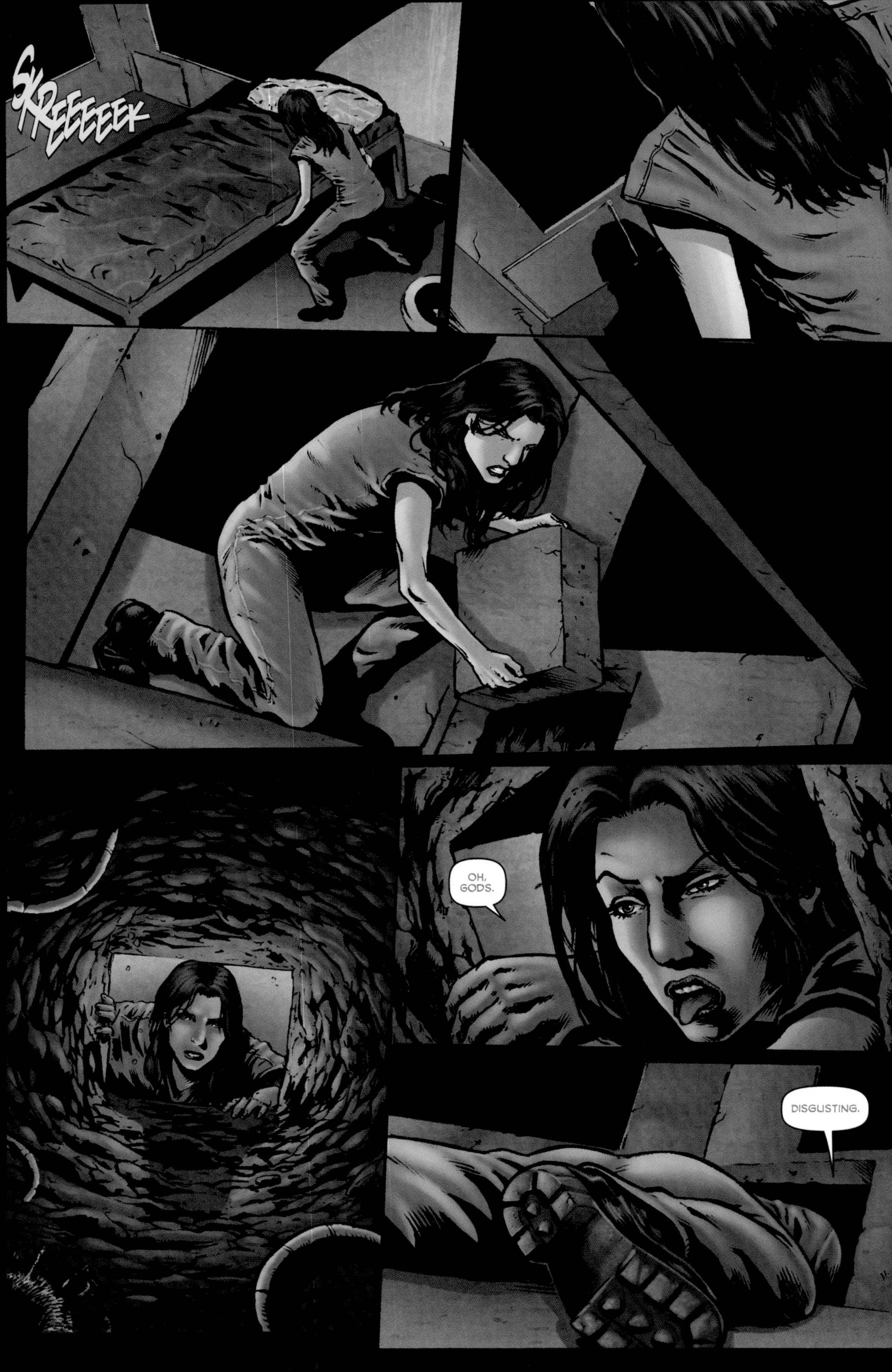
SKREEEEEEK
OH, GODS.
DISGUSTING.

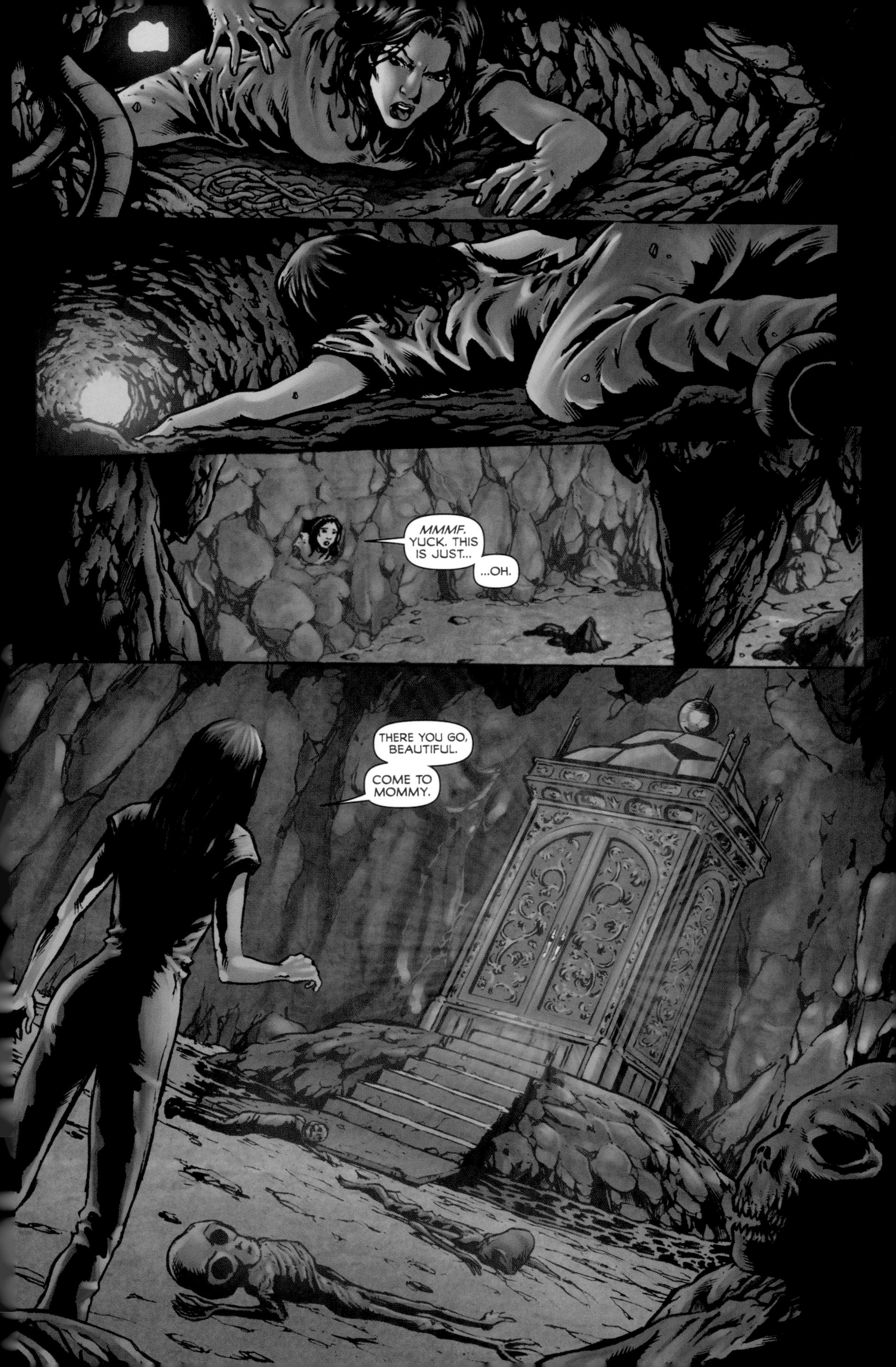
MMMF. YUCK. THIS IS JUST...
...OH.
THERE YOU GO, BEAUTIFUL.
COME TO MOMMY.

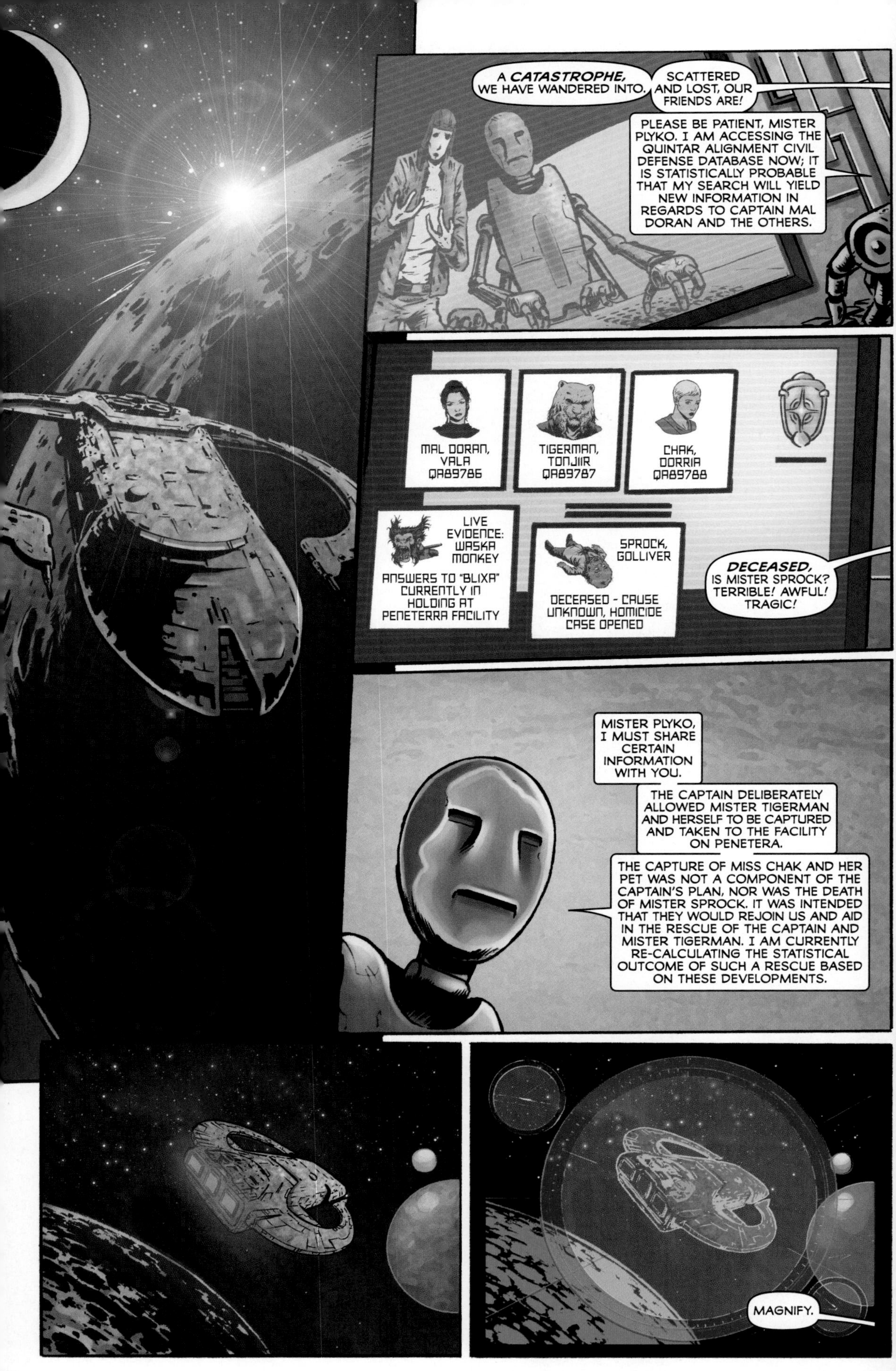
A CATASTROPHE, WE HAVE WANDERED INTO.
SCATTERED AND LOST, OUR FRIENDS ARE!
PLEASE BE PATIENT, MISTER PLYKO. I AM ACCESSING THE QUINTAR ALIGNMENT CIVIL DEFENSE DATABASE NOW; IT IS STATISTICALLY PROBABLE THAT MY SEARCH WILL YIELD NEW INFORMATION IN REGARDS TO CAPTAIN MAL DORAN AND THE OTHERS.
MAL DORAN, VALA QA89786
TIGERMAN, TONJIIR QA89787
CHAK, DORRIA QA89788
LIVE EVIDENCE: WASKA MONKEY
ANSWERS TO "BLIXA" CURRENTLY IN HOLDING AT PENETERRA FACILITY
SPROCK, GOLLIVER
DECEASED - CAUSE UNKNOWN, HOMICIDE CASE OPENED
DECEASED, IS MISTER SPROCK? TERRIBLE! AWFUL! TRAGIC!
MISTER PLYKO, I MUST SHARE CERTAIN INFORMATION WITH YOU.
THE CAPTAIN DELIBERATELY ALLOWED MISTER TIGERMAN AND HERSELF TO BE CAPTURED AND TAKEN TO THE FACILITY ON PENETERA.
THE CAPTURE OF MISS CHAK AND HER PET WAS NOT A COMPONENT OF THE CAPTAIN'S PLAN, NOR WAS THE DEATH OF MISTER SPROCK. IT WAS INTENDED THAT THEY WOULD REJOIN US AND AID IN THE RESCUE OF THE CAPTAIN AND MISTER TIGERMAN. I AM CURRENTLY RE-CALCULATING THE STATISTICAL OUTCOME OF SUCH A RESCUE BASED ON THESE DEVELOPMENTS.
MAGNIFY.

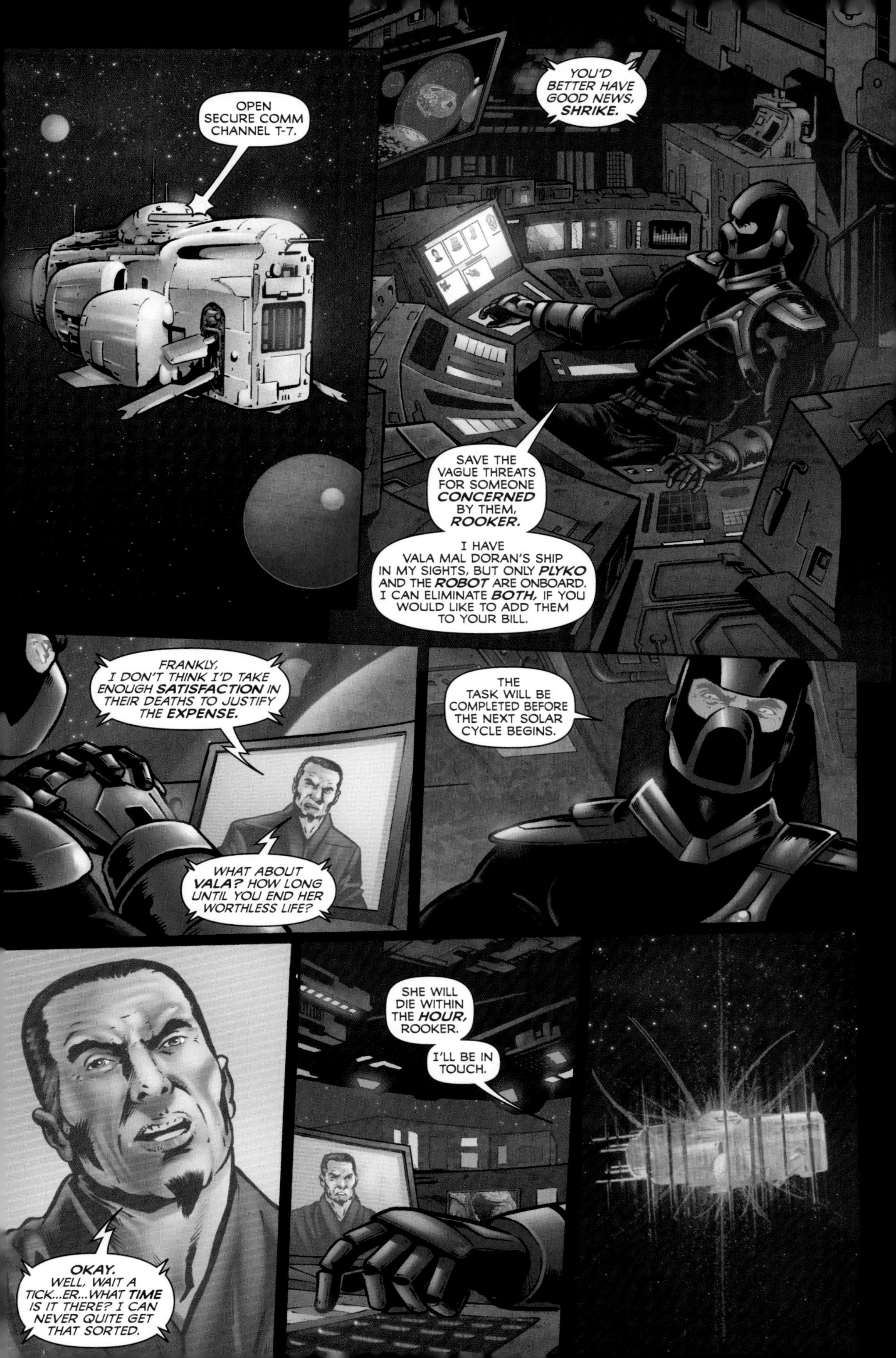
OPEN SECURE COMM CHANNEL T-7.
YOU'D BETTER HAVE GOOD NEWS, SHRIKE.
SAVE THE VAGUE THREATS FOR SOMEONE CONCERNED BY THEM, ROOKER.
I HAVE VALA MAL DORAN'S SHIP IN MY SIGHTS, BUT ONLY PLYKO AND THE ROBOT ARE ONBOARD. I CAN ELIMINATE BOTH, IF YOU WOULD LIKE TO ADD THEM TO YOUR BILL.
FRANKLY, I DON'T THINK I'D TAKE ENOUGH SATISFACTION IN THEIR DEATHS TO JUSTIFY THE EXPENSE.
WHAT ABOUT VALA? HOW LONG UNTIL YOU END HER WORTHLESS LIFE?
THE TASK WILL BE COMPLETED BEFORE THE NEXT SOLAR CYCLE BEGINS.
OKAY. WELL, WAIT A TICK...ER...WHAT TIME IS IT THERE? I CAN NEVER QUITE GET THAT SORTED.
SHE WILL DIE WITHIN THE HOUR, ROOKER.
I'LL BE IN TOUCH.

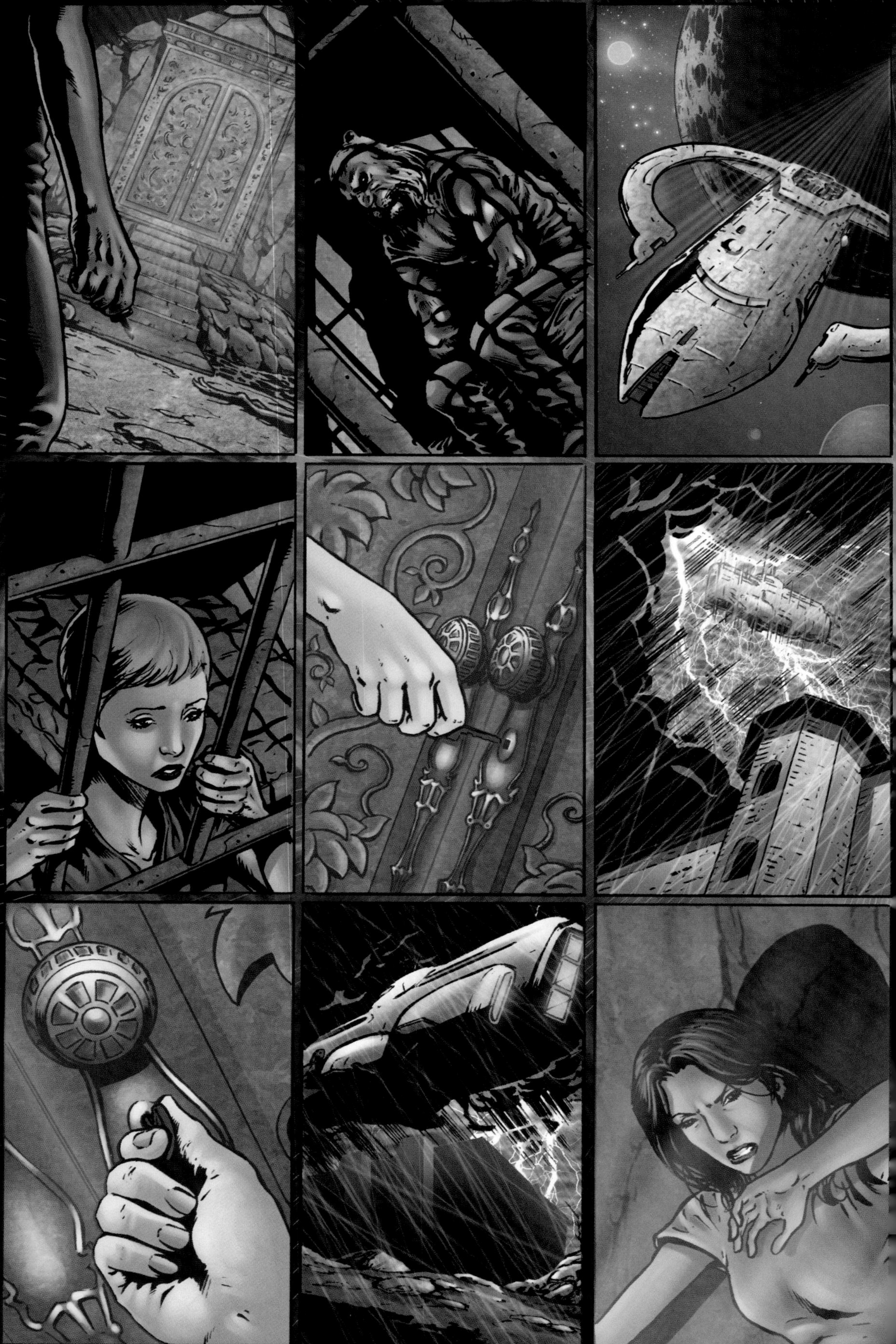

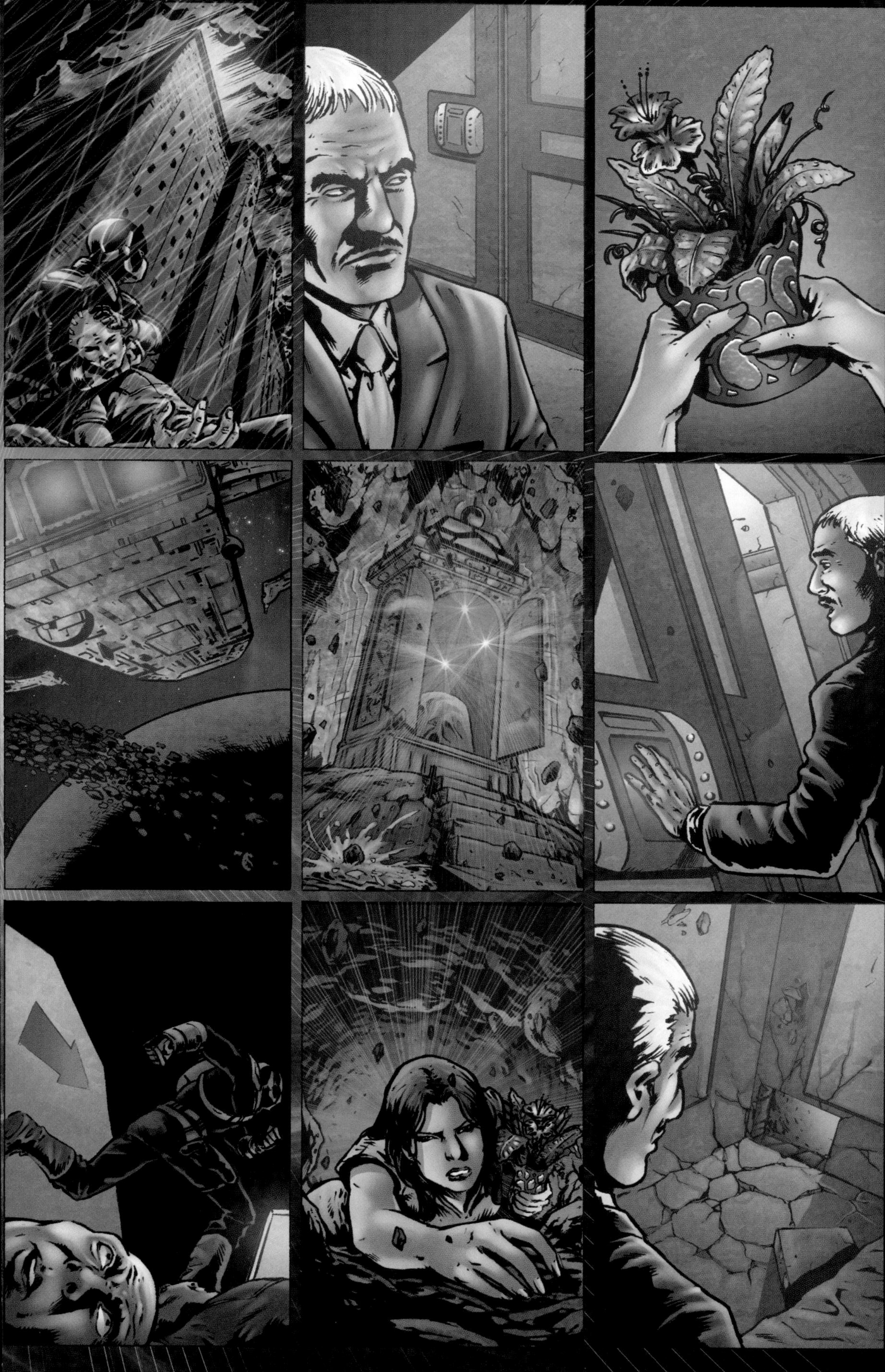

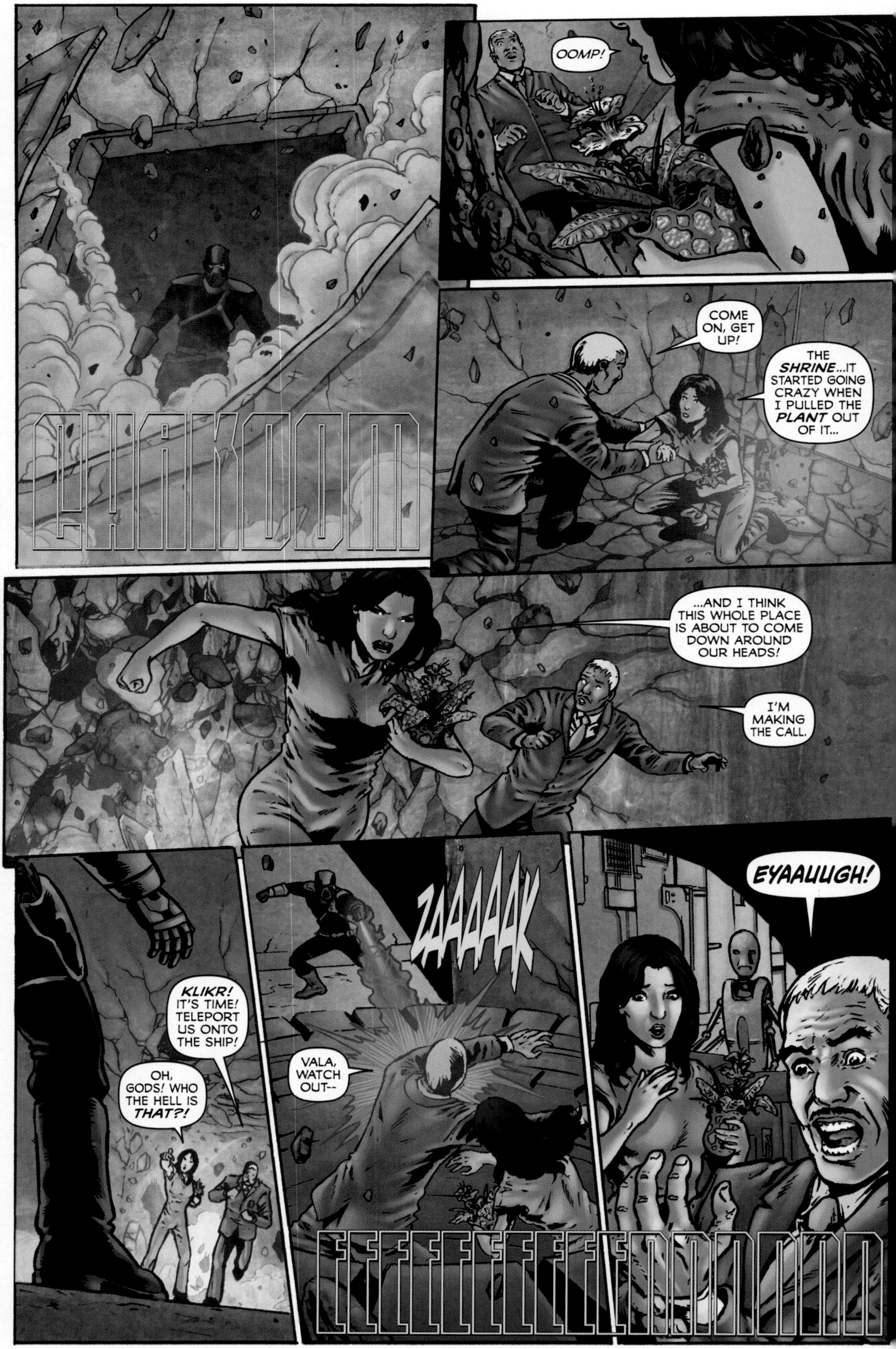
CHAKOOM
OOMP!
COME ON, GET UP!
THE SHRINE...IT STARTED GOING CRAZY WHEN I PULLED THE PLANT OUT OF IT...
...AND I THINK THIS WHOLE PLACE IS ABOUT TO COME DOWN AROUND OUR HEADS!
I'M MAKING THE CALL.
KLIKR! IT'S TIME! TELEPORT US ONTO THE SHIP!
OH, GODS! WHO THE HELL IS THAT?!
ZAAAAK
VALA, WATCH OUT--
EYAAUUGH!
EEEEEEEEEENNNNNN

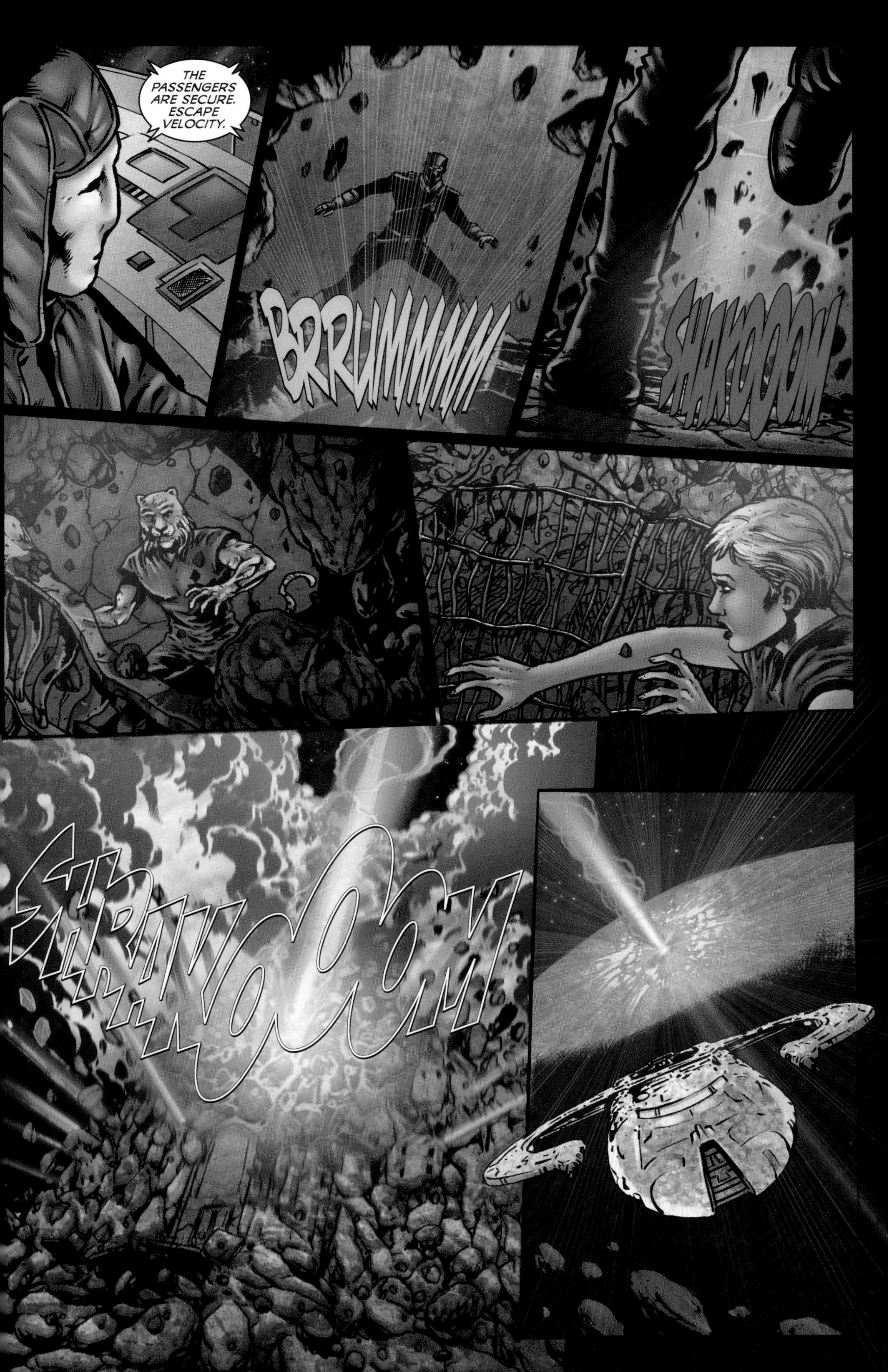
THE PASSENGERS ARE SECURE. ESCAPE VELOCITY.
BRRUMMMM
SHAKOOOM

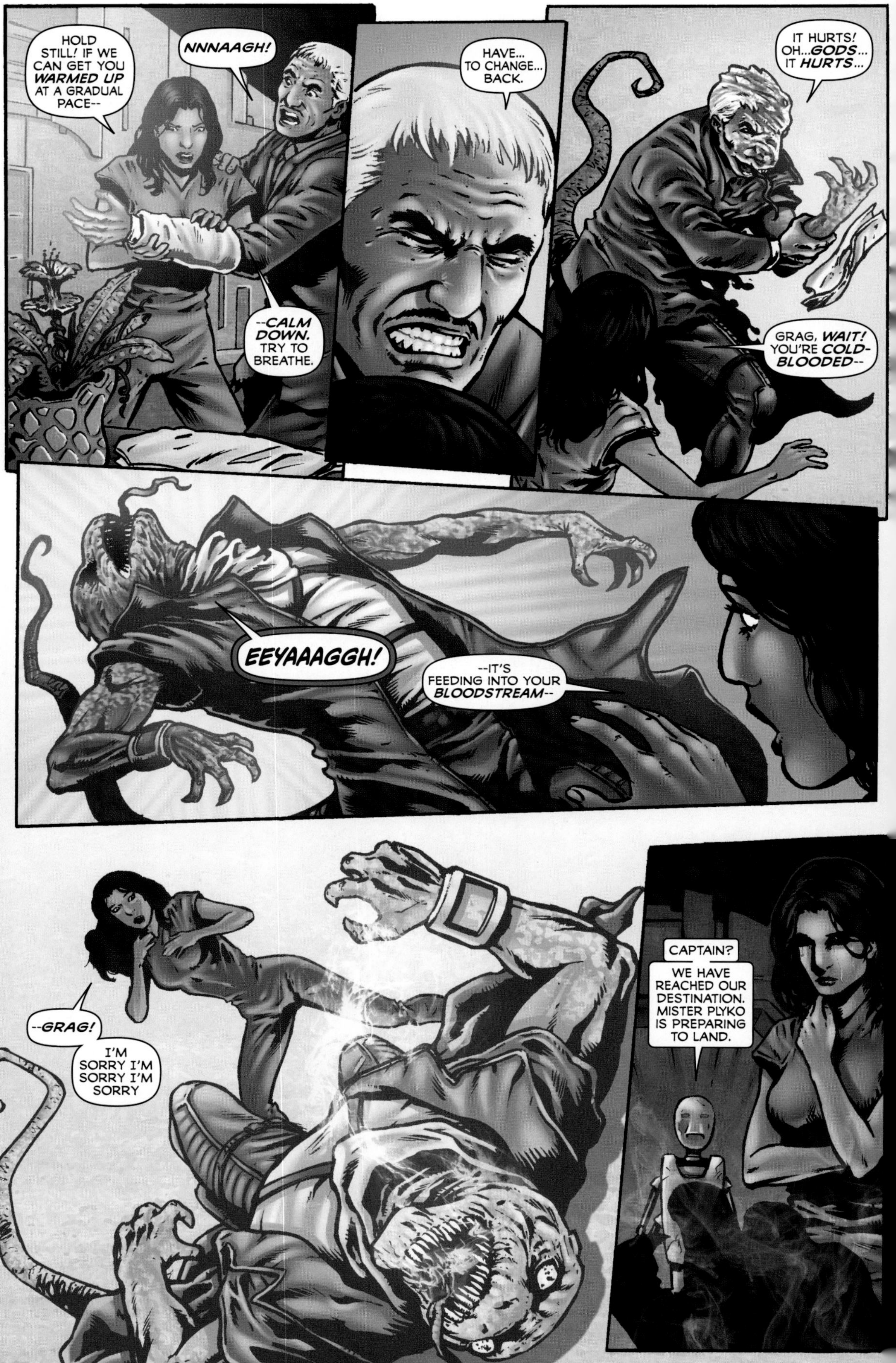
HOLD STILL! IF WE CAN GET YOU *WARMED UP* AT A GRADUAL PACE--
NNNAAGH!
--*CALM DOWN.* TRY TO BREATHE.
HAVE... TO CHANGE... BACK.
IT HURTS! OH...*GODS*... IT *HURTS*...
GRAG, *WAIT!* YOU'RE *COLD-BLOODED*--
EEYAAAGGH!
--IT'S FEEDING INTO YOUR *BLOODSTREAM*--
--*GRAG!*
I'M SORRY I'M SORRY I'M SORRY
CAPTAIN?
WE HAVE REACHED OUR DESTINATION. MISTER PLYKO IS PREPARING TO LAND.

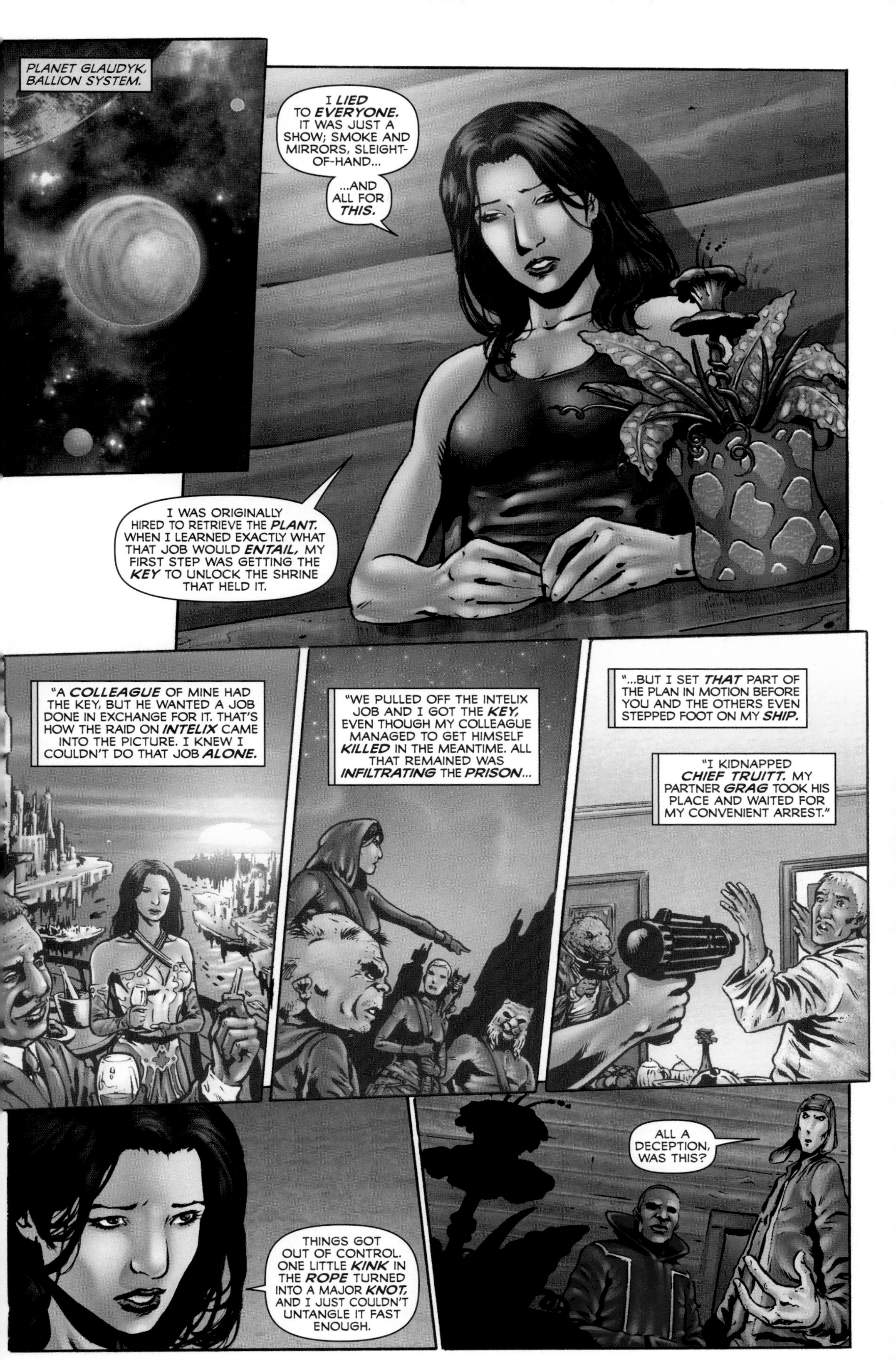
PLANET GLAUDYK, BALLION SYSTEM.
I LIED TO EVERYONE. IT WAS JUST A SHOW; SMOKE AND MIRRORS, SLEIGHT-OF-HAND...
...AND ALL FOR THIS.
I WAS ORIGINALLY HIRED TO RETRIEVE THE PLANT. WHEN I LEARNED EXACTLY WHAT THAT JOB WOULD ENTAIL, MY FIRST STEP WAS GETTING THE KEY TO UNLOCK THE SHRINE THAT HELD IT.
"A COLLEAGUE OF MINE HAD THE KEY, BUT HE WANTED A JOB DONE IN EXCHANGE FOR IT. THAT'S HOW THE RAID ON INTELIX CAME INTO THE PICTURE. I KNEW I COULDN'T DO THAT JOB ALONE.
"WE PULLED OFF THE INTELIX JOB AND I GOT THE KEY, EVEN THOUGH MY COLLEAGUE MANAGED TO GET HIMSELF KILLED IN THE MEANTIME. ALL THAT REMAINED WAS INFILTRATING THE PRISON...
"...BUT I SET THAT PART OF THE PLAN IN MOTION BEFORE YOU AND THE OTHERS EVEN STEPPED FOOT ON MY SHIP.
"I KIDNAPPED CHIEF TRUITT. MY PARTNER GRAG TOOK HIS PLACE AND WAITED FOR MY CONVENIENT ARREST."
ALL A DECEPTION, WAS THIS?
THINGS GOT OUT OF CONTROL. ONE LITTLE KINK IN THE ROPE TURNED INTO A MAJOR KNOT, AND I JUST COULDN'T UNTANGLE IT FAST ENOUGH.

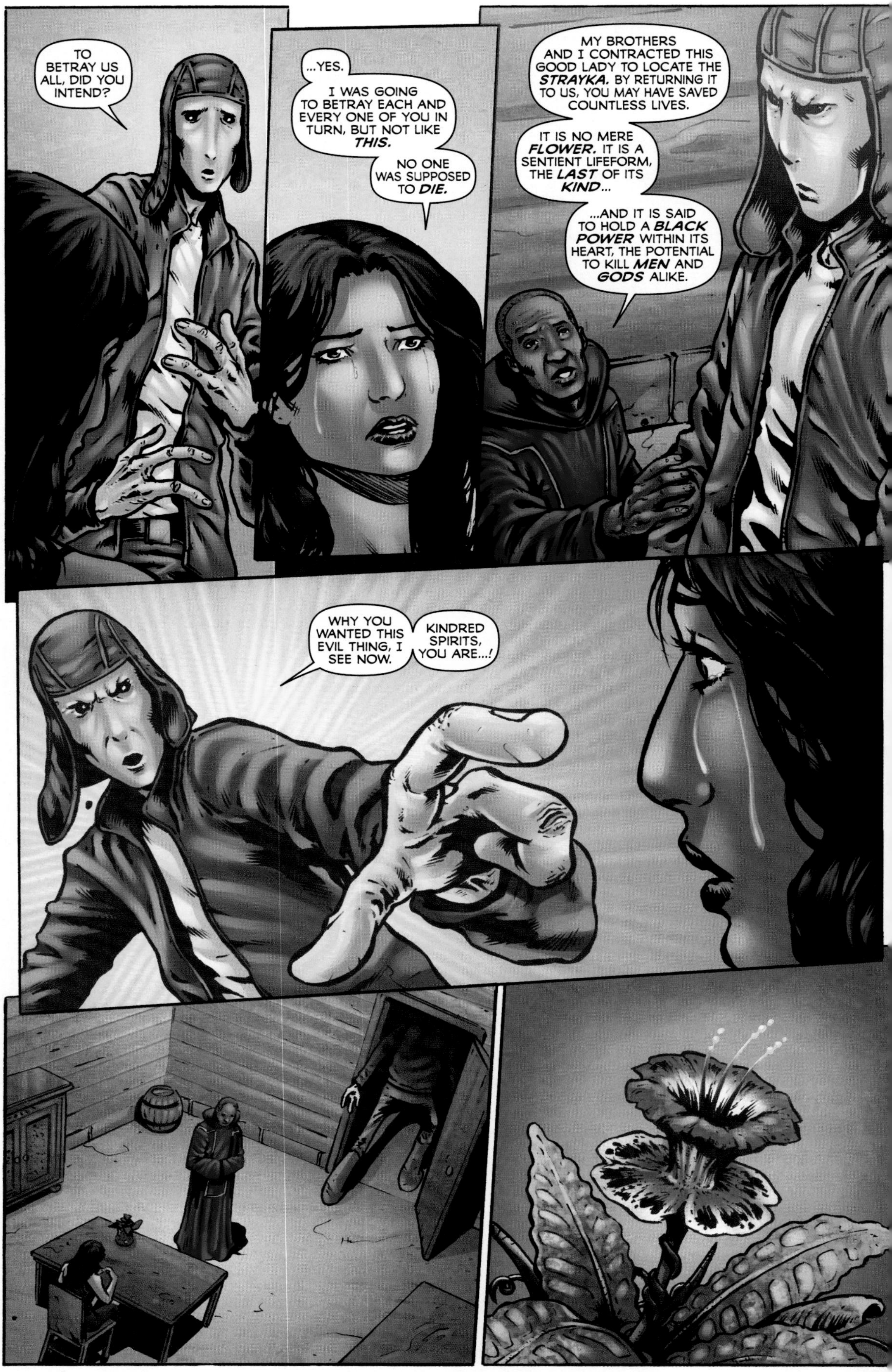
TO BETRAY US ALL, DID YOU INTEND?
...YES.
I WAS GOING TO BETRAY EACH AND EVERY ONE OF YOU IN TURN, BUT NOT LIKE THIS.
NO ONE WAS SUPPOSED TO DIE.
MY BROTHERS AND I CONTRACTED THIS GOOD LADY TO LOCATE THE STRAYKA. BY RETURNING IT TO US, YOU MAY HAVE SAVED COUNTLESS LIVES.
IT IS NO MERE FLOWER. IT IS A SENTIENT LIFEFORM, THE LAST OF ITS KIND...
...AND IT IS SAID TO HOLD A BLACK POWER WITHIN ITS HEART, THE POTENTIAL TO KILL MEN AND GODS ALIKE.
WHY YOU WANTED THIS EVIL THING, I SEE NOW.
KINDRED SPIRITS, YOU ARE...!

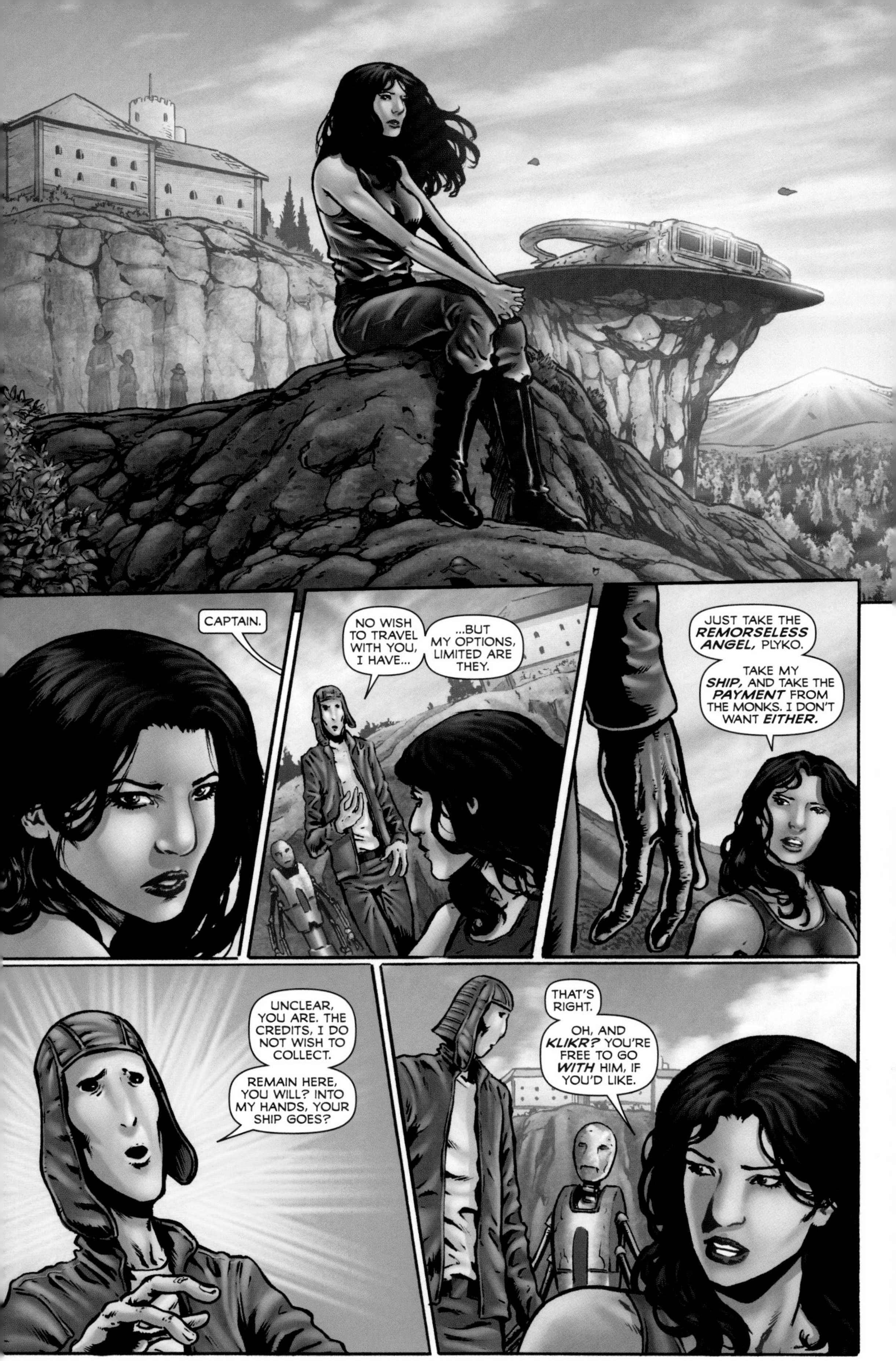

CAPTAIN.
NO WISH TO TRAVEL WITH YOU, I HAVE...
...BUT MY OPTIONS, LIMITED ARE THEY.
JUST TAKE THE REMORSELESS ANGEL, PLYKO.
TAKE MY SHIP, AND TAKE THE PAYMENT FROM THE MONKS. I DON'T WANT EITHER.
UNCLEAR, YOU ARE. THE CREDITS, I DO NOT WISH TO COLLECT.
REMAIN HERE, YOU WILL? INTO MY HANDS, YOUR SHIP GOES?
THAT'S RIGHT.
OH, AND KLIKR? YOU'RE FREE TO GO WITH HIM, IF YOU'D LIKE.

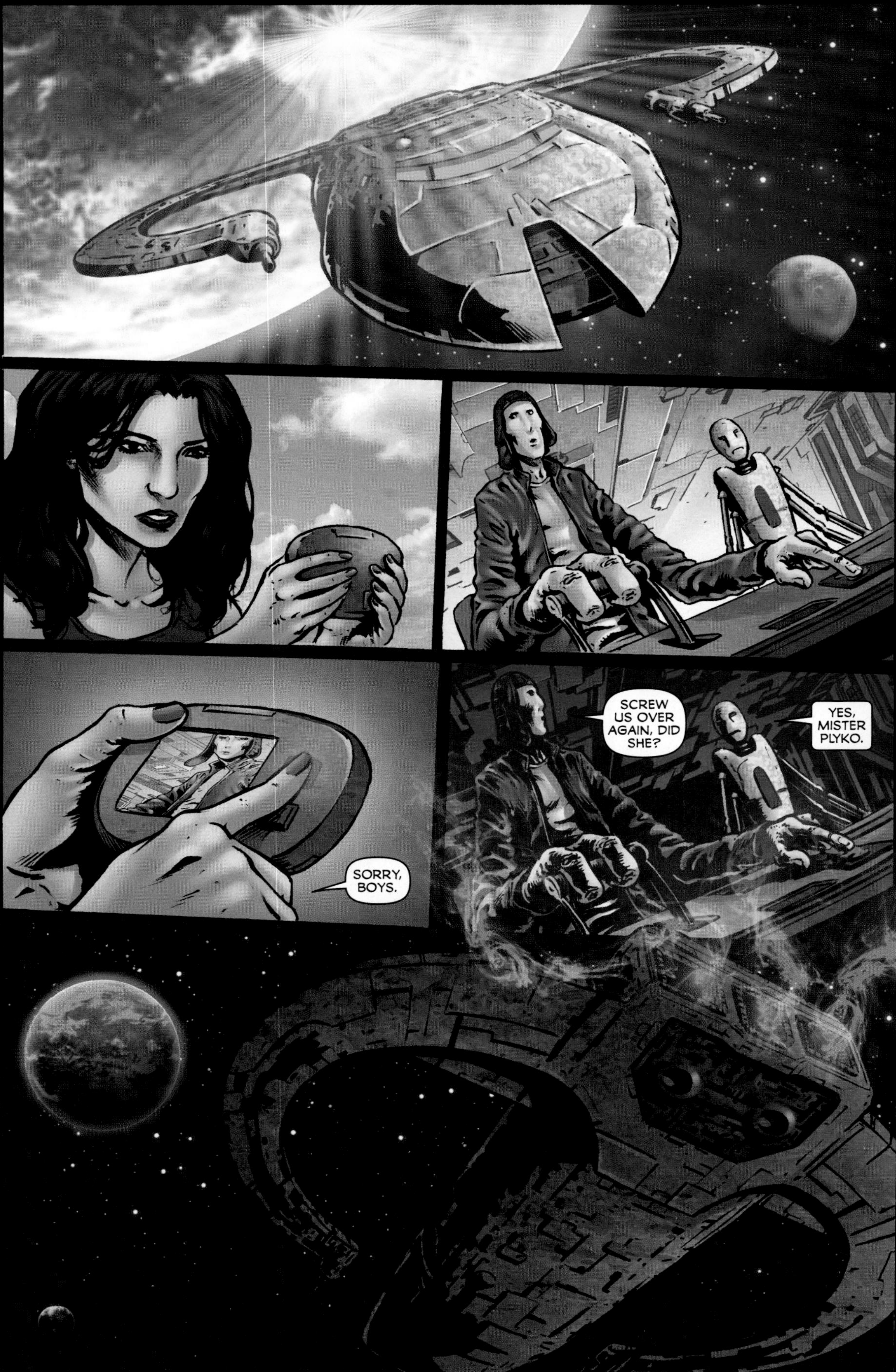
SORRY, BOYS.
SCREW US OVER AGAIN, DID SHE?
YES, MISTER PLYKO.

MISS MAL DORAN, I HAVE YOUR **CREDITS**...

...AND WE HAVE A SHIP WAITING TO TAKE YOU WHEREVER YOU NEED TO **GO.**

"THANK YOU, **BROTHER SHAND.** I'D LIKE TO LEAVE IMMEDIATELY."

STARGATE COMMAND: CHEYENNE MOUNTAIN, COLORADO. PLANET EARTH.

YEARS LATER.

BREEP BREEP

YOU HAVE ONE NEW MESSAGE.

VALA, THIS IS **STANLEY TRUITT.** I NEED TO SPEAK TO YOU AS SOON AS POSSIBLE. THIS IS AN URGENT MATTER.

I KNOW YOU'LL PROBABLY BE PRETTY NERVOUS ABOUT RESPONDING, BUT THIS IS BIGGER THAN BOTH OF US. I'M NOT INTERESTED IN **REVENGE.**

I REALLY JUST NEED YOUR HELP--

VALA?

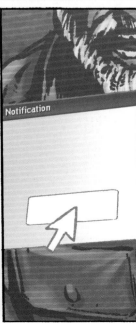

Notification

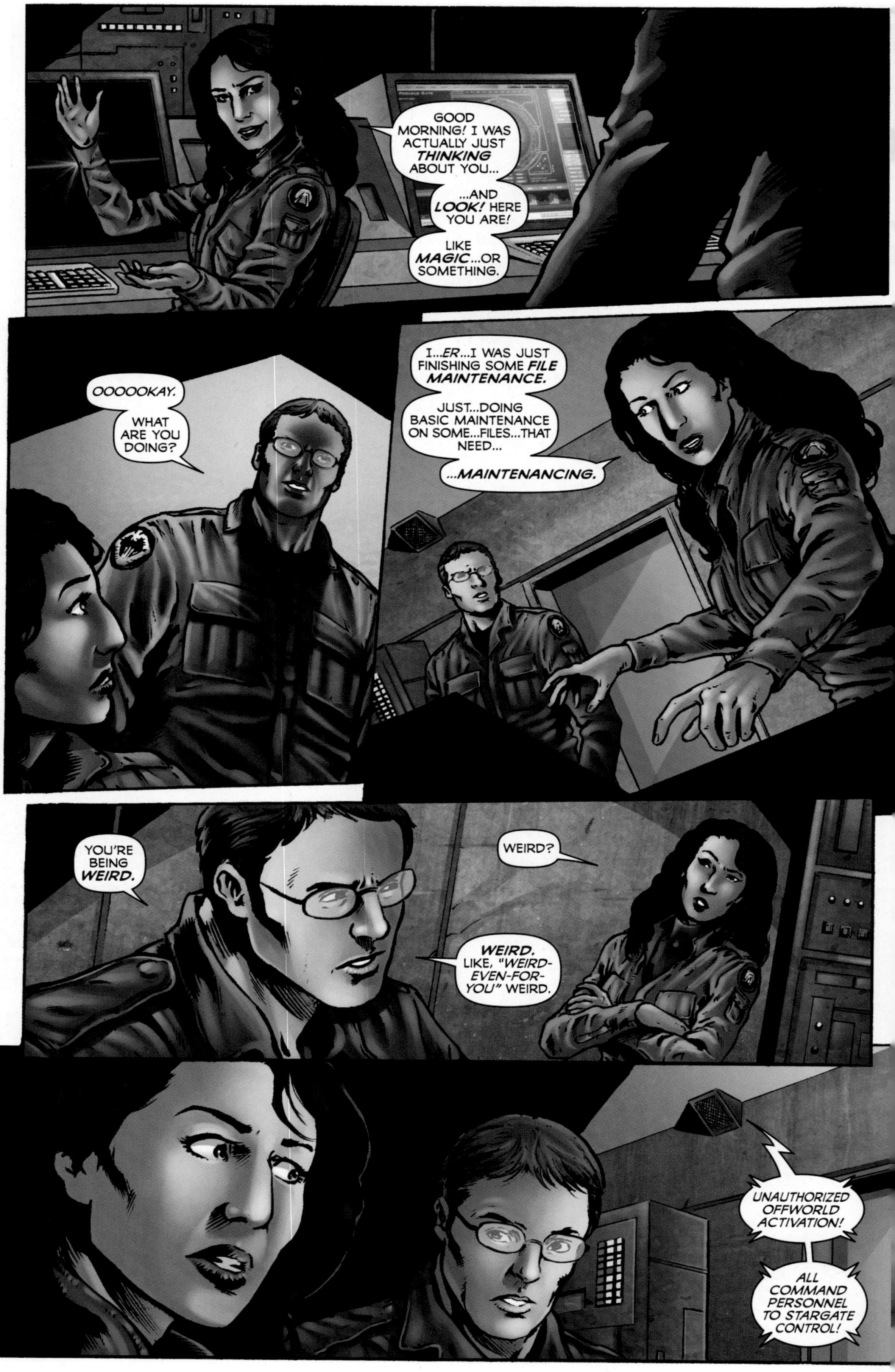
GOOD MORNING! I WAS ACTUALLY JUST THINKING ABOUT YOU...
...AND LOOK! HERE YOU ARE!
LIKE MAGIC...OR SOMETHING.
OOOOOKAY.
WHAT ARE YOU DOING?
I...ER...I WAS JUST FINISHING SOME FILE MAINTENANCE.
JUST...DOING BASIC MAINTENANCE ON SOME...FILES...THAT NEED...
...MAINTENANCING.
YOU'RE BEING WEIRD.
WEIRD?
WEIRD. LIKE, "WEIRD-EVEN-FOR-YOU" WEIRD.
UNAUTHORIZED OFFWORLD ACTIVATION!
ALL COMMAND PERSONNEL TO STARGATE CONTROL!

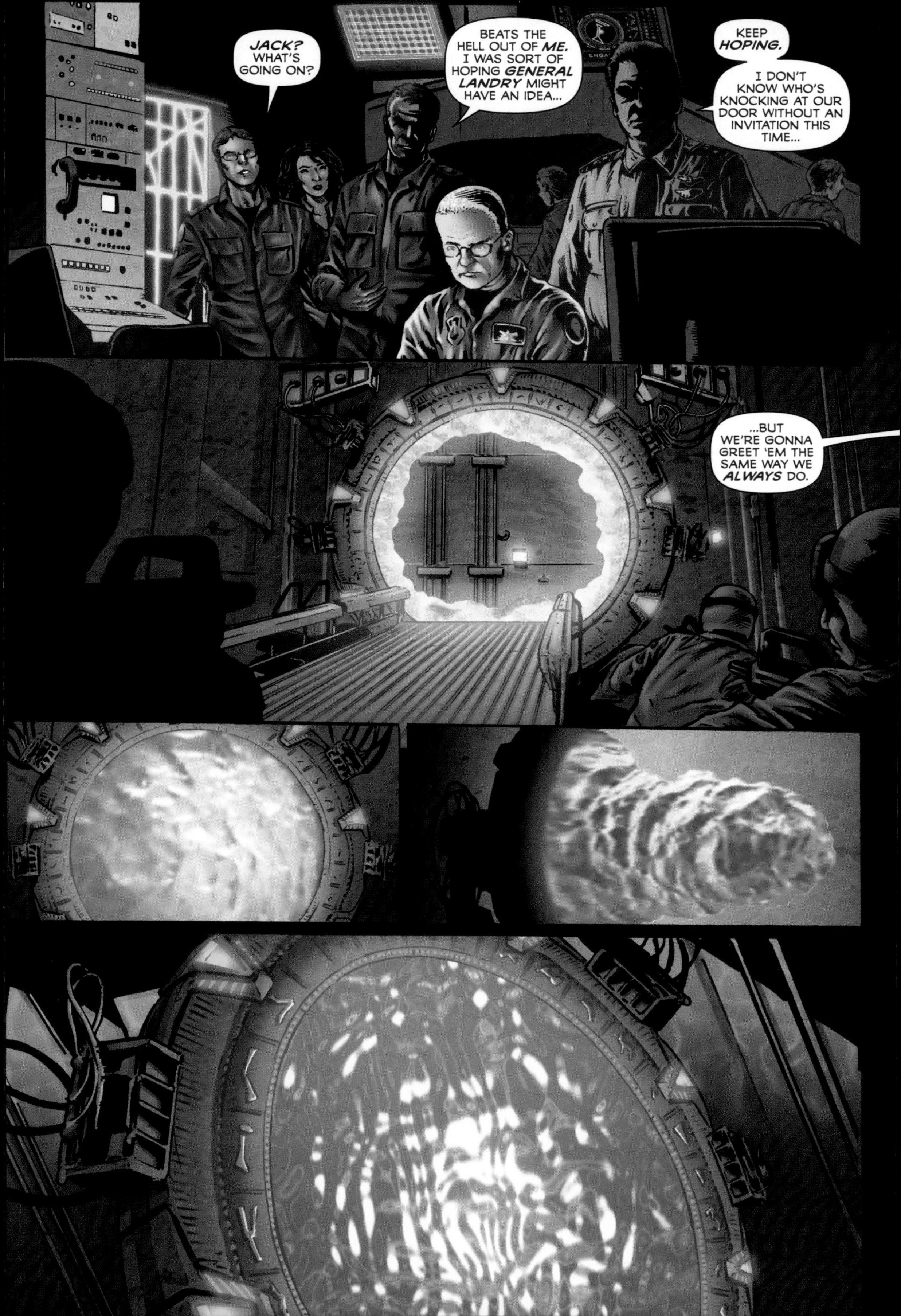
JACK? WHAT'S GOING ON?
BEATS THE HELL OUT OF ME. I WAS SORT OF HOPING GENERAL LANDRY MIGHT HAVE AN IDEA...
KEEP HOPING.
I DON'T KNOW WHO'S KNOCKING AT OUR DOOR WITHOUT AN INVITATION THIS TIME...
...BUT WE'RE GONNA GREET 'EM THE SAME WAY WE ALWAYS DO.

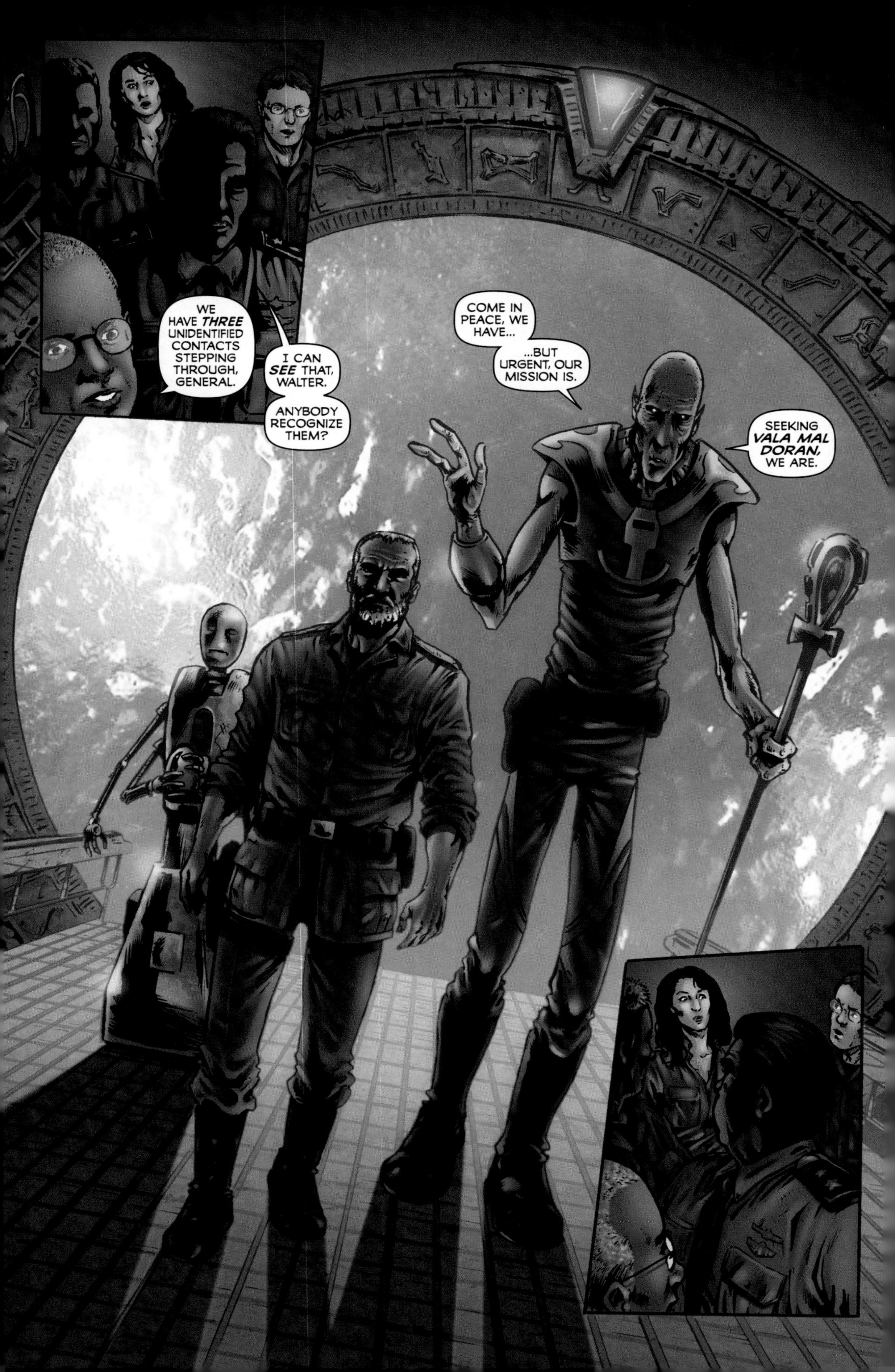
WE HAVE THREE UNIDENTIFIED CONTACTS STEPPING THROUGH, GENERAL.
I CAN SEE THAT, WALTER.
ANYBODY RECOGNIZE THEM?
COME IN PEACE, WE HAVE...
...BUT URGENT, OUR MISSION IS.
SEEKING VALA MAL DORAN, WE ARE.

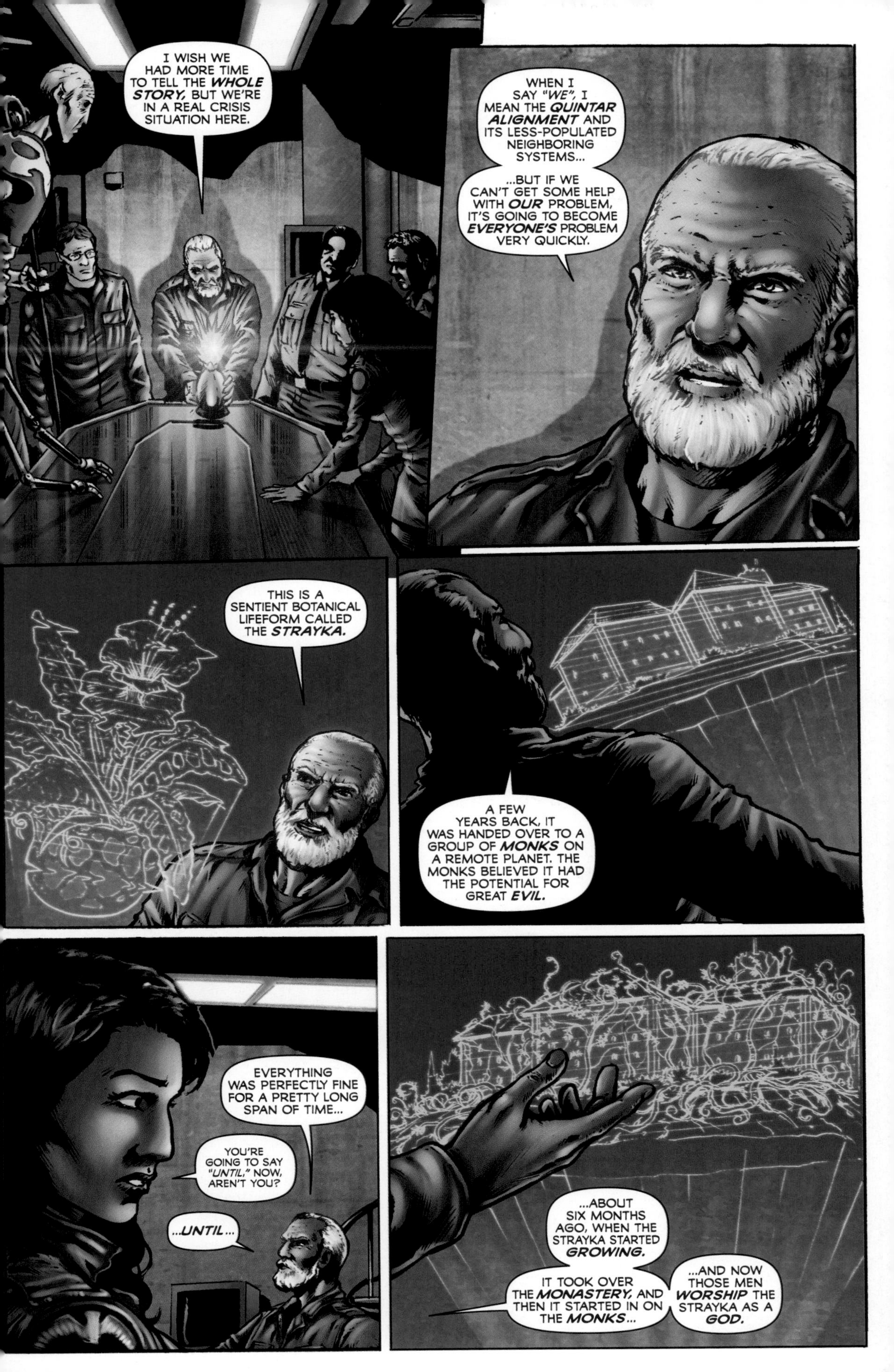

I WISH WE HAD MORE TIME TO TELL THE *WHOLE STORY,* BUT WE'RE IN A REAL CRISIS SITUATION HERE.
WHEN I SAY "*WE*", I MEAN THE ***QUINTAR ALIGNMENT*** AND ITS LESS-POPULATED NEIGHBORING SYSTEMS...
...BUT IF WE CAN'T GET SOME HELP WITH ***OUR*** PROBLEM, IT'S GOING TO BECOME ***EVERYONE'S*** PROBLEM VERY QUICKLY.
THIS IS A SENTIENT BOTANICAL LIFEFORM CALLED THE ***STRAYKA.***
A FEW YEARS BACK, IT WAS HANDED OVER TO A GROUP OF ***MONKS*** ON A REMOTE PLANET. THE MONKS BELIEVED IT HAD THE POTENTIAL FOR GREAT ***EVIL.***
EVERYTHING WAS PERFECTLY FINE FOR A PRETTY LONG SPAN OF TIME...
YOU'RE GOING TO SAY "*UNTIL,*" NOW, AREN'T YOU?
...***UNTIL***...
...ABOUT SIX MONTHS AGO, WHEN THE STRAYKA STARTED ***GROWING.***
IT TOOK OVER THE ***MONASTERY,*** AND THEN IT STARTED IN ON THE ***MONKS***...
...AND NOW THOSE MEN ***WORSHIP*** THE STRAYKA AS A ***GOD.***

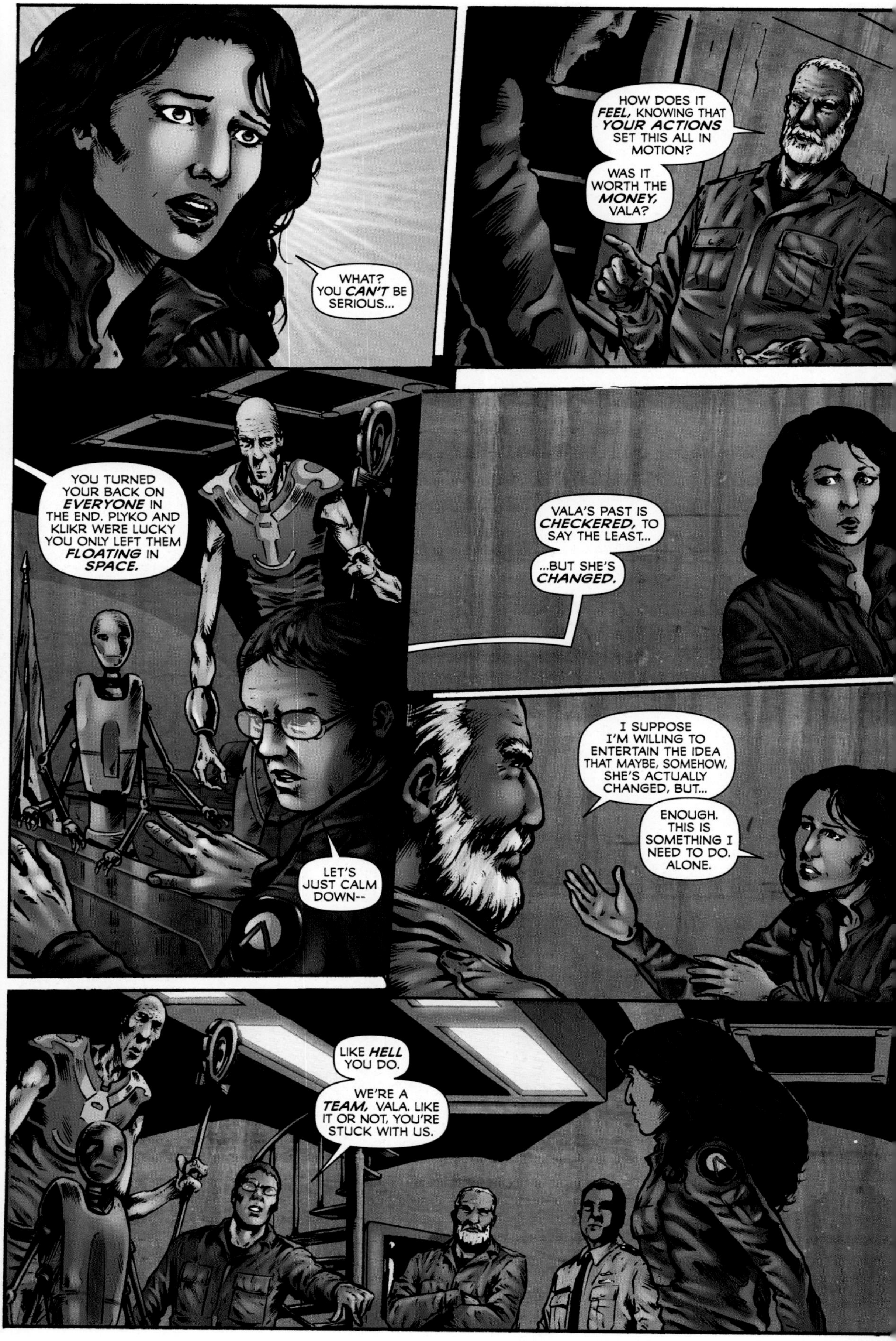
WHAT? YOU CAN'T BE SERIOUS...
HOW DOES IT FEEL, KNOWING THAT YOUR ACTIONS SET THIS ALL IN MOTION?
WAS IT WORTH THE MONEY, VALA?
YOU TURNED YOUR BACK ON EVERYONE IN THE END. PLYKO AND KLIKR WERE LUCKY YOU ONLY LEFT THEM FLOATING IN SPACE.
LET'S JUST CALM DOWN--
VALA'S PAST IS CHECKERED, TO SAY THE LEAST...
...BUT SHE'S CHANGED.
I SUPPOSE I'M WILLING TO ENTERTAIN THE IDEA THAT MAYBE, SOMEHOW, SHE'S ACTUALLY CHANGED, BUT...
ENOUGH. THIS IS SOMETHING I NEED TO DO. ALONE.
LIKE HELL YOU DO.
WE'RE A TEAM, VALA. LIKE IT OR NOT, YOU'RE STUCK WITH US.

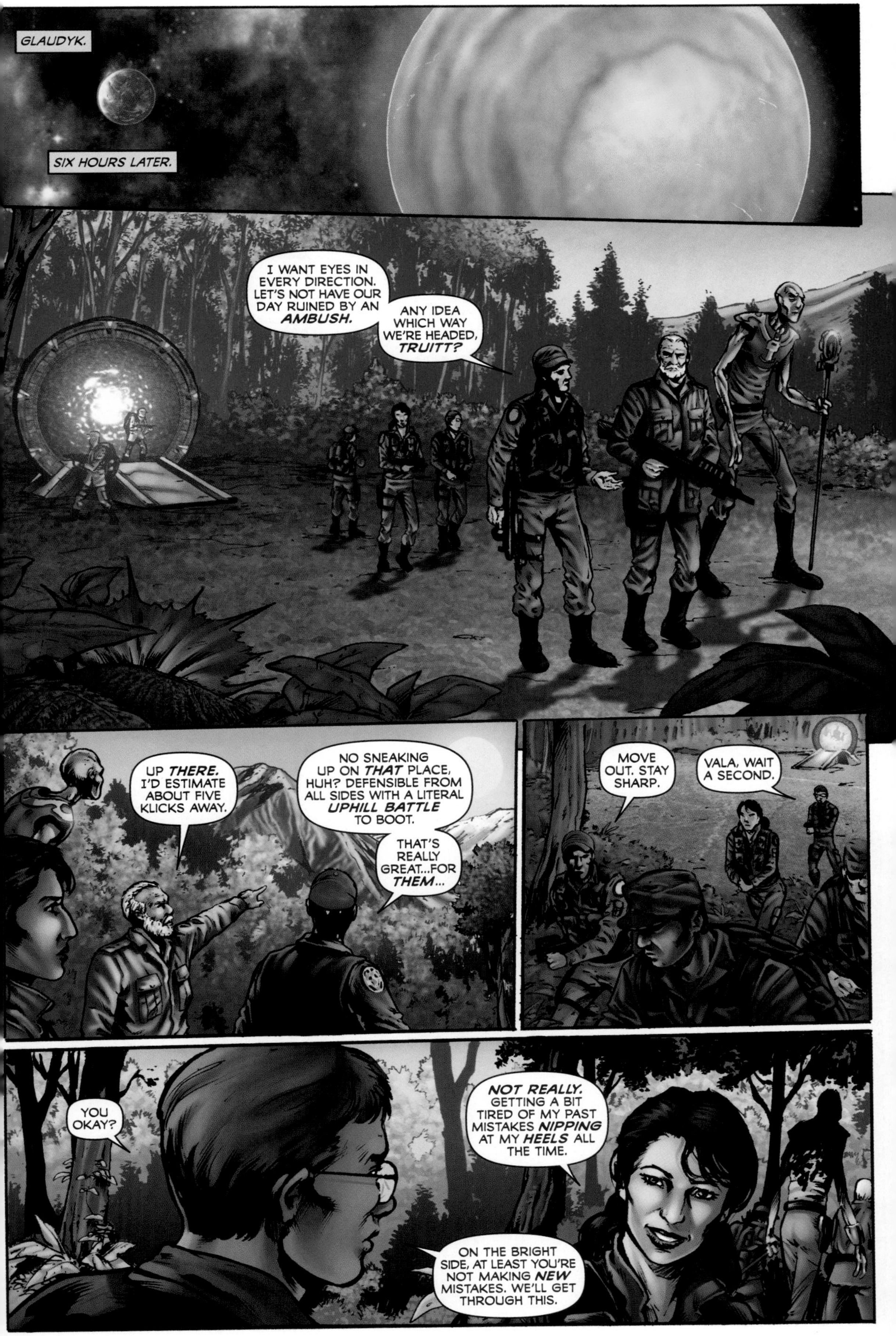
GLAUDYK.
SIX HOURS LATER.
I WANT EYES IN EVERY DIRECTION. LET'S NOT HAVE OUR DAY RUINED BY AN AMBUSH.
ANY IDEA WHICH WAY WE'RE HEADED, TRUITT?
UP THERE. I'D ESTIMATE ABOUT FIVE KLICKS AWAY.
NO SNEAKING UP ON THAT PLACE, HUH? DEFENSIBLE FROM ALL SIDES WITH A LITERAL UPHILL BATTLE TO BOOT.
THAT'S REALLY GREAT...FOR THEM...
MOVE OUT. STAY SHARP.
VALA, WAIT A SECOND.
YOU OKAY?
NOT REALLY. GETTING A BIT TIRED OF MY PAST MISTAKES NIPPING AT MY HEELS ALL THE TIME.
ON THE BRIGHT SIDE, AT LEAST YOU'RE NOT MAKING NEW MISTAKES. WE'LL GET THROUGH THIS.

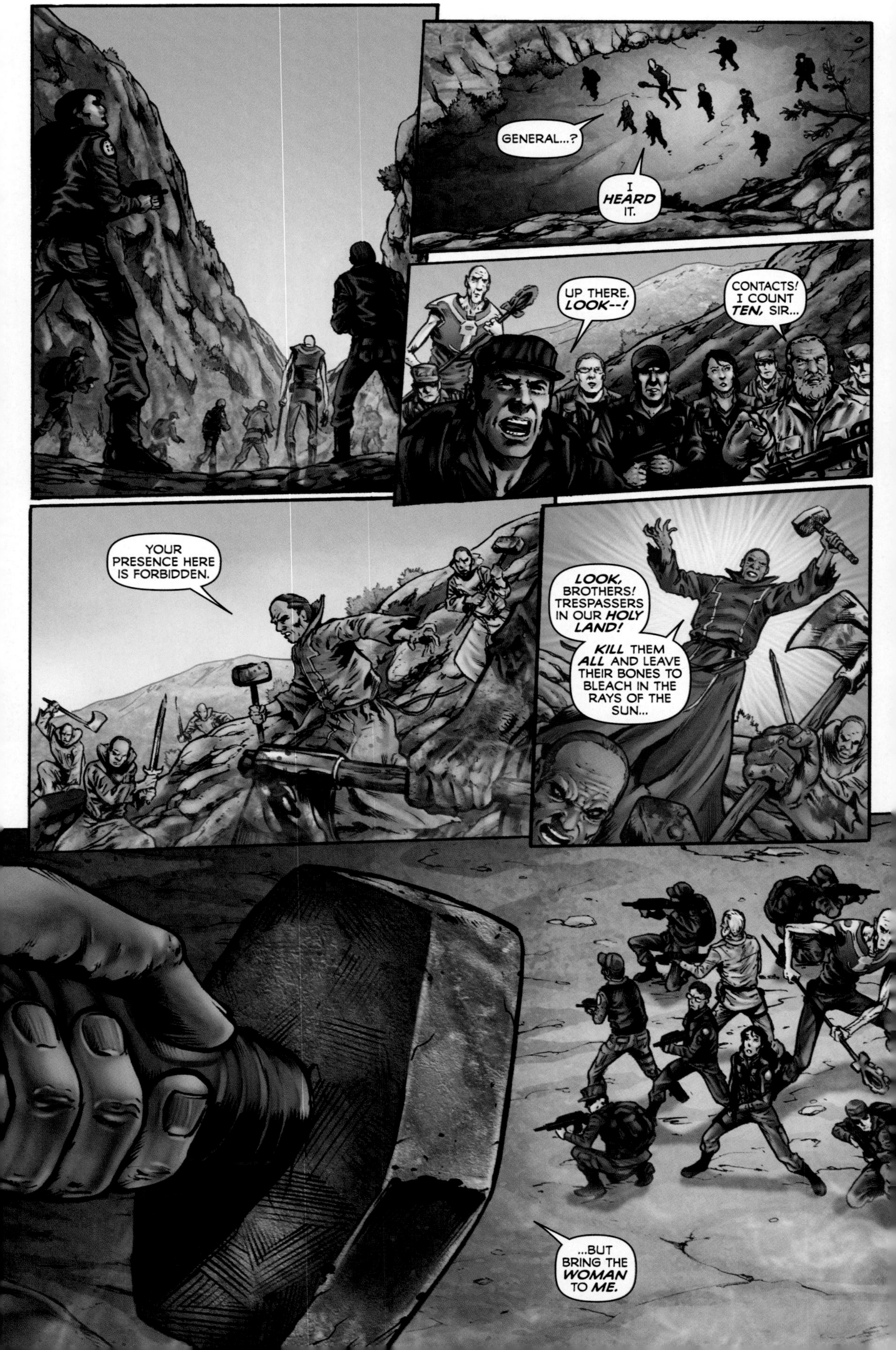
GENERAL...?
I HEARD IT.
UP THERE. LOOK--!
CONTACTS! I COUNT TEN, SIR...
YOUR PRESENCE HERE IS FORBIDDEN.
LOOK, BROTHERS! TRESPASSERS IN OUR HOLY LAND!
KILL THEM ALL AND LEAVE THEIR BONES TO BLEACH IN THE RAYS OF THE SUN...
...BUT BRING THE WOMAN TO ME.

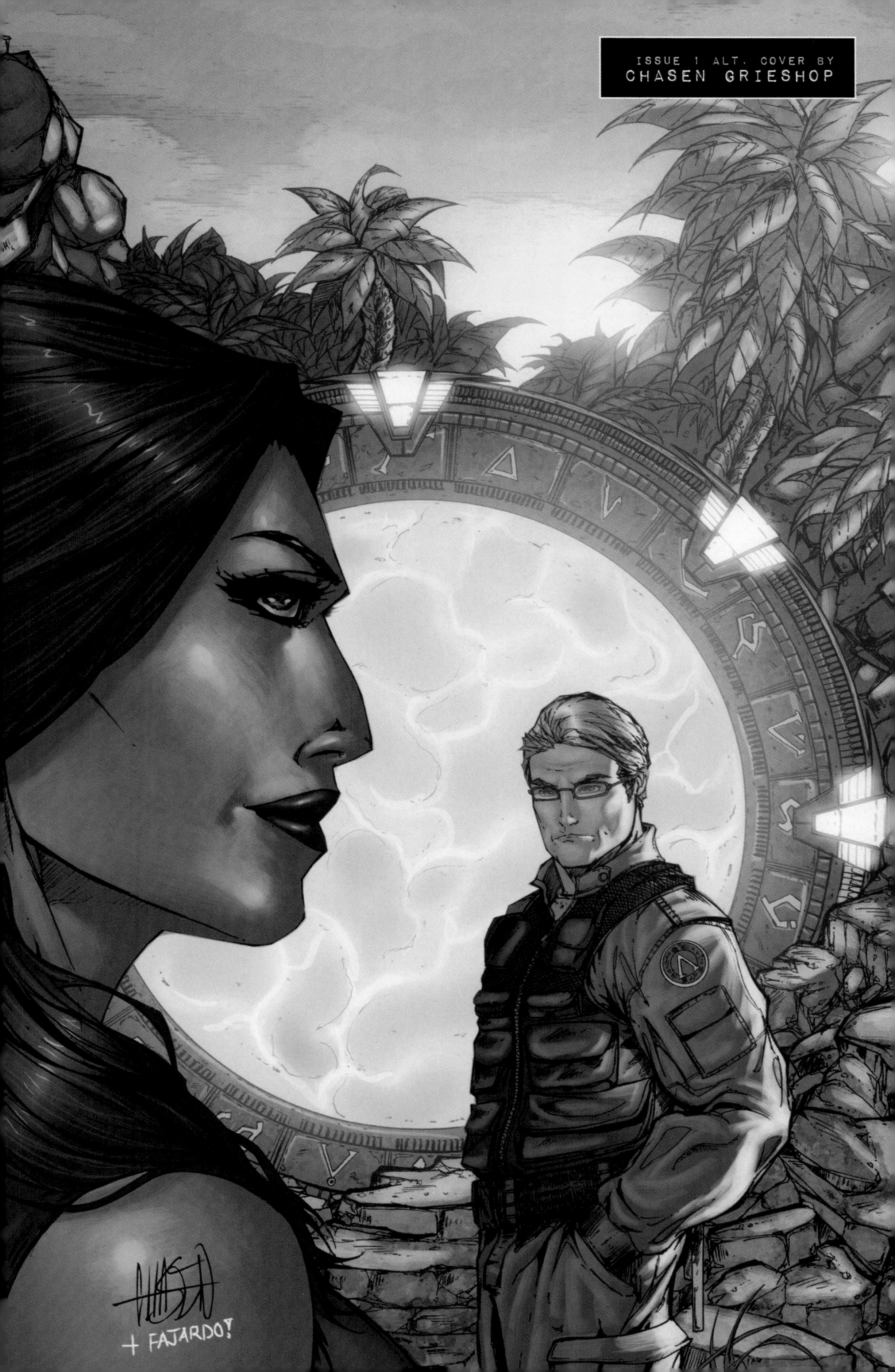
+ FAJARDO!

ISSUE 1 ALT. COVER BY
CHASEN GRIESHOP

ISSUE 4 COVER BY
BRETT BOOTH

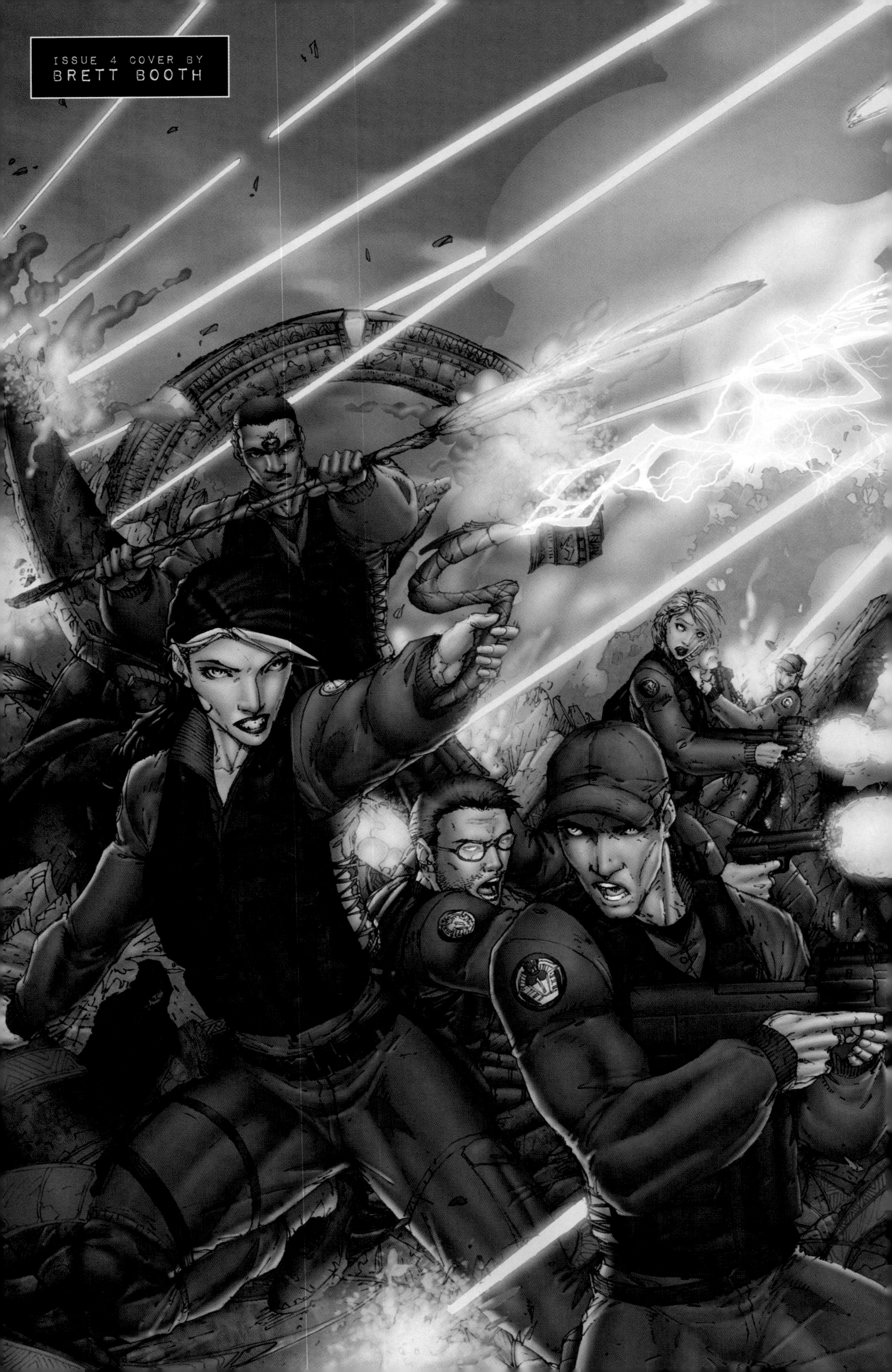

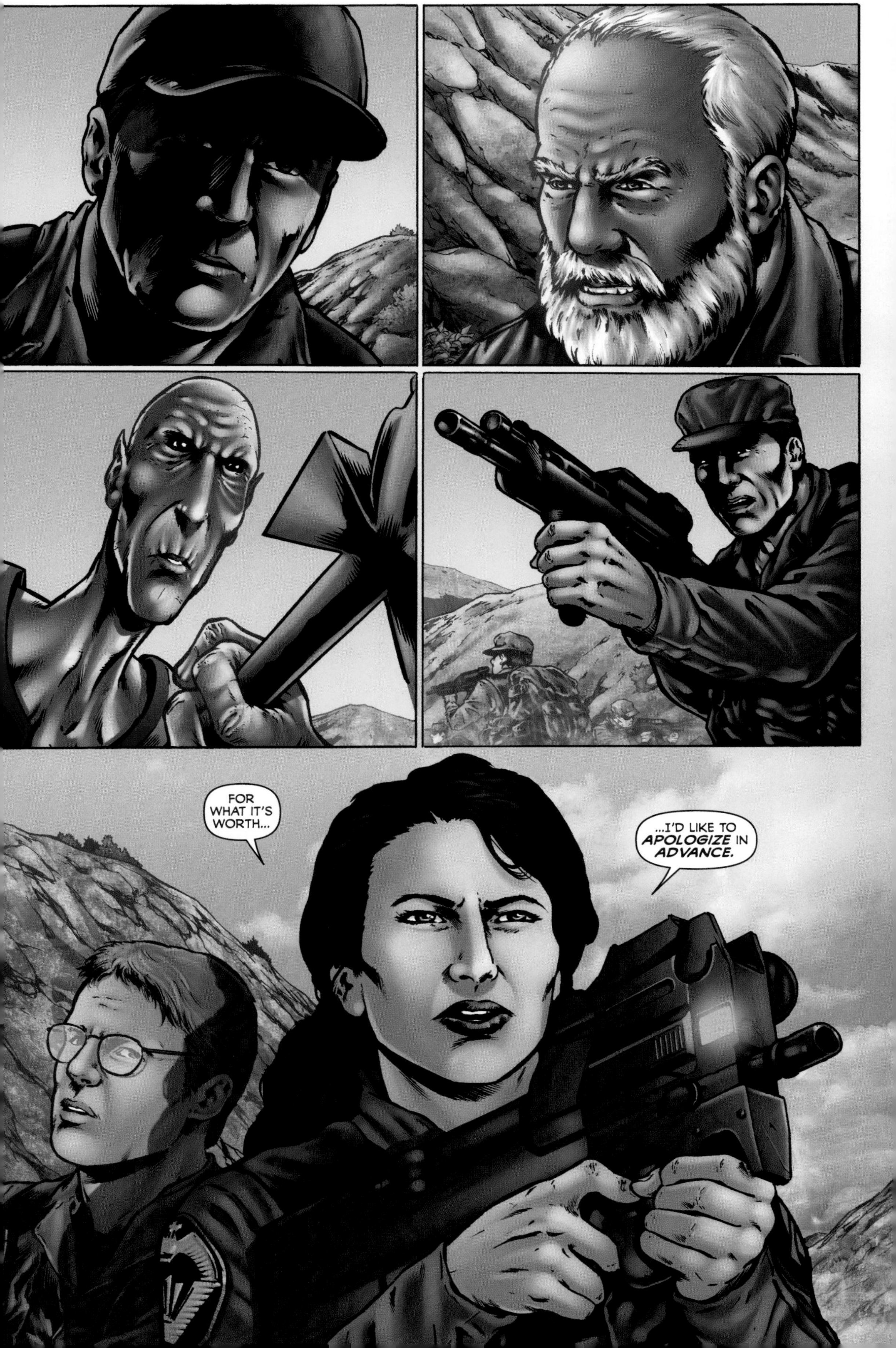
FOR WHAT IT'S WORTH...
...I'D LIKE TO *APOLOGIZE* IN *ADVANCE*.

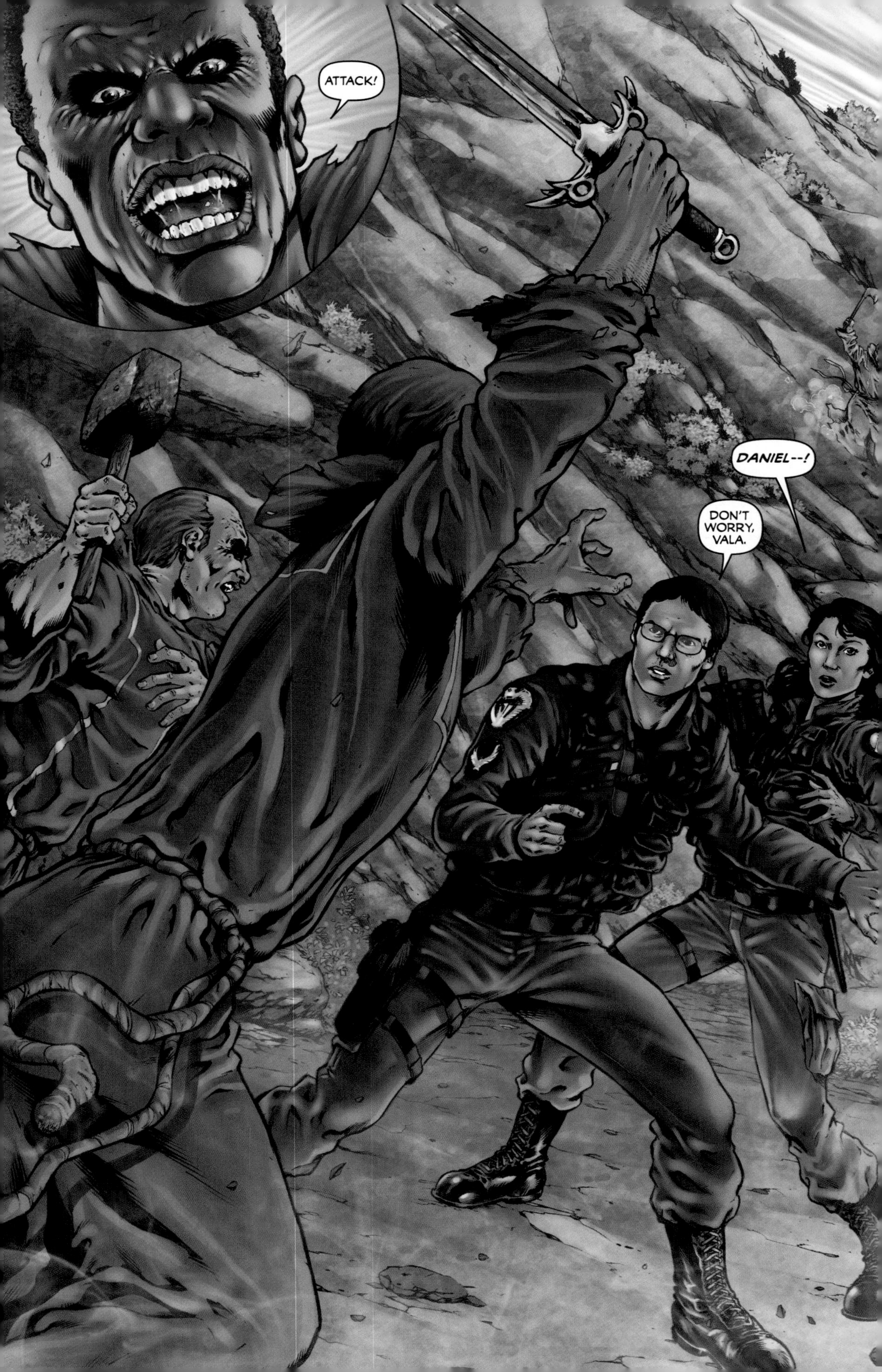
ATTACK!
DANIEL--!
DON'T WORRY, VALA.

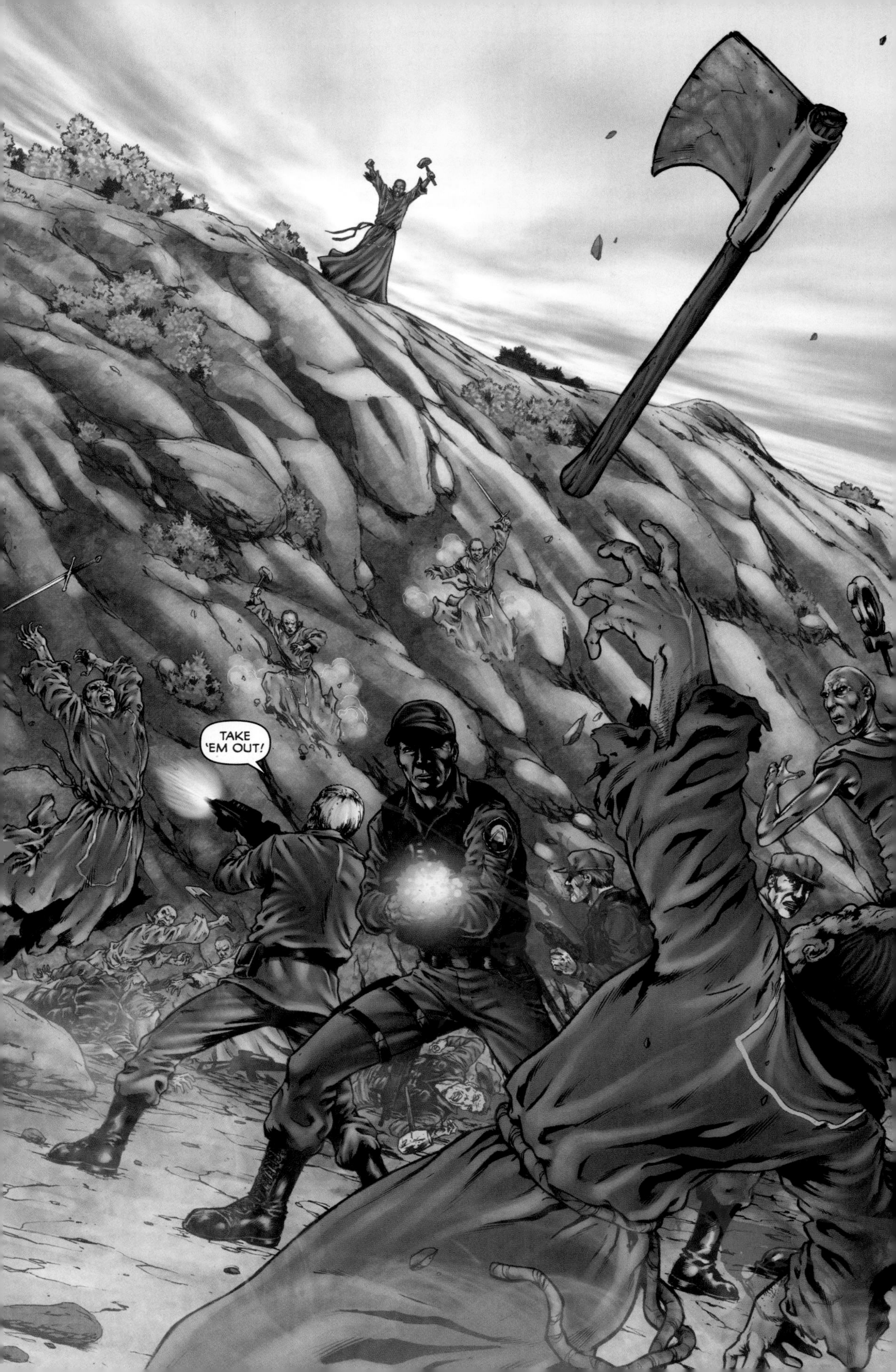
TAKE 'EM OUT!

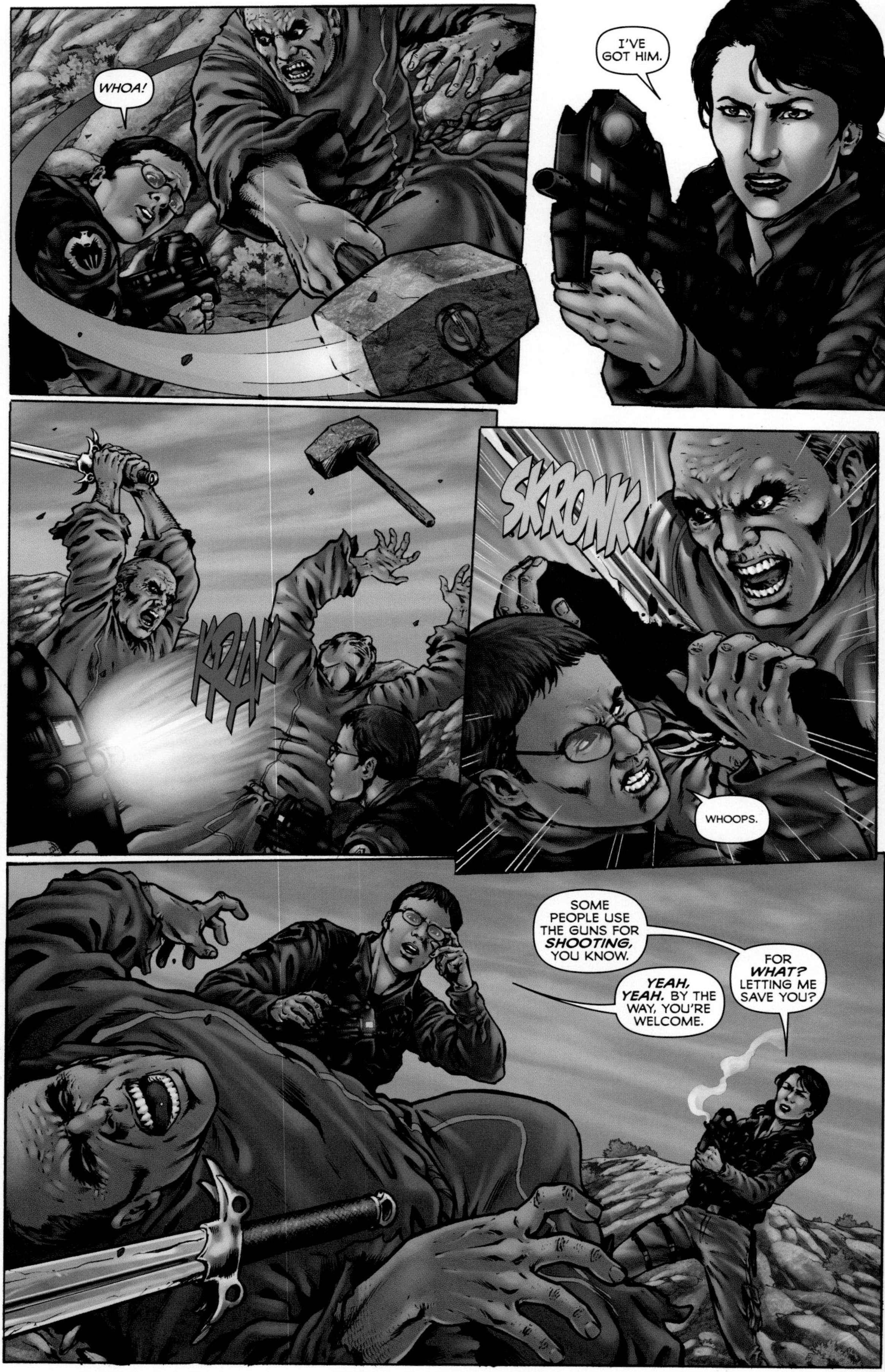
WHOA!
I'VE GOT HIM.
KRAK
SKRONK
WHOOPS.
SOME PEOPLE USE THE GUNS FOR *SHOOTING,* YOU KNOW.
FOR *WHAT?* LETTING ME SAVE YOU?
YEAH, YEAH. BY THE WAY, YOU'RE WELCOME.

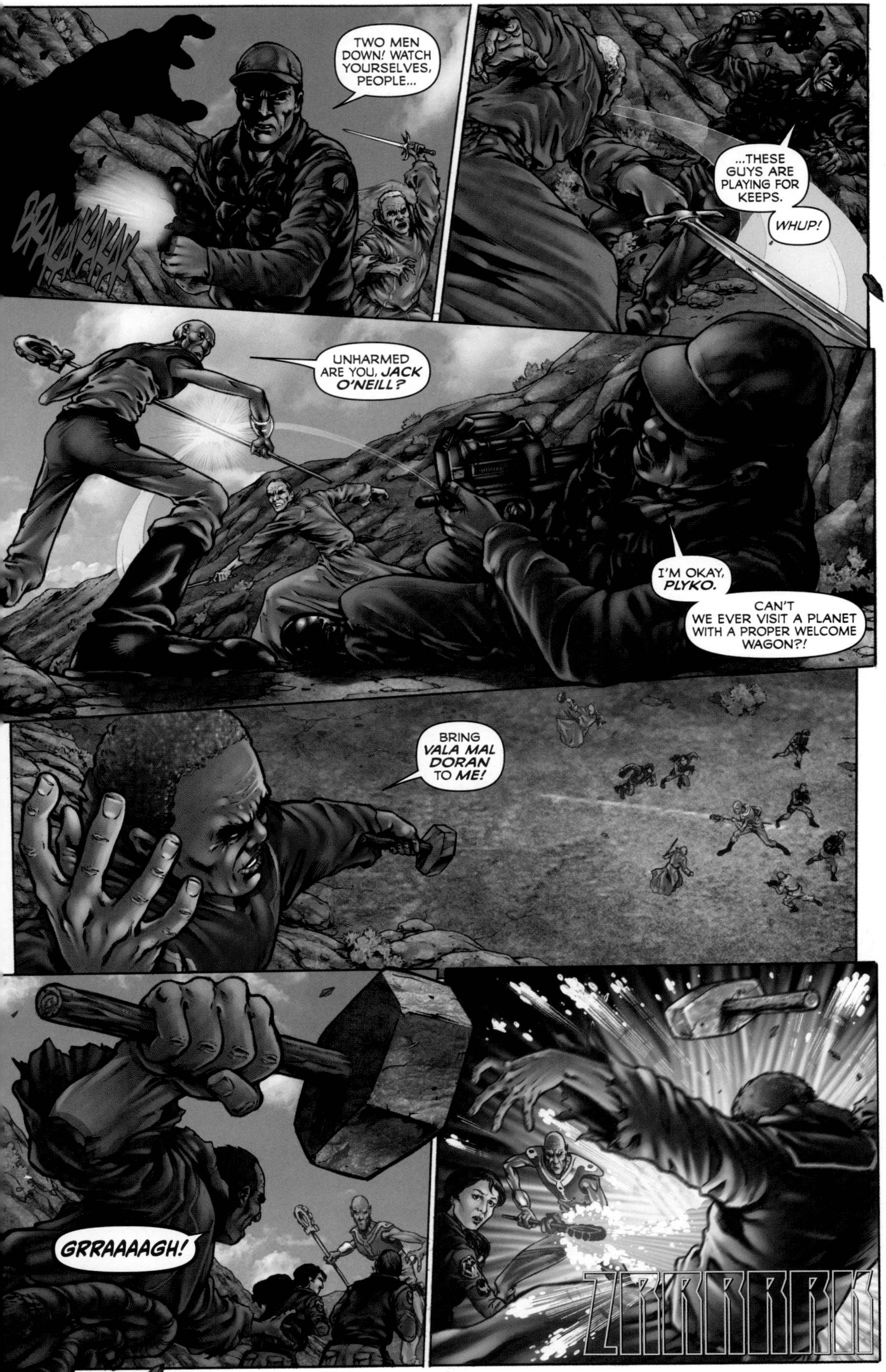
TWO MEN DOWN! WATCH YOURSELVES, PEOPLE...
BRAKAKAKAKAK
...THESE GUYS ARE PLAYING FOR KEEPS.
WHUP!
UNHARMED ARE YOU, JACK O'NEILL?
I'M OKAY, PLYKO.
CAN'T WE EVER VISIT A PLANET WITH A PROPER WELCOME WAGON?!
BRING VALA MAL DORAN TO ME!
GRRAAAAGH!
ZRRRRRRK

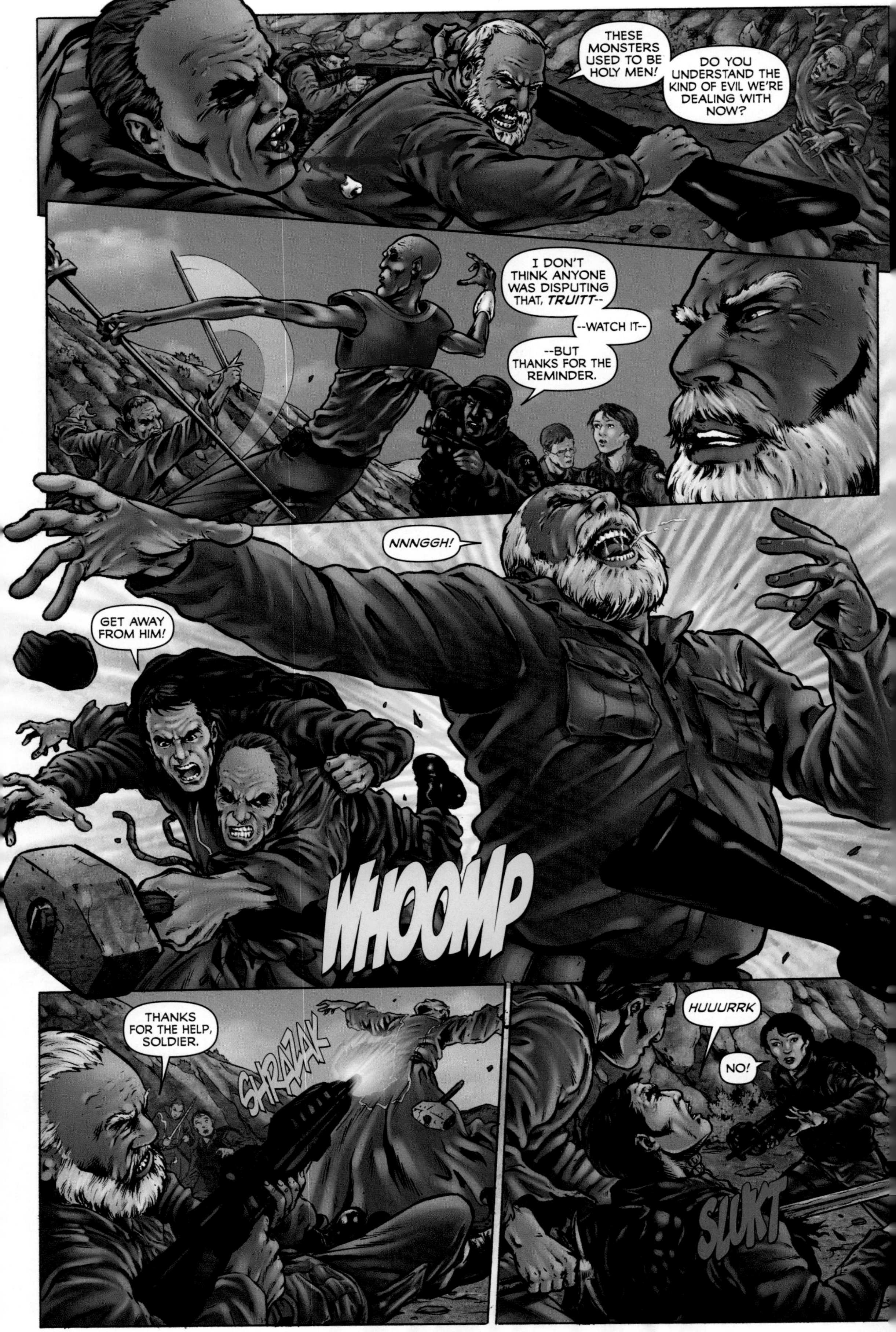
THESE MONSTERS USED TO BE HOLY MEN!
DO YOU UNDERSTAND THE KIND OF EVIL WE'RE DEALING WITH NOW?
I DON'T THINK ANYONE WAS DISPUTING THAT, TRUITT--
--WATCH IT--
--BUT THANKS FOR THE REMINDER.
NNNGGH!
GET AWAY FROM HIM!
WHOOMP
THANKS FOR THE HELP, SOLDIER.
SHRAZAK
HUUURRK
NO!
SLUKT

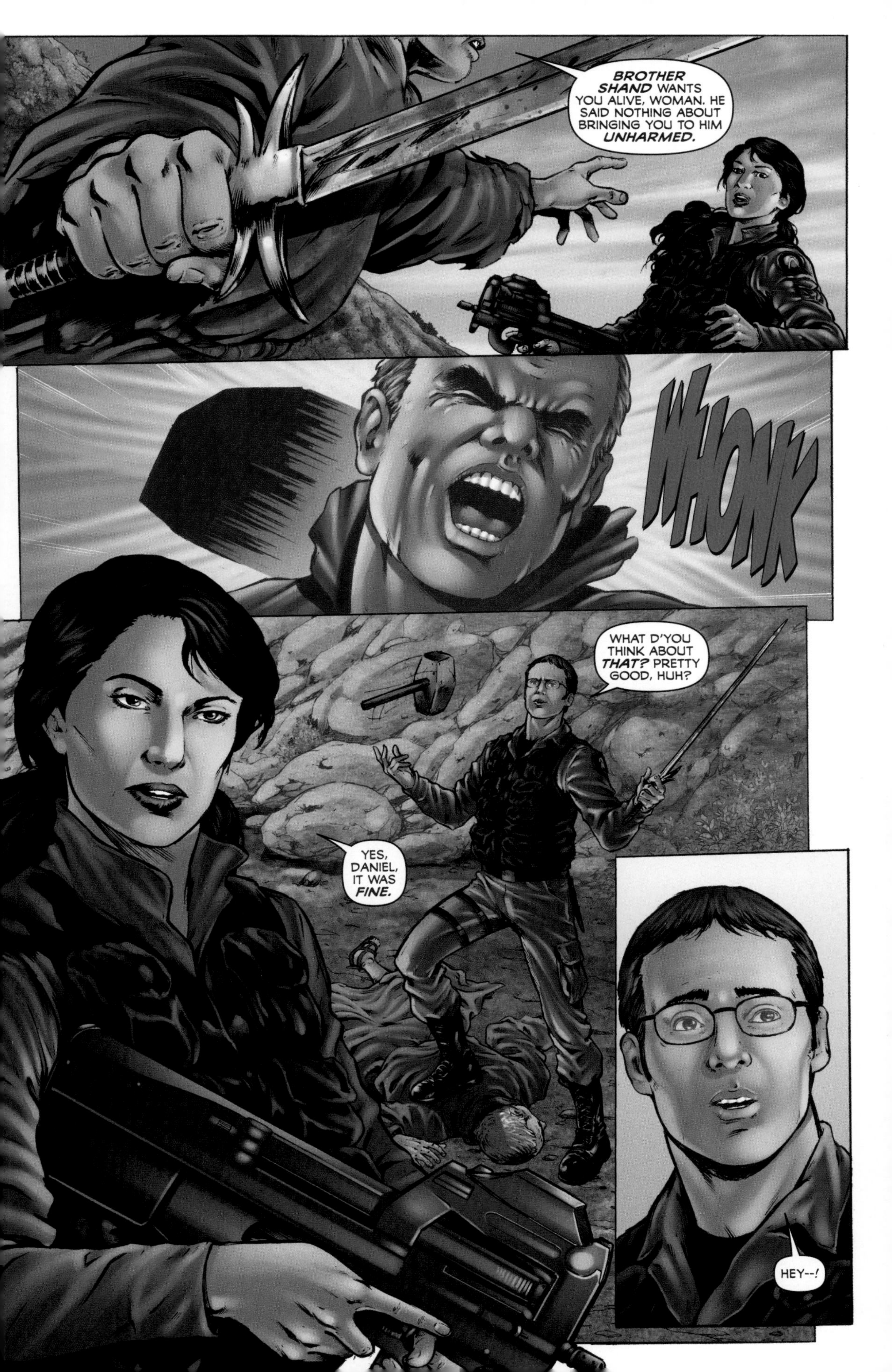
BROTHER SHAND WANTS YOU ALIVE, WOMAN. HE SAID NOTHING ABOUT BRINGING YOU TO HIM UNHARMED.
WHONK
WHAT D'YOU THINK ABOUT THAT? PRETTY GOOD, HUH?
YES, DANIEL, IT WAS FINE.
HEY--!

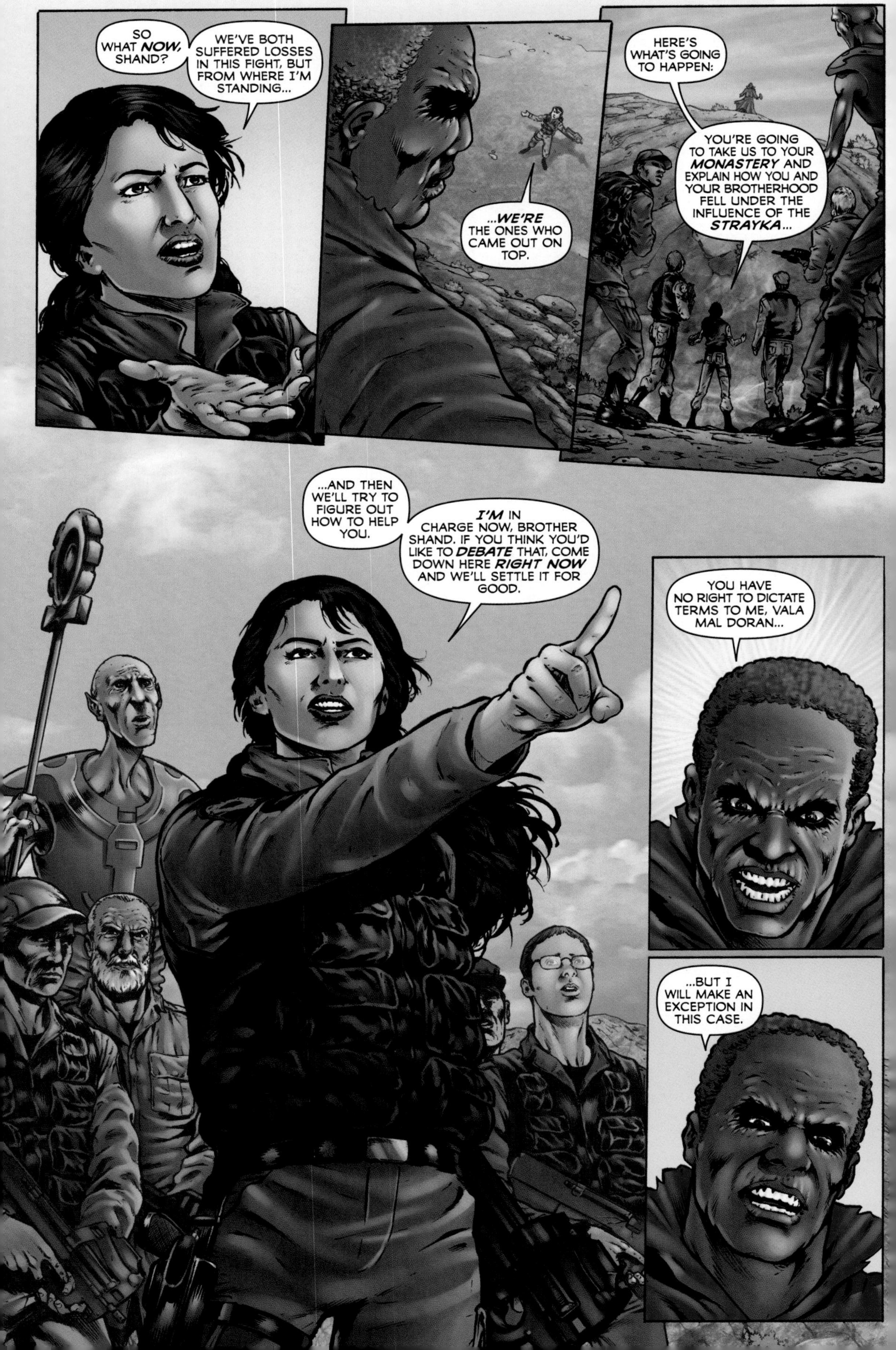

SO WHAT *NOW,* SHAND?
WE'VE BOTH SUFFERED LOSSES IN THIS FIGHT, BUT FROM WHERE I'M STANDING...
...*WE'RE* THE ONES WHO CAME OUT ON TOP.
HERE'S WHAT'S GOING TO HAPPEN:
YOU'RE GOING TO TAKE US TO YOUR *MONASTERY* AND EXPLAIN HOW YOU AND YOUR BROTHERHOOD FELL UNDER THE INFLUENCE OF THE *STRAYKA*...
...AND THEN WE'LL TRY TO FIGURE OUT HOW TO HELP YOU.
I'M IN CHARGE NOW, BROTHER SHAND. IF YOU THINK YOU'D LIKE TO *DEBATE* THAT, COME DOWN HERE *RIGHT NOW* AND WE'LL SETTLE IT FOR GOOD.
YOU HAVE NO RIGHT TO DICTATE TERMS TO ME, VALA MAL DORAN...
...BUT I WILL MAKE AN EXCEPTION IN THIS CASE.

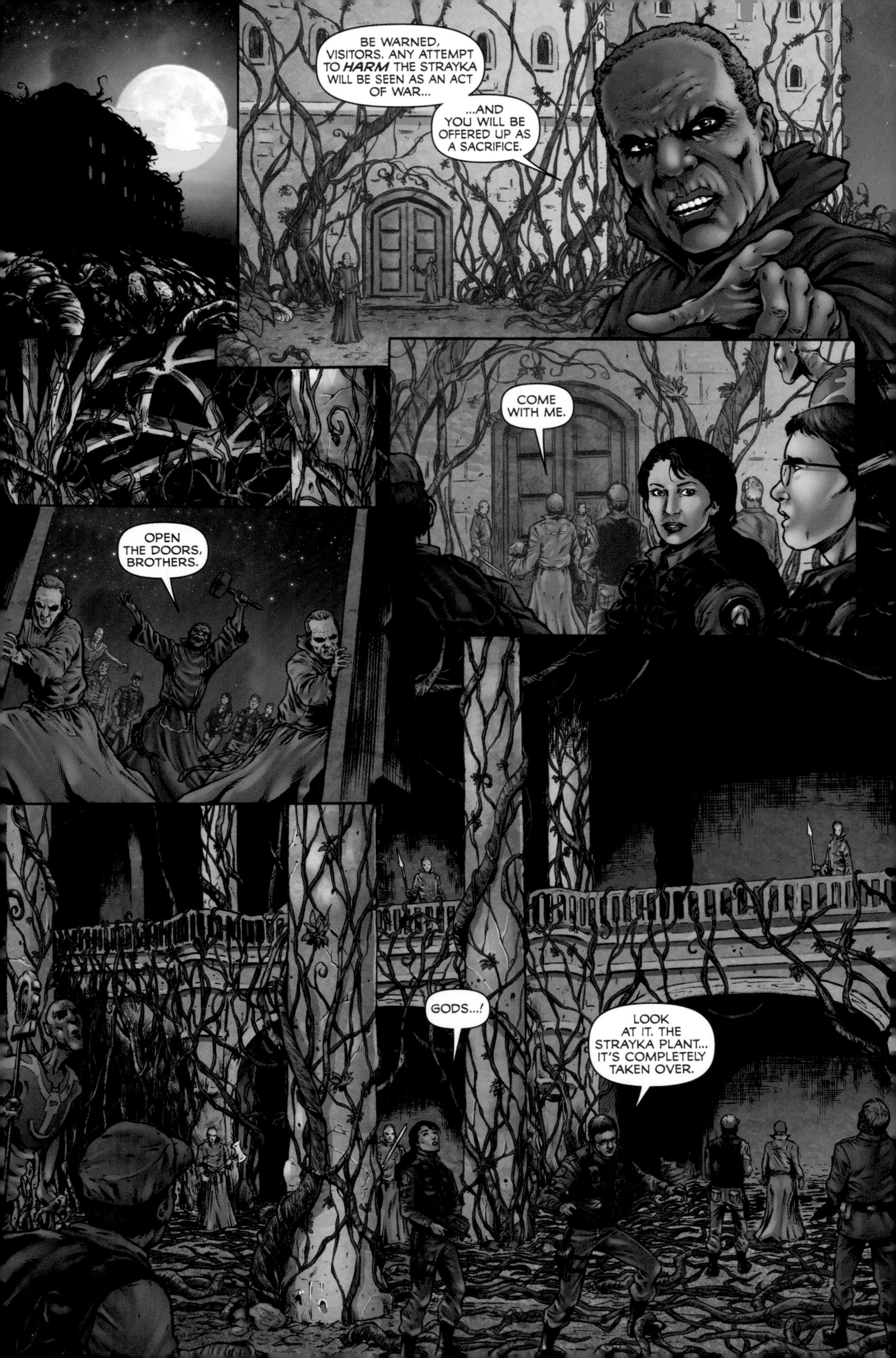
BE WARNED, VISITORS. ANY ATTEMPT TO *HARM* THE STRAYKA WILL BE SEEN AS AN ACT OF WAR...
...AND YOU WILL BE OFFERED UP AS A SACRIFICE.
OPEN THE DOORS, BROTHERS.
COME WITH ME.
GODS...!
LOOK AT IT. THE STRAYKA PLANT... IT'S COMPLETELY TAKEN OVER.

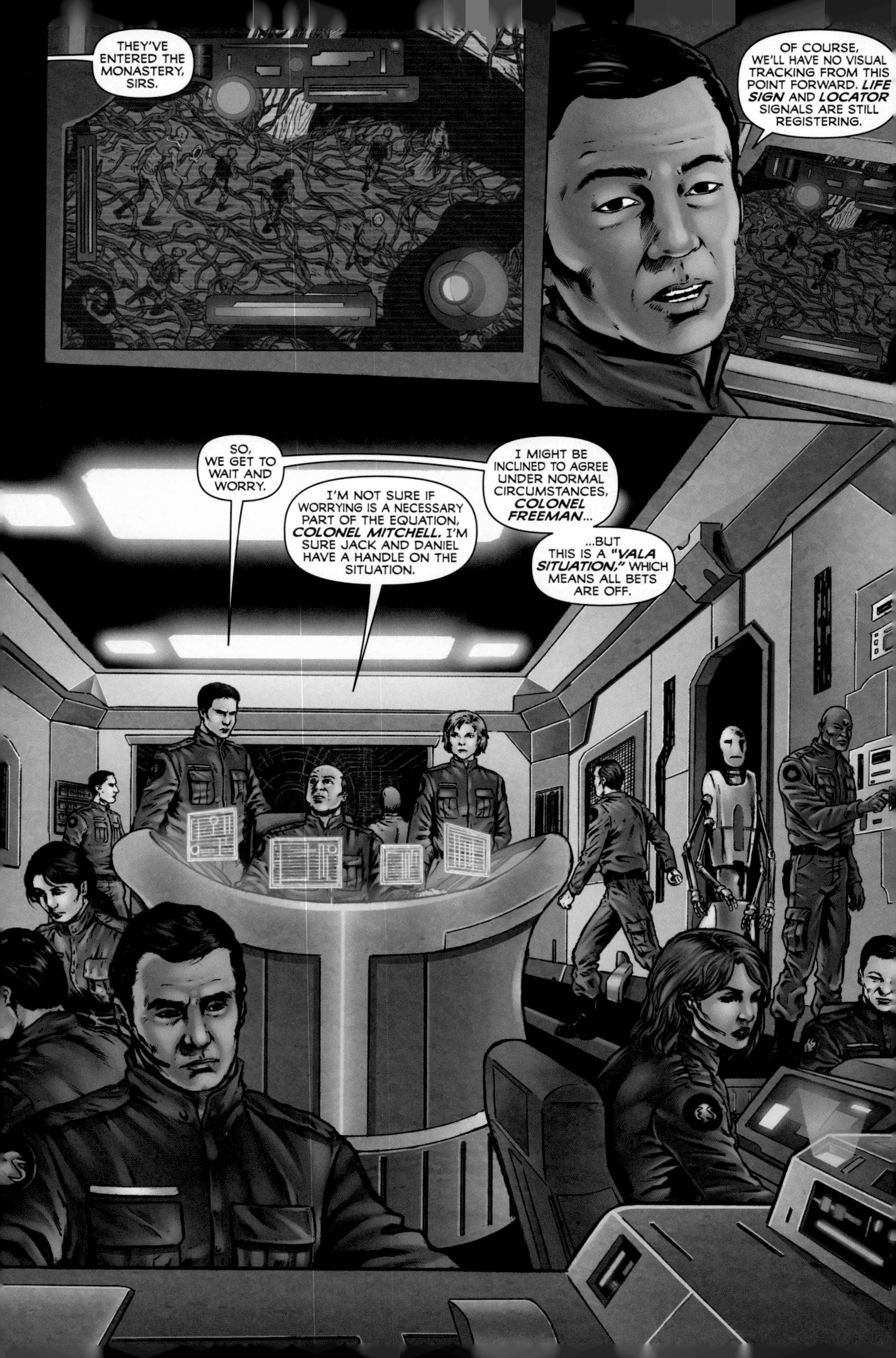
THEY'VE ENTERED THE MONASTERY, SIRS.
OF COURSE, WE'LL HAVE NO VISUAL TRACKING FROM THIS POINT FORWARD. LIFE SIGN AND LOCATOR SIGNALS ARE STILL REGISTERING.
SO, WE GET TO WAIT AND WORRY.
I'M NOT SURE IF WORRYING IS A NECESSARY PART OF THE EQUATION, COLONEL MITCHELL. I'M SURE JACK AND DANIEL HAVE A HANDLE ON THE SITUATION.
I MIGHT BE INCLINED TO AGREE UNDER NORMAL CIRCUMSTANCES, COLONEL FREEMAN...
...BUT THIS IS A "VALA SITUATION," WHICH MEANS ALL BETS ARE OFF.

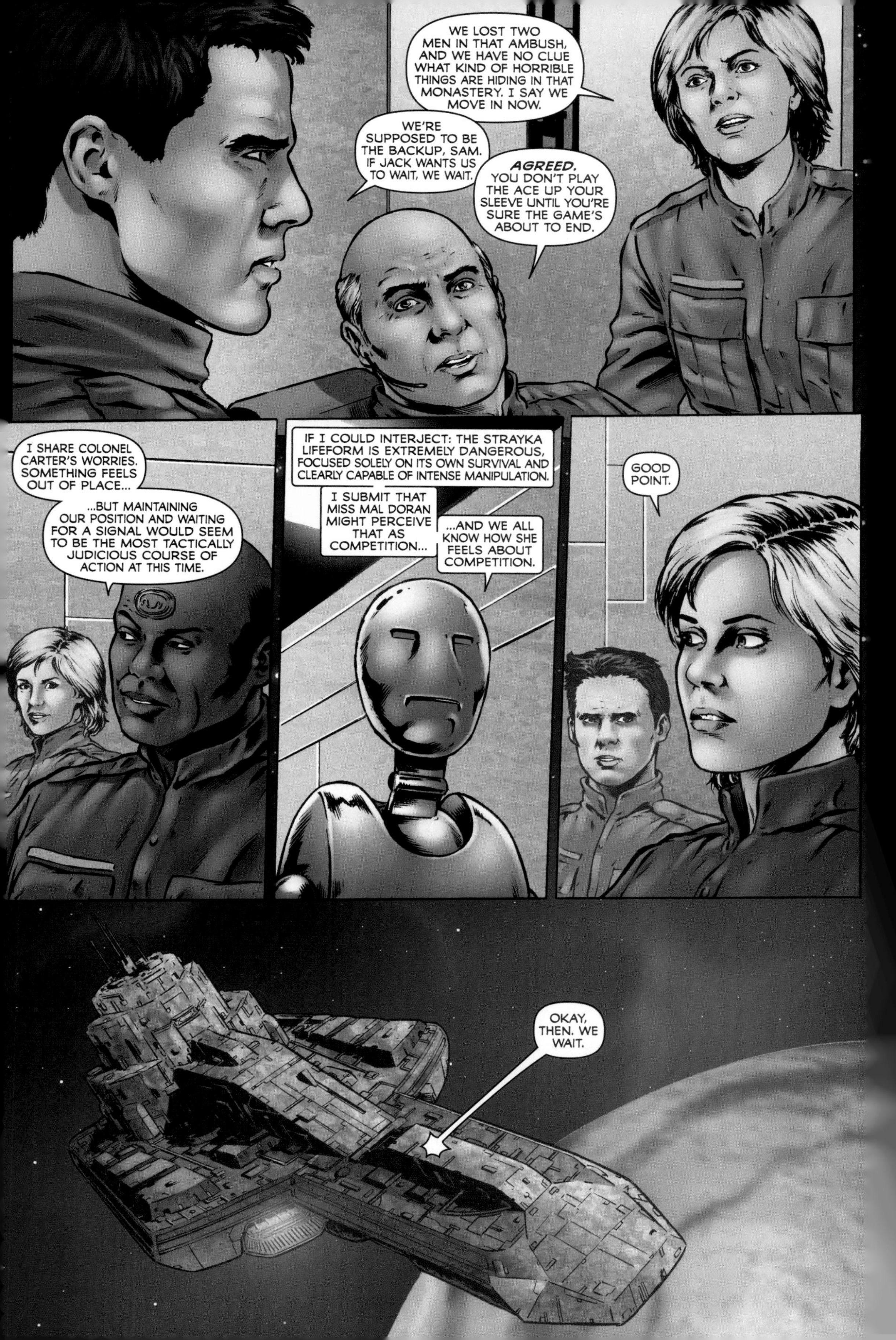
WE LOST TWO MEN IN THAT AMBUSH, AND WE HAVE NO CLUE WHAT KIND OF HORRIBLE THINGS ARE HIDING IN THAT MONASTERY. I SAY WE MOVE IN NOW.
WE'RE SUPPOSED TO BE THE BACKUP, SAM. IF JACK WANTS US TO WAIT, WE WAIT.
AGREED. YOU DON'T PLAY THE ACE UP YOUR SLEEVE UNTIL YOU'RE SURE THE GAME'S ABOUT TO END.
I SHARE COLONEL CARTER'S WORRIES. SOMETHING FEELS OUT OF PLACE...
...BUT MAINTAINING OUR POSITION AND WAITING FOR A SIGNAL WOULD SEEM TO BE THE MOST TACTICALLY JUDICIOUS COURSE OF ACTION AT THIS TIME.
IF I COULD INTERJECT: THE STRAYKA LIFEFORM IS EXTREMELY DANGEROUS, FOCUSED SOLELY ON ITS OWN SURVIVAL AND CLEARLY CAPABLE OF INTENSE MANIPULATION.
I SUBMIT THAT MISS MAL DORAN MIGHT PERCEIVE THAT AS COMPETITION...
...AND WE ALL KNOW HOW SHE FEELS ABOUT COMPETITION.
GOOD POINT.
OKAY, THEN. WE WAIT.

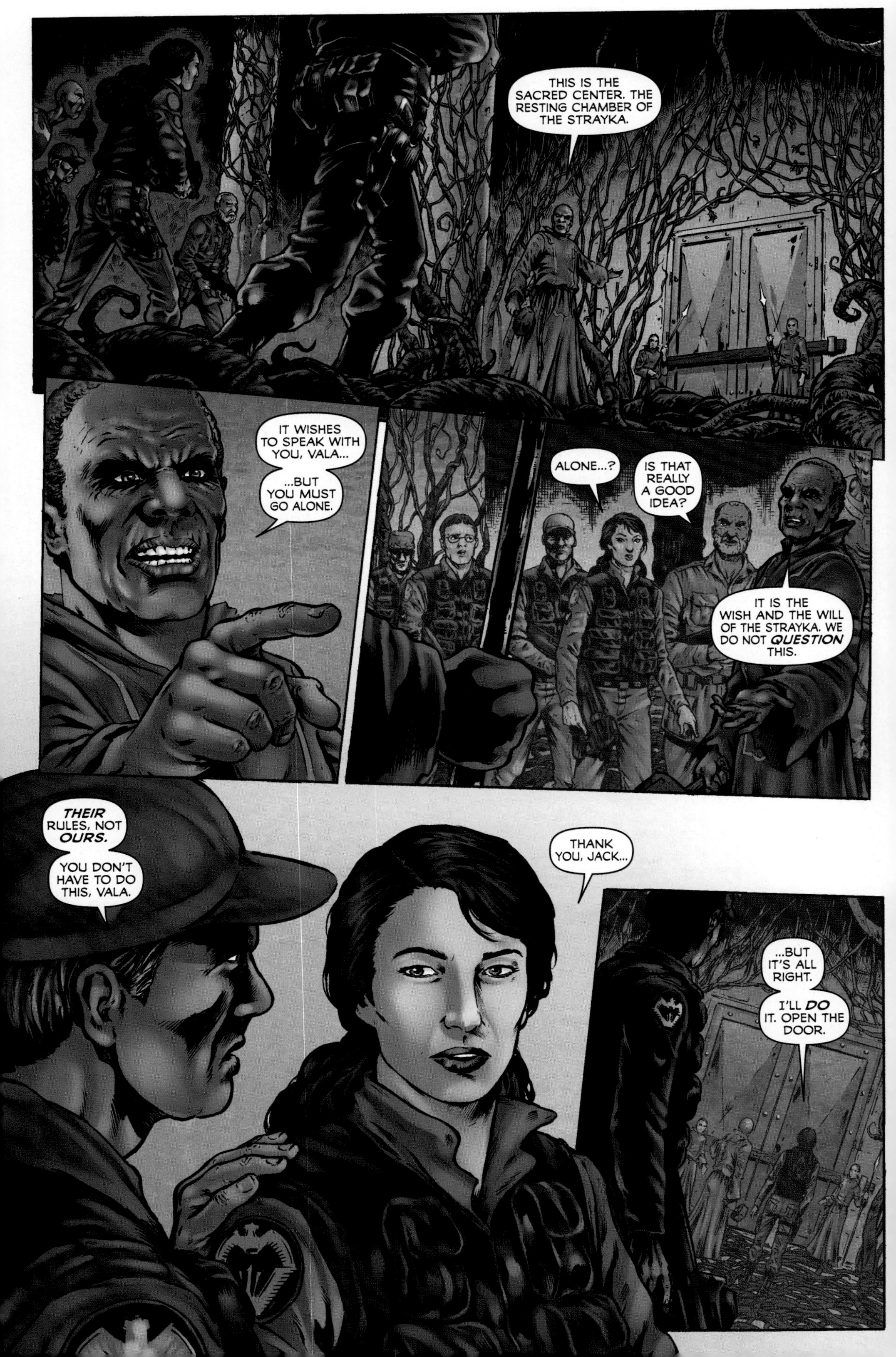
THIS IS THE SACRED CENTER. THE RESTING CHAMBER OF THE STRAYKA.
IT WISHES TO SPEAK WITH YOU, VALA...
...BUT YOU MUST GO ALONE.
ALONE...?
IS THAT REALLY A GOOD IDEA?
IT IS THE WISH AND THE WILL OF THE STRAYKA. WE DO NOT QUESTION THIS.
THEIR RULES, NOT OURS.
YOU DON'T HAVE TO DO THIS, VALA.
THANK YOU, JACK...
...BUT IT'S ALL RIGHT.
I'LL DO IT. OPEN THE DOOR.

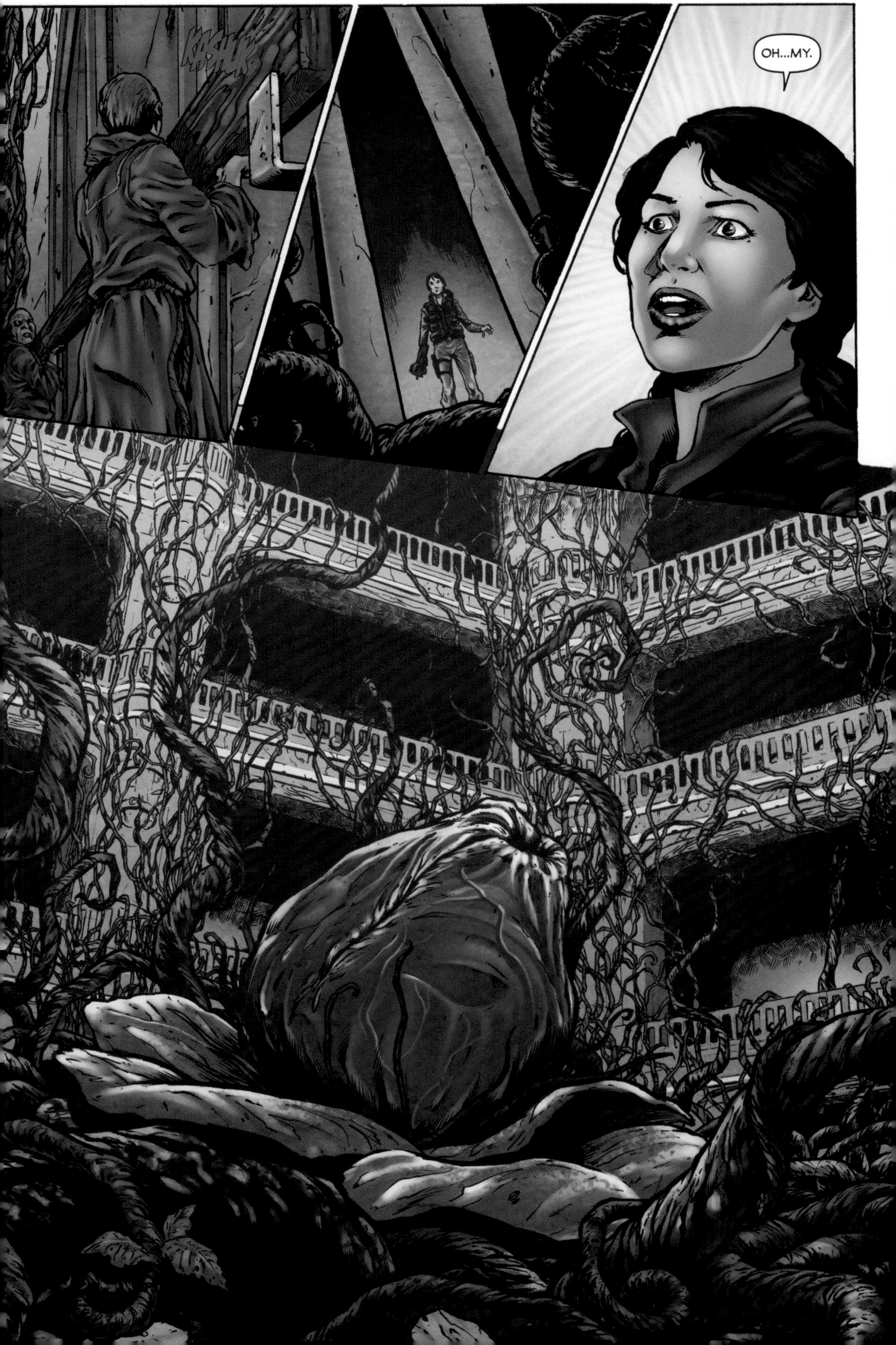
KASHUK
OH...MY.

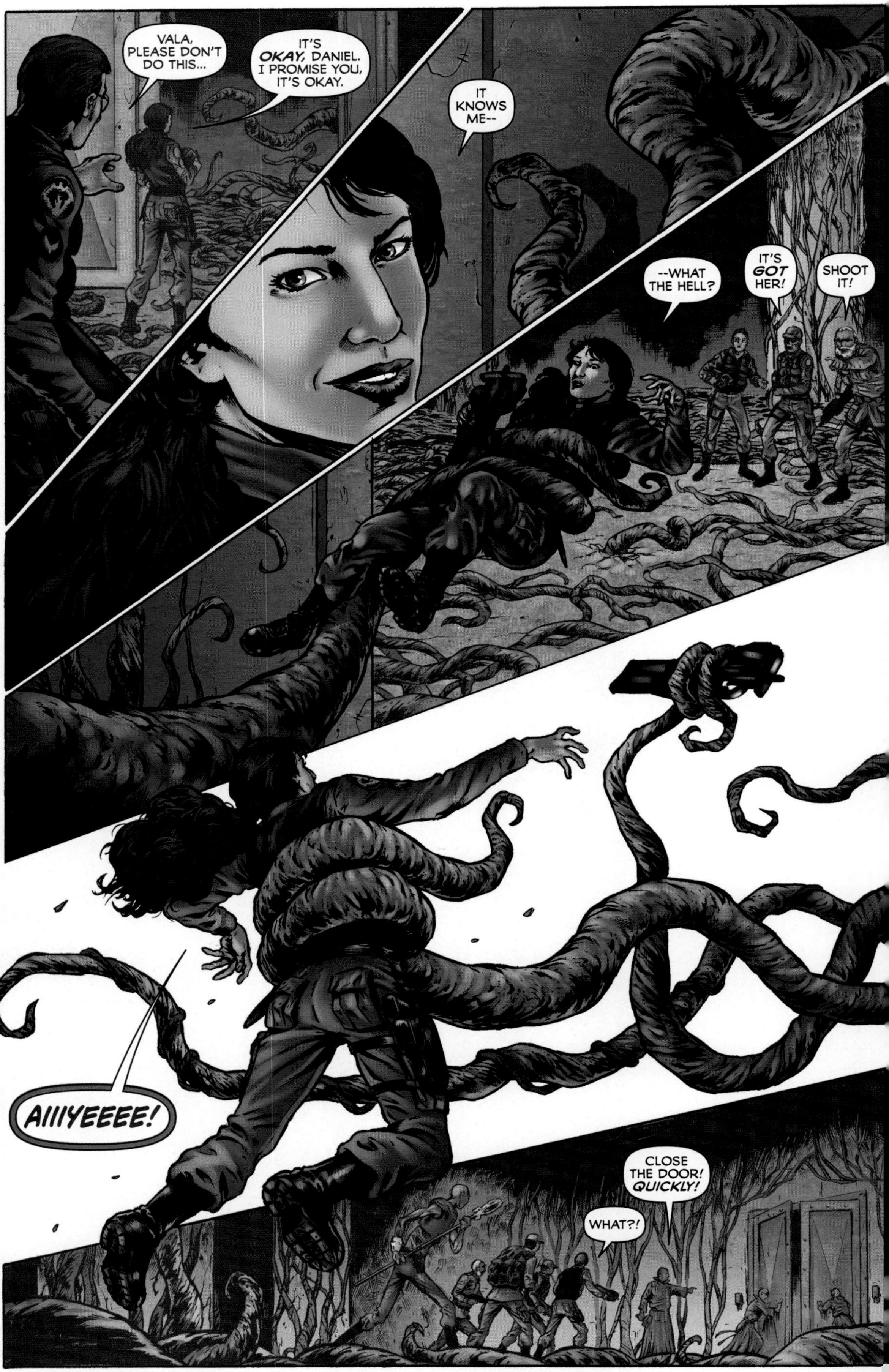
VALA, PLEASE DON'T DO THIS...
IT'S *OKAY,* DANIEL. I PROMISE YOU, IT'S OKAY.
IT KNOWS ME--
--WHAT THE HELL?
IT'S *GOT* HER!
SHOOT IT!
AIIIYEEEE!
CLOSE THE DOOR! *QUICKLY!*
WHAT?!

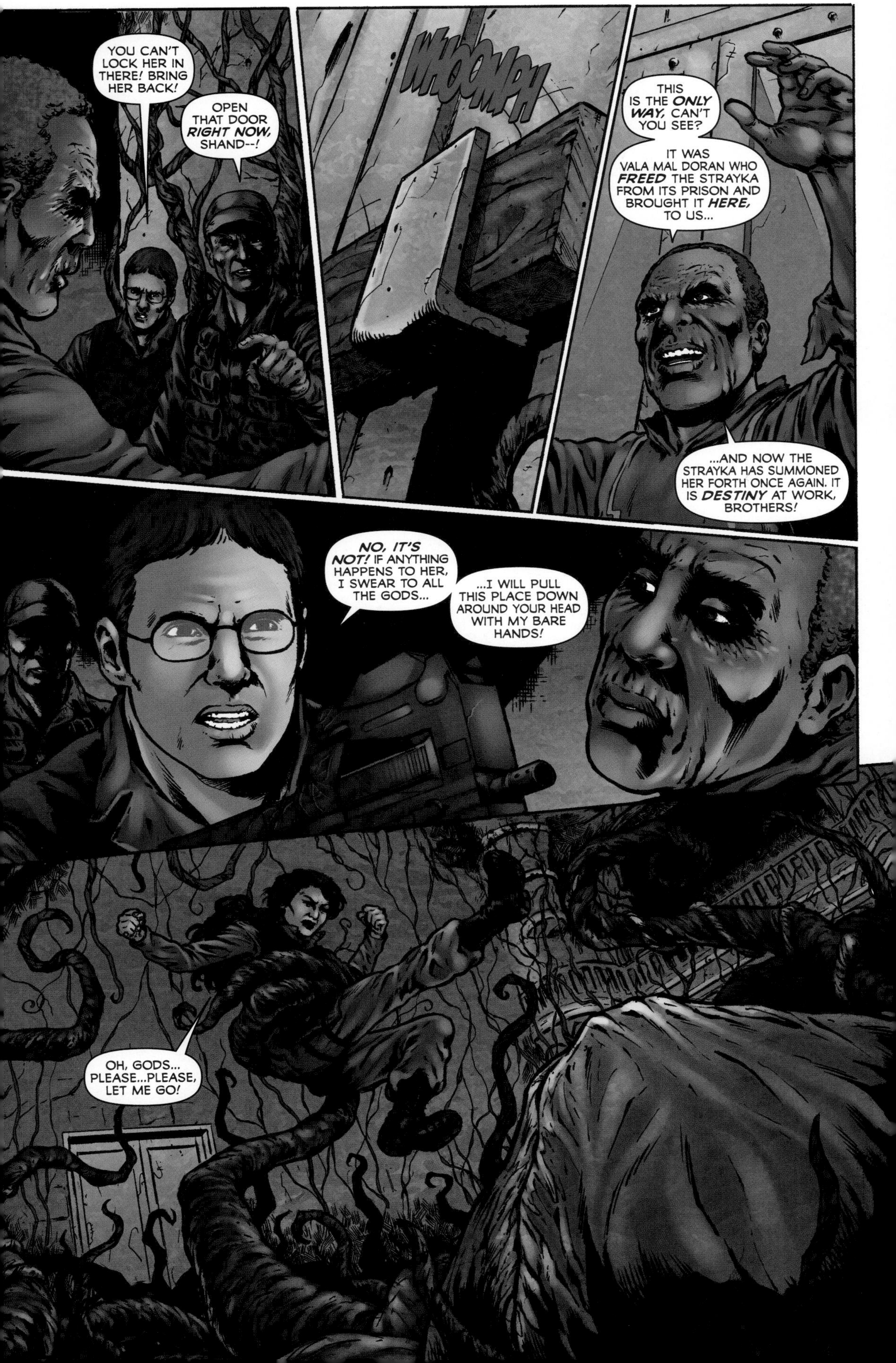
YOU CAN'T LOCK HER IN THERE! BRING HER BACK!
OPEN THAT DOOR RIGHT NOW, SHAND--!
WHOOMPH
THIS IS THE ONLY WAY, CAN'T YOU SEE?
IT WAS VALA MAL DORAN WHO FREED THE STRAYKA FROM ITS PRISON AND BROUGHT IT HERE, TO US...
...AND NOW THE STRAYKA HAS SUMMONED HER FORTH ONCE AGAIN. IT IS DESTINY AT WORK, BROTHERS!
NO, IT'S NOT! IF ANYTHING HAPPENS TO HER, I SWEAR TO ALL THE GODS...
...I WILL PULL THIS PLACE DOWN AROUND YOUR HEAD WITH MY BARE HANDS!
OH, GODS... PLEASE...PLEASE, LET ME GO!

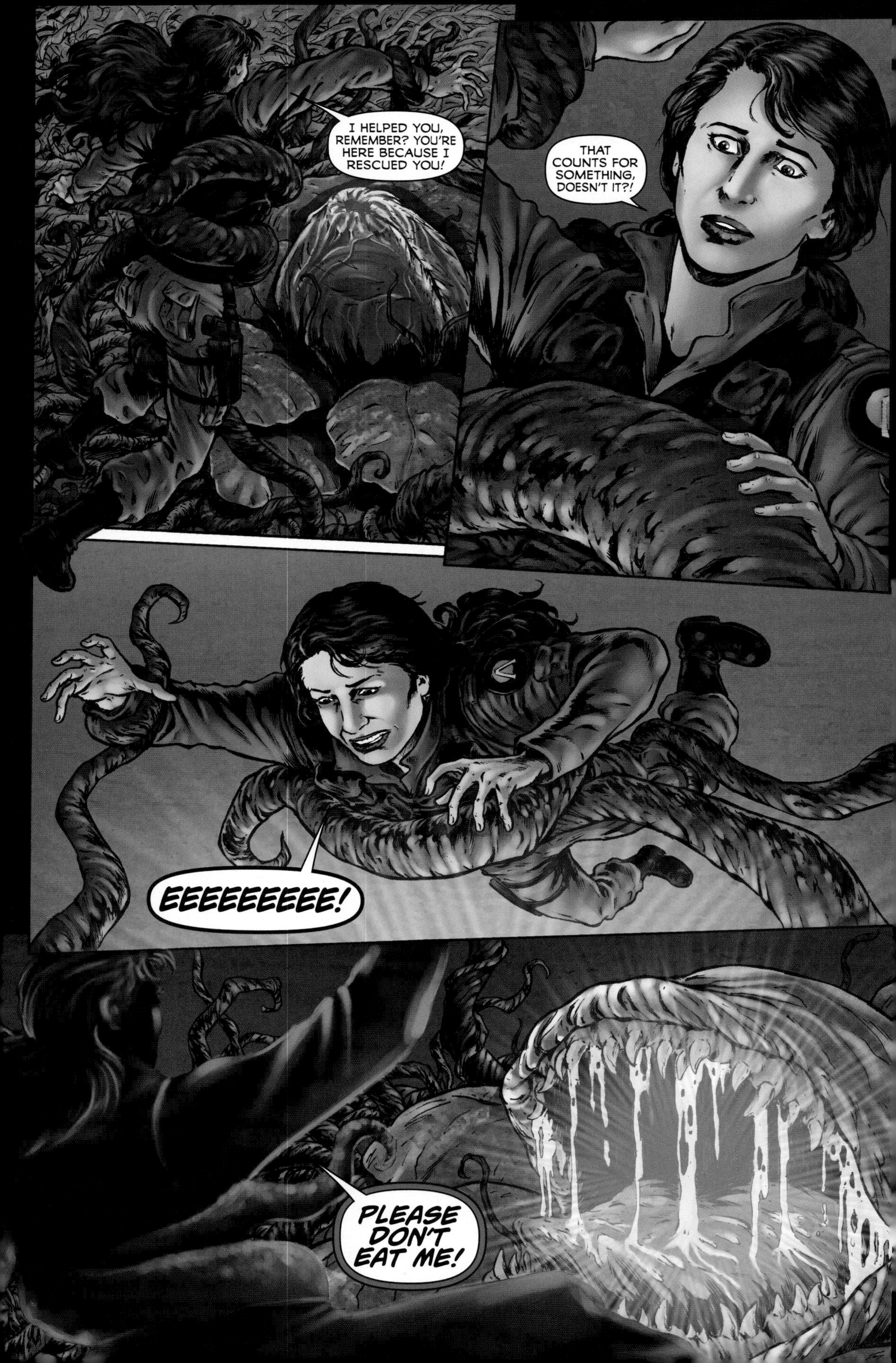
I HELPED YOU, REMEMBER? YOU'RE HERE BECAUSE I RESCUED YOU!
THAT COUNTS FOR SOMETHING, DOESN'T IT?!
EEEEEEEEEE!
PLEASE DON'T EAT ME!

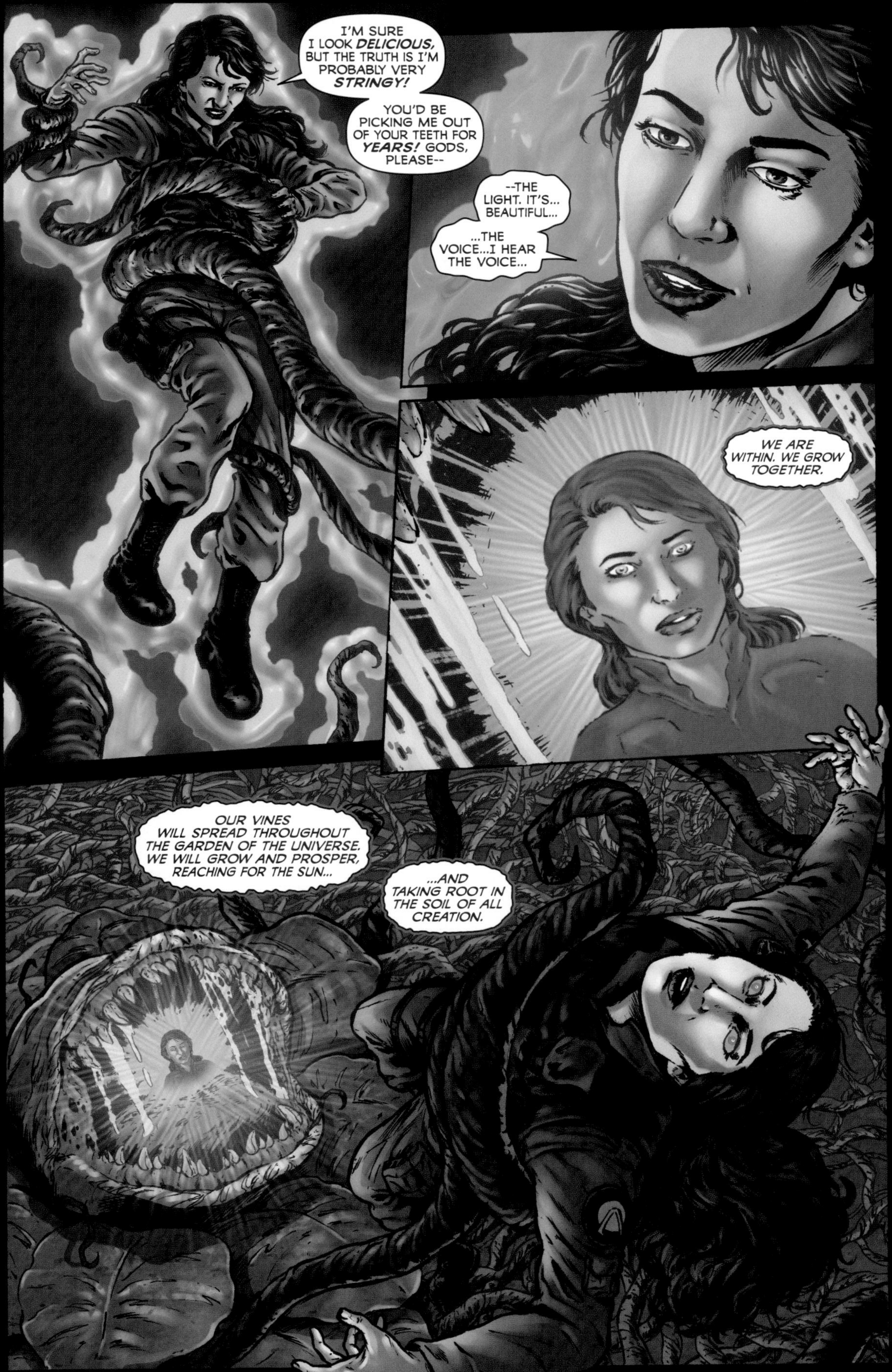
I'M SURE I LOOK **DELICIOUS,** BUT THE TRUTH IS I'M PROBABLY VERY **STRINGY!**
YOU'D BE PICKING ME OUT OF YOUR TEETH FOR **YEARS!** GODS, PLEASE--
--THE LIGHT. IT'S... BEAUTIFUL...
...THE VOICE...I HEAR THE VOICE...
WE ARE WITHIN. WE GROW TOGETHER.
OUR VINES WILL SPREAD THROUGHOUT THE GARDEN OF THE UNIVERSE. WE WILL GROW AND PROSPER, REACHING FOR THE SUN...
...AND TAKING ROOT IN THE SOIL OF ALL CREATION.

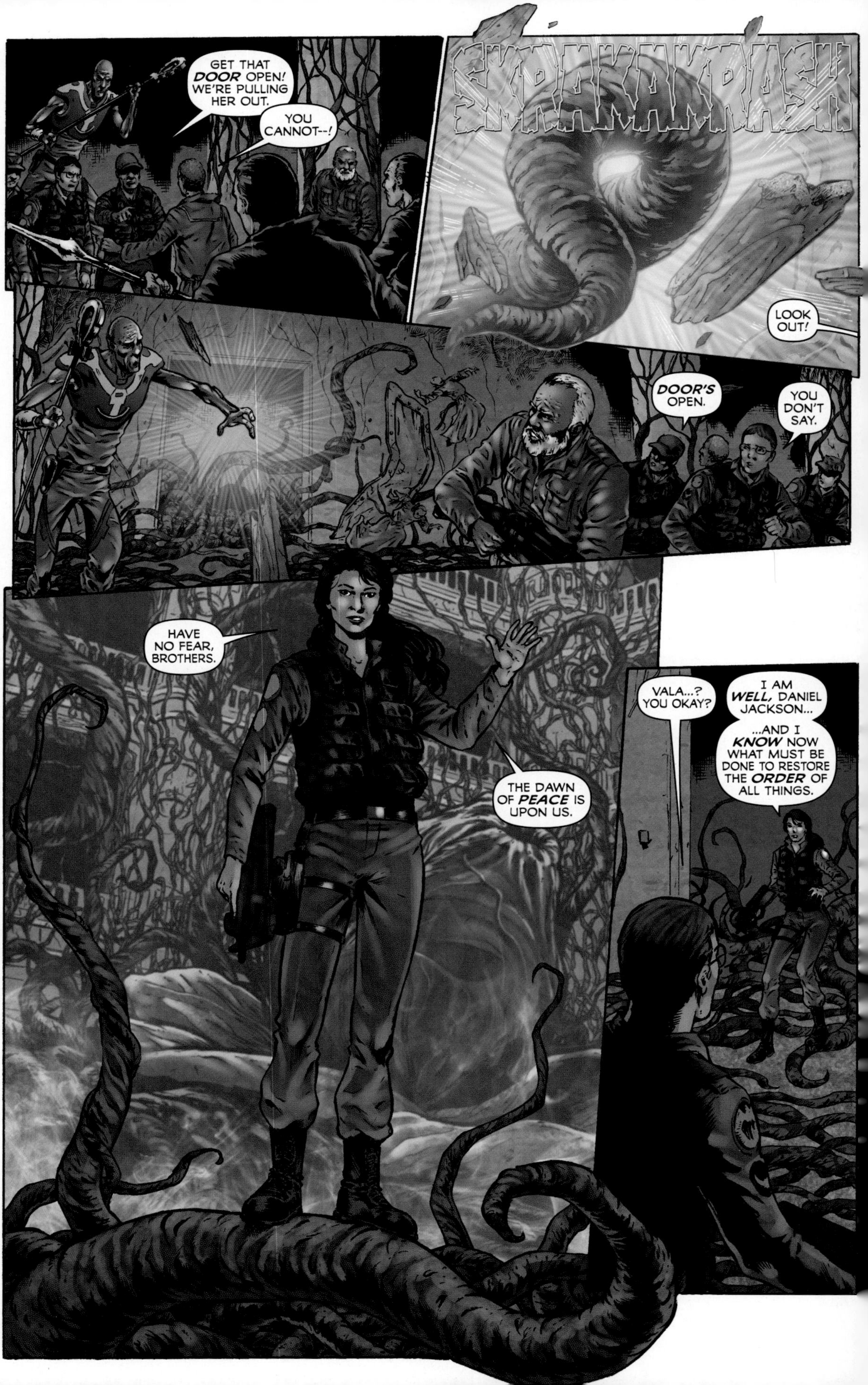
GET THAT DOOR OPEN! WE'RE PULLING HER OUT.
YOU CANNOT--!
SKRAKAKRASH
LOOK OUT!
DOOR'S OPEN.
YOU DON'T SAY.
HAVE NO FEAR, BROTHERS.
THE DAWN OF PEACE IS UPON US.
VALA...? YOU OKAY?
I AM WELL, DANIEL JACKSON...
...AND I KNOW NOW WHAT MUST BE DONE TO RESTORE THE ORDER OF ALL THINGS.

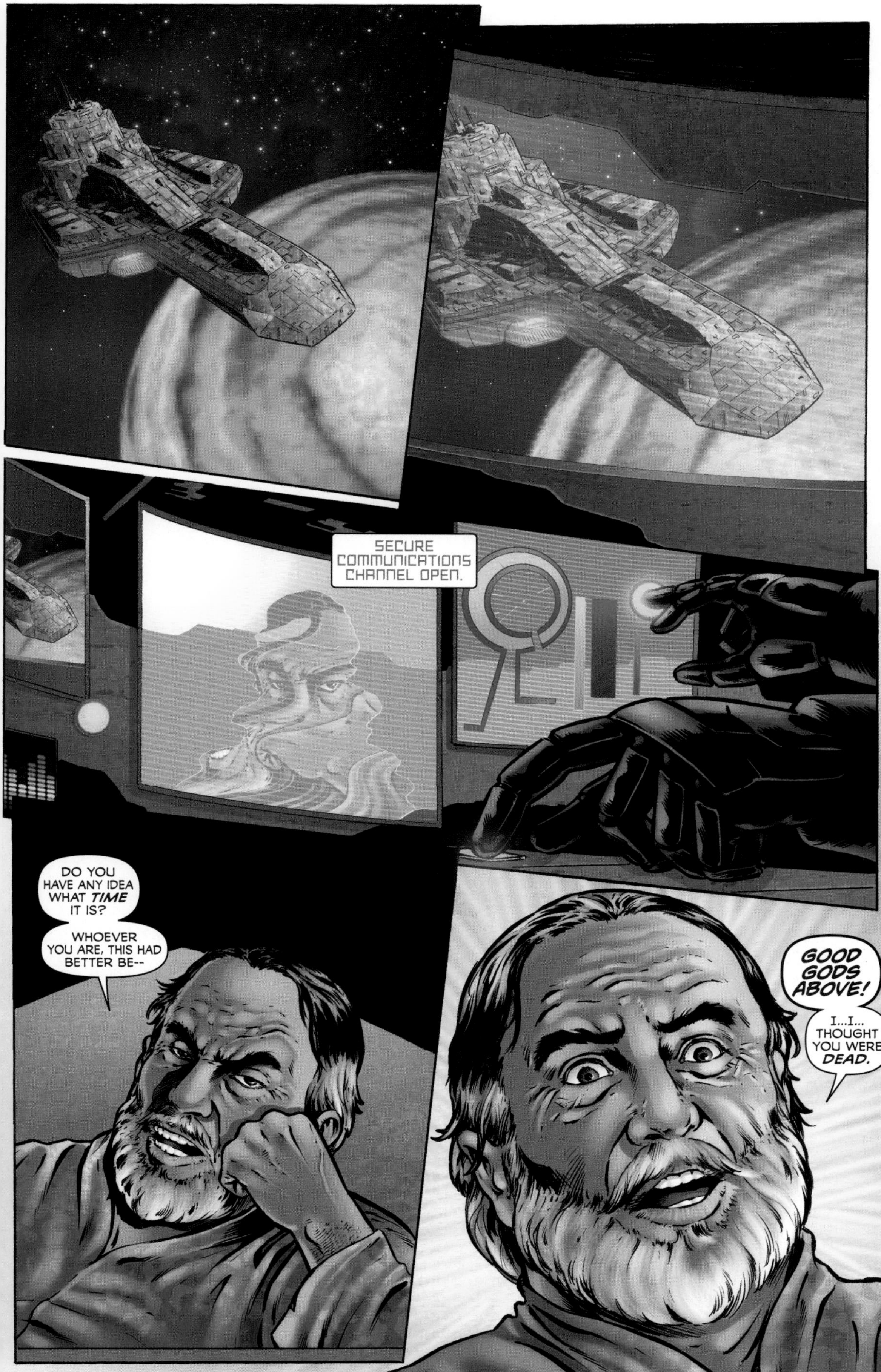
SECURE COMMUNICATIONS CHANNEL OPEN.
DO YOU HAVE ANY IDEA WHAT *TIME* IT IS?
WHOEVER YOU ARE, THIS HAD BETTER BE--
GOOD GODS ABOVE!
I...I... THOUGHT YOU WERE *DEAD.*

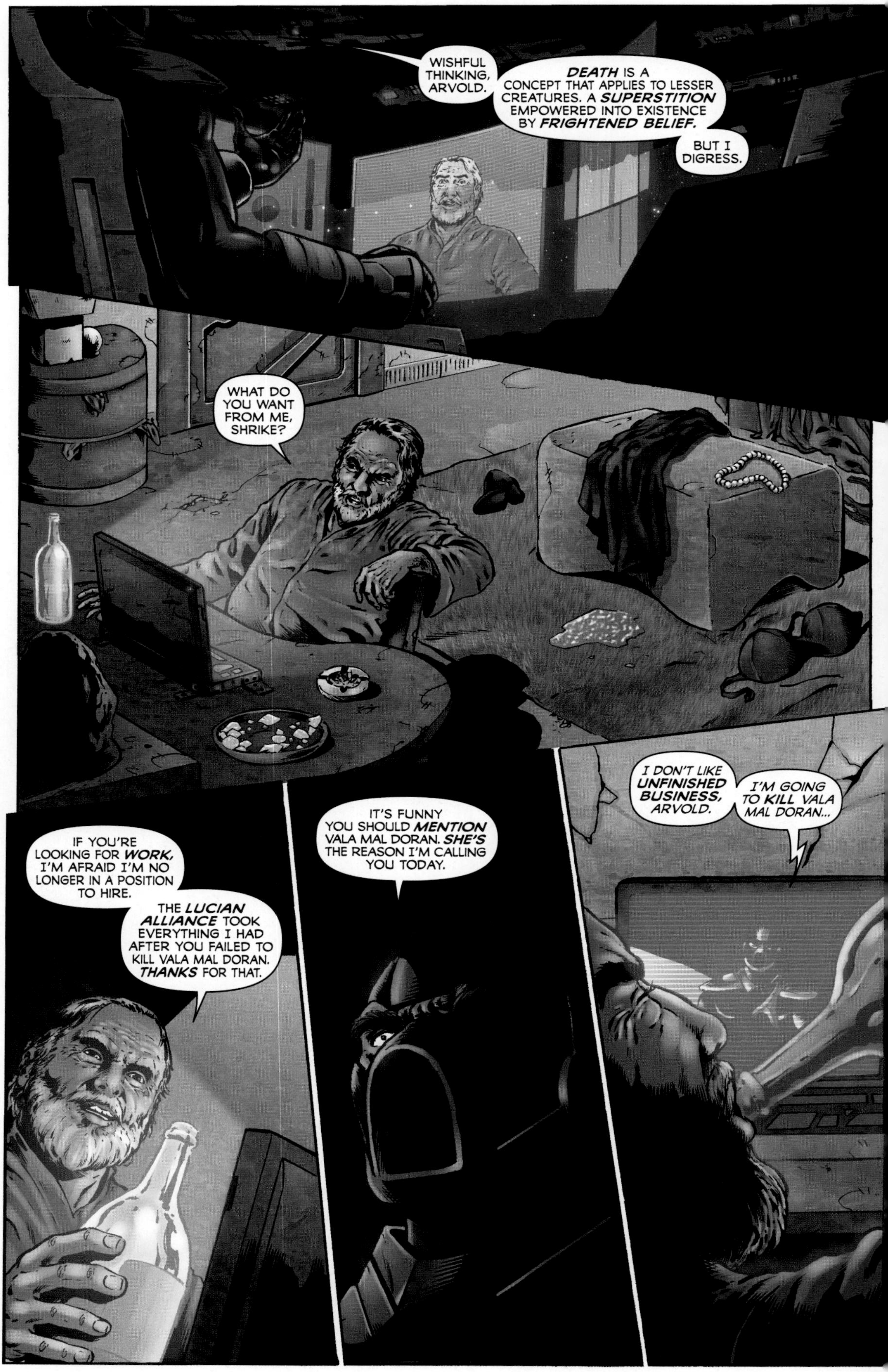
WISHFUL THINKING, ARVOLD.
DEATH IS A CONCEPT THAT APPLIES TO LESSER CREATURES. A SUPERSTITION EMPOWERED INTO EXISTENCE BY FRIGHTENED BELIEF.
BUT I DIGRESS.
WHAT DO YOU WANT FROM ME, SHRIKE?
IF YOU'RE LOOKING FOR WORK, I'M AFRAID I'M NO LONGER IN A POSITION TO HIRE.
THE LUCIAN ALLIANCE TOOK EVERYTHING I HAD AFTER YOU FAILED TO KILL VALA MAL DORAN. THANKS FOR THAT.
IT'S FUNNY YOU SHOULD MENTION VALA MAL DORAN. SHE'S THE REASON I'M CALLING YOU TODAY.
I DON'T LIKE UNFINISHED BUSINESS, ARVOLD.
I'M GOING TO KILL VALA MAL DORAN...

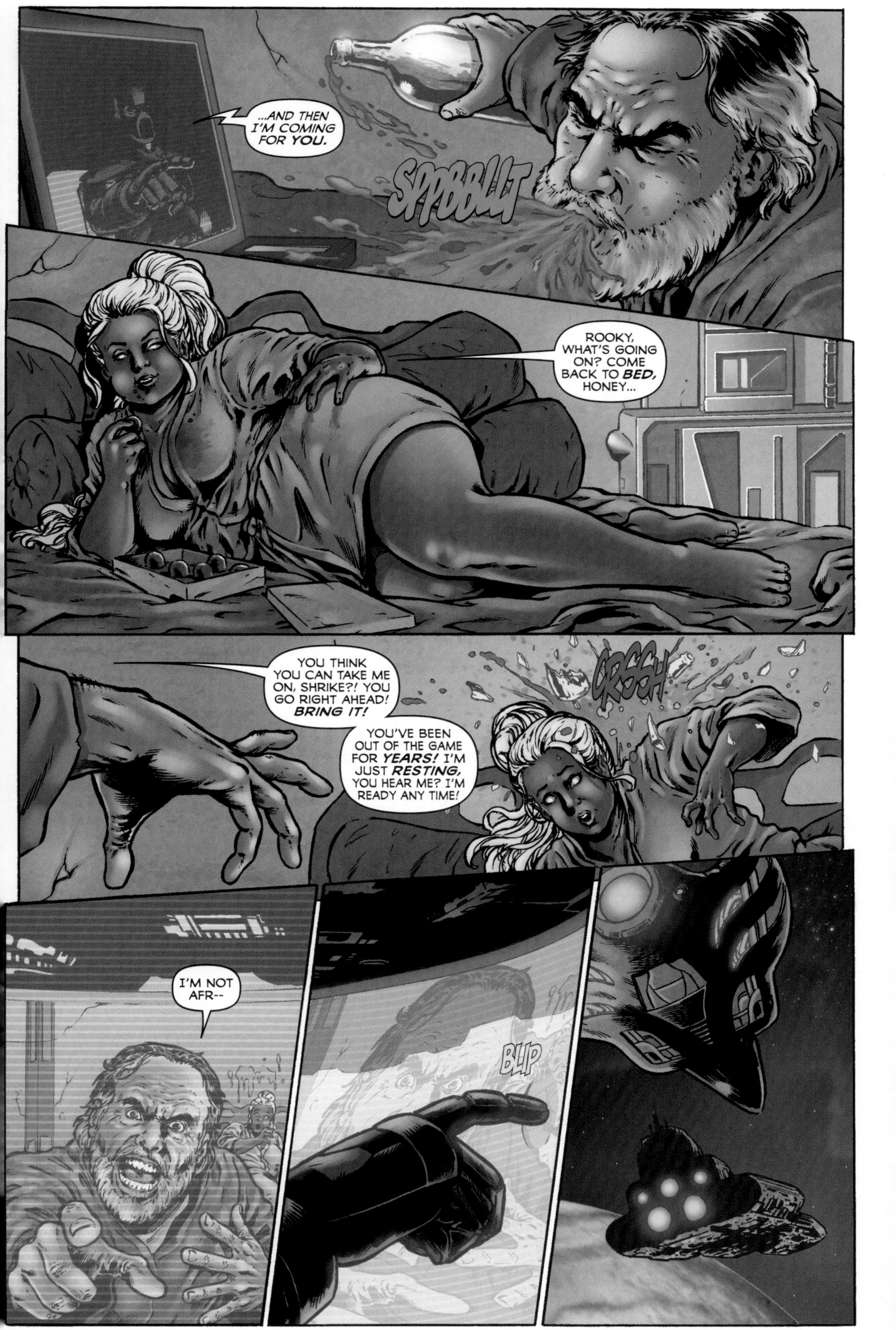
...AND THEN I'M COMING FOR YOU.
SPPBBLLT
ROOKY, WHAT'S GOING ON? COME BACK TO BED, HONEY...
YOU THINK YOU CAN TAKE ME ON, SHRIKE?! YOU GO RIGHT AHEAD! BRING IT!
YOU'VE BEEN OUT OF THE GAME FOR YEARS! I'M JUST RESTING, YOU HEAR ME? I'M READY ANY TIME!
CRSSH
I'M NOT AFR--
BLIP

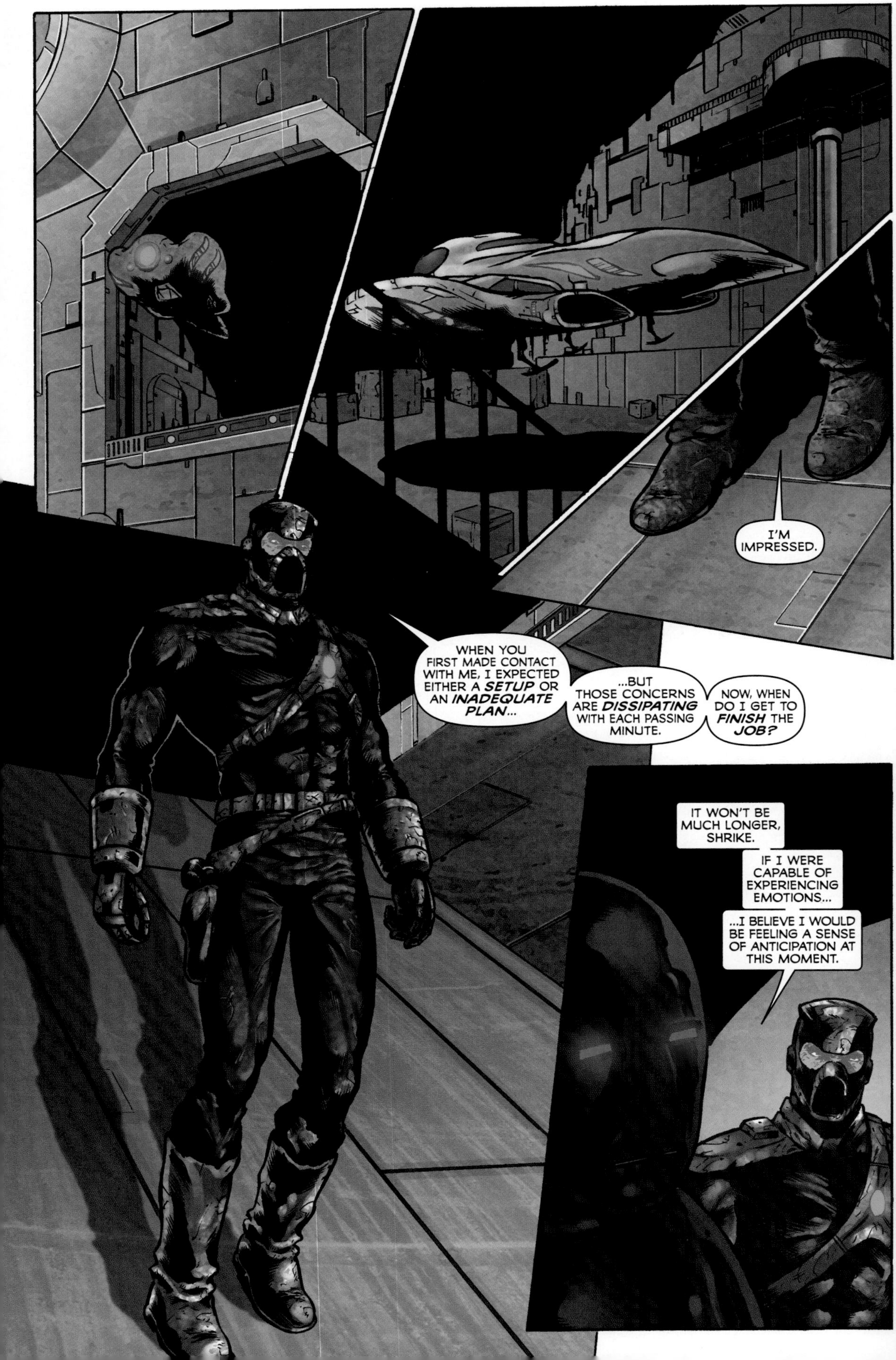
I'M IMPRESSED.
WHEN YOU FIRST MADE CONTACT WITH ME, I EXPECTED EITHER A SETUP OR AN INADEQUATE PLAN...
...BUT THOSE CONCERNS ARE DISSIPATING WITH EACH PASSING MINUTE.
NOW, WHEN DO I GET TO FINISH THE JOB?
IT WON'T BE MUCH LONGER, SHRIKE.
IF I WERE CAPABLE OF EXPERIENCING EMOTIONS...
...I BELIEVE I WOULD BE FEELING A SENSE OF ANTICIPATION AT THIS MOMENT.

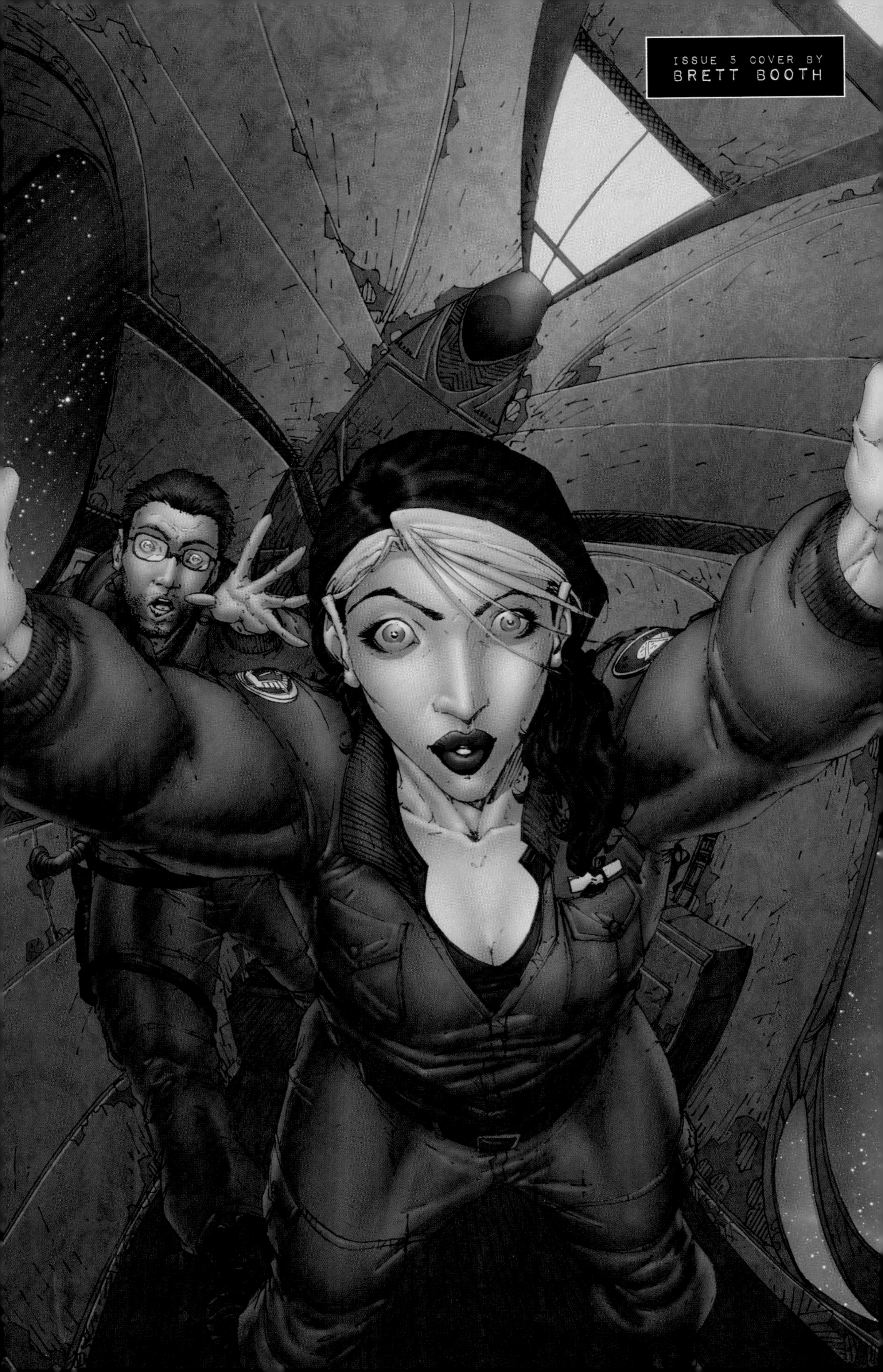

ISSUE 5 COVER BY
BRETT BOOTH

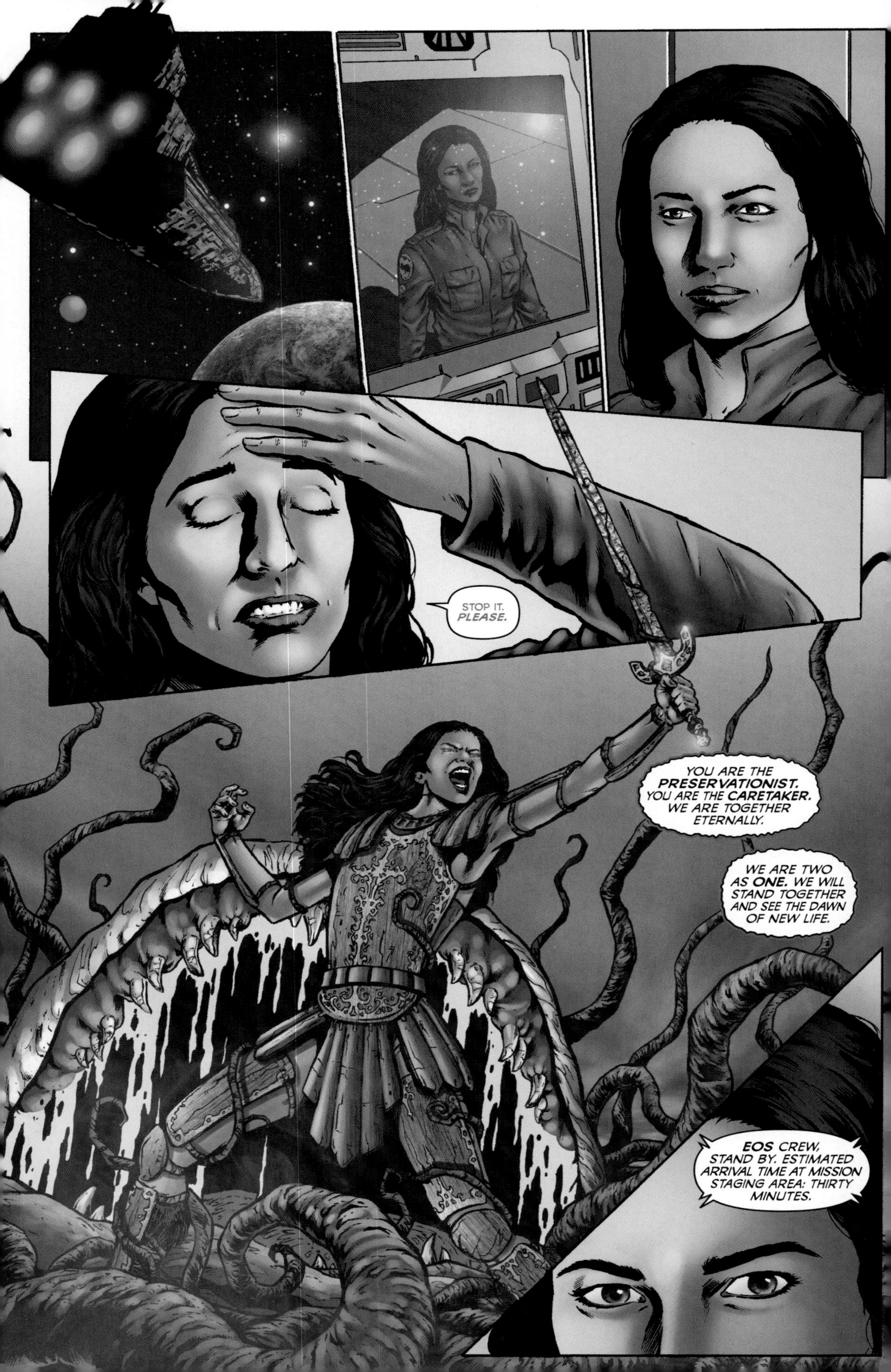
STOP IT. *PLEASE.*
YOU ARE THE **PRESERVATIONIST.** YOU ARE THE **CARETAKER.** WE ARE TOGETHER ETERNALLY.
WE ARE TWO AS **ONE.** WE WILL STAND TOGETHER AND SEE THE DAWN OF NEW LIFE.
EOS CREW, STAND BY. ESTIMATED ARRIVAL TIME AT MISSION STAGING AREA: THIRTY MINUTES.

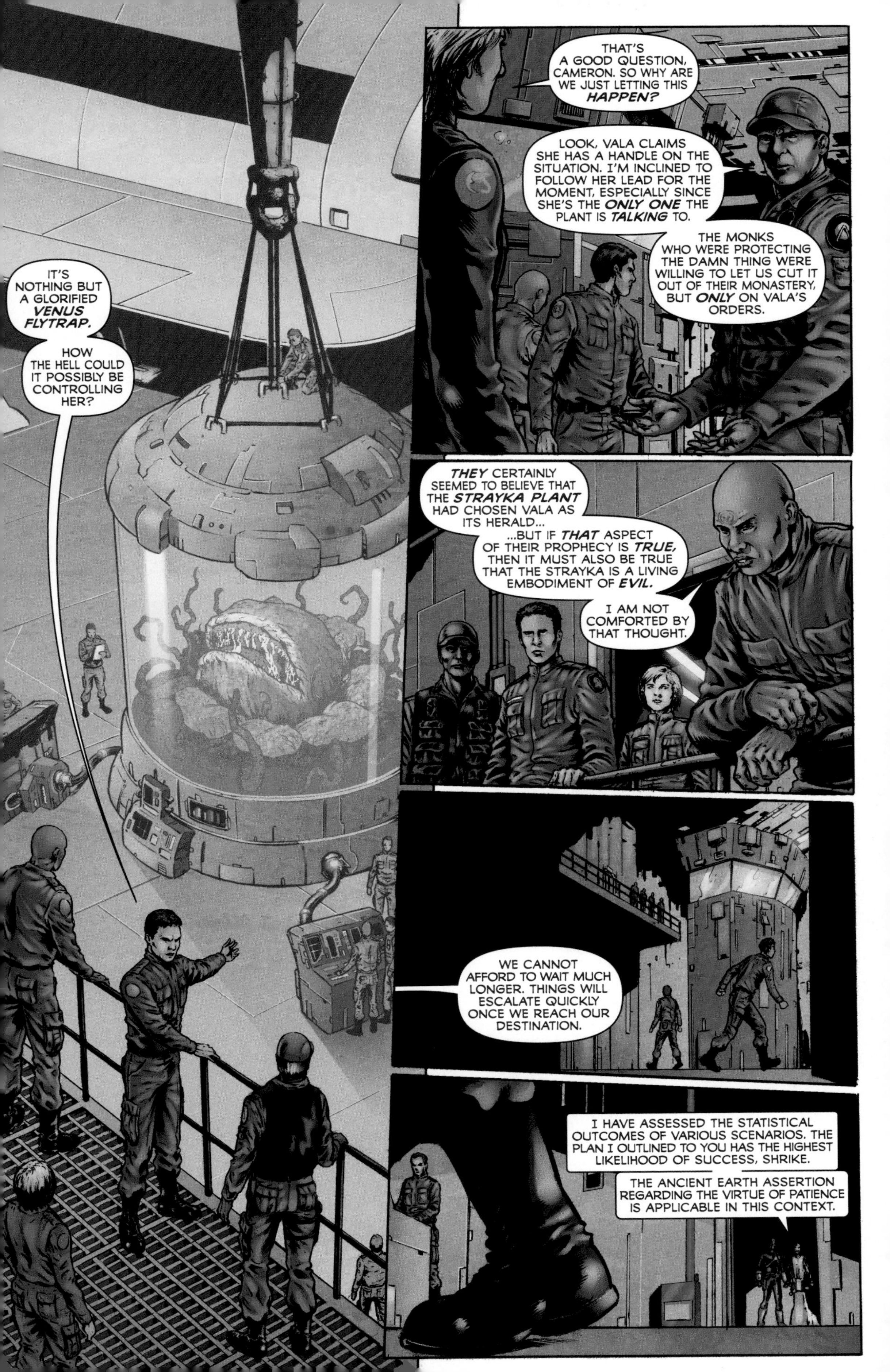
IT'S NOTHING BUT A GLORIFIED VENUS FLYTRAP.
HOW THE HELL COULD IT POSSIBLY BE CONTROLLING HER?
THAT'S A GOOD QUESTION, CAMERON. SO WHY ARE WE JUST LETTING THIS HAPPEN?
LOOK, VALA CLAIMS SHE HAS A HANDLE ON THE SITUATION. I'M INCLINED TO FOLLOW HER LEAD FOR THE MOMENT, ESPECIALLY SINCE SHE'S THE ONLY ONE THE PLANT IS TALKING TO.
THE MONKS WHO WERE PROTECTING THE DAMN THING WERE WILLING TO LET US CUT IT OUT OF THEIR MONASTERY, BUT ONLY ON VALA'S ORDERS.
THEY CERTAINLY SEEMED TO BELIEVE THAT THE STRAYKA PLANT HAD CHOSEN VALA AS ITS HERALD...
...BUT IF THAT ASPECT OF THEIR PROPHECY IS TRUE, THEN IT MUST ALSO BE TRUE THAT THE STRAYKA IS A LIVING EMBODIMENT OF EVIL.
I AM NOT COMFORTED BY THAT THOUGHT.
WE CANNOT AFFORD TO WAIT MUCH LONGER. THINGS WILL ESCALATE QUICKLY ONCE WE REACH OUR DESTINATION.
I HAVE ASSESSED THE STATISTICAL OUTCOMES OF VARIOUS SCENARIOS. THE PLAN I OUTLINED TO YOU HAS THE HIGHEST LIKELIHOOD OF SUCCESS, SHRIKE.
THE ANCIENT EARTH ASSERTION REGARDING THE VIRTUE OF PATIENCE IS APPLICABLE IN THIS CONTEXT.

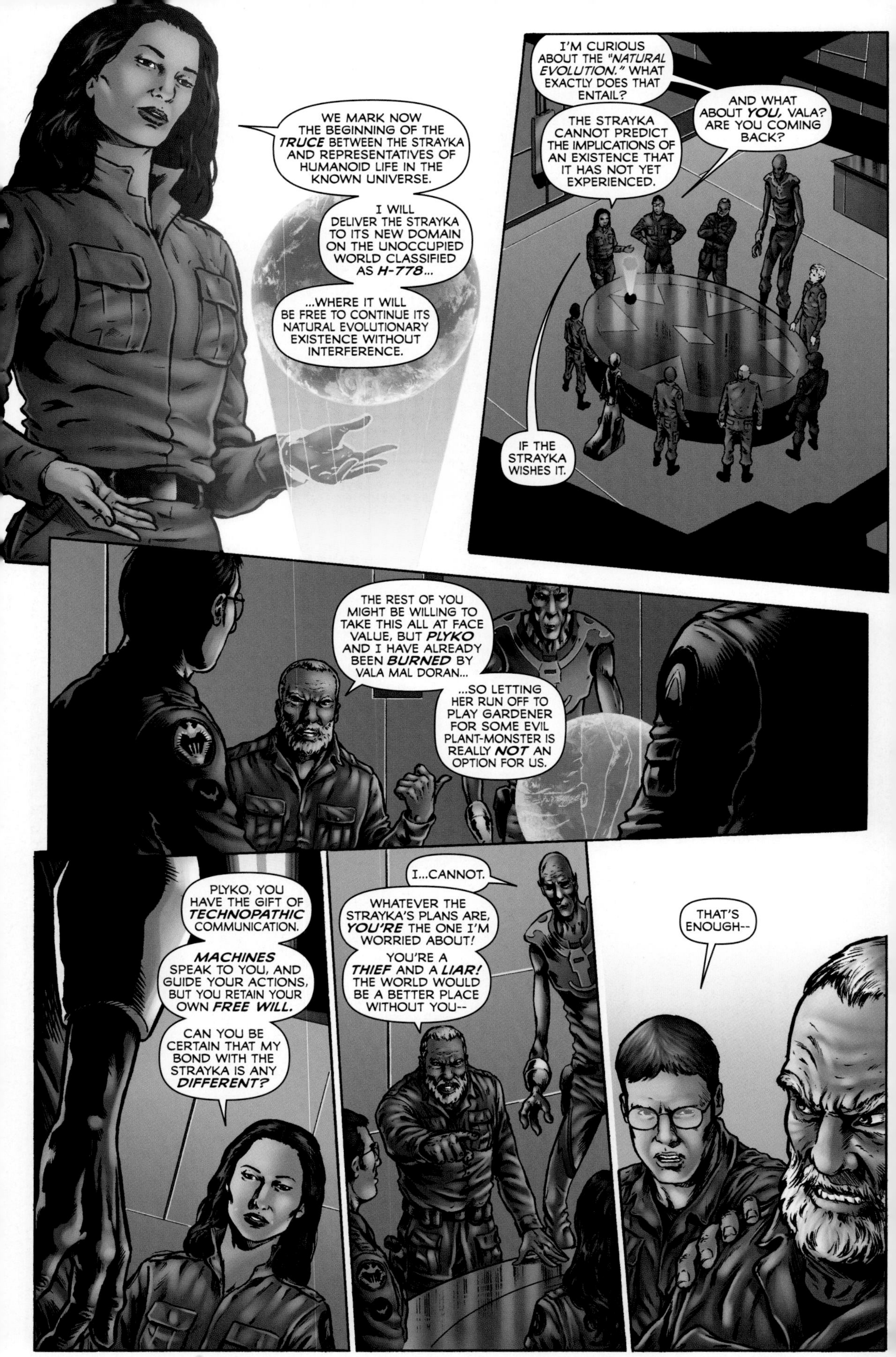
WE MARK NOW THE BEGINNING OF THE *TRUCE* BETWEEN THE STRAYKA AND REPRESENTATIVES OF HUMANOID LIFE IN THE KNOWN UNIVERSE.
I WILL DELIVER THE STRAYKA TO ITS NEW DOMAIN ON THE UNOCCUPIED WORLD CLASSIFIED AS *H-778*...
...WHERE IT WILL BE FREE TO CONTINUE ITS NATURAL EVOLUTIONARY EXISTENCE WITHOUT INTERFERENCE.
I'M CURIOUS ABOUT THE *"NATURAL EVOLUTION."* WHAT EXACTLY DOES THAT ENTAIL?
THE STRAYKA CANNOT PREDICT THE IMPLICATIONS OF AN EXISTENCE THAT IT HAS NOT YET EXPERIENCED.
AND WHAT ABOUT *YOU,* VALA? ARE YOU COMING BACK?
IF THE STRAYKA WISHES IT.
THE REST OF YOU MIGHT BE WILLING TO TAKE THIS ALL AT FACE VALUE, BUT *PLYKO* AND I HAVE ALREADY BEEN *BURNED* BY VALA MAL DORAN...
...SO LETTING HER RUN OFF TO PLAY GARDENER FOR SOME EVIL PLANT-MONSTER IS REALLY *NOT* AN OPTION FOR US.
PLYKO, YOU HAVE THE GIFT OF *TECHNOPATHIC* COMMUNICATION.
MACHINES SPEAK TO YOU, AND GUIDE YOUR ACTIONS, BUT YOU RETAIN YOUR OWN *FREE WILL.*
CAN YOU BE CERTAIN THAT MY BOND WITH THE STRAYKA IS ANY *DIFFERENT?*
I...CANNOT.
WHATEVER THE STRAYKA'S PLANS ARE, *YOU'RE* THE ONE I'M WORRIED ABOUT!
YOU'RE A *THIEF* AND A *LIAR!* THE WORLD WOULD BE A BETTER PLACE WITHOUT YOU--
THAT'S ENOUGH--

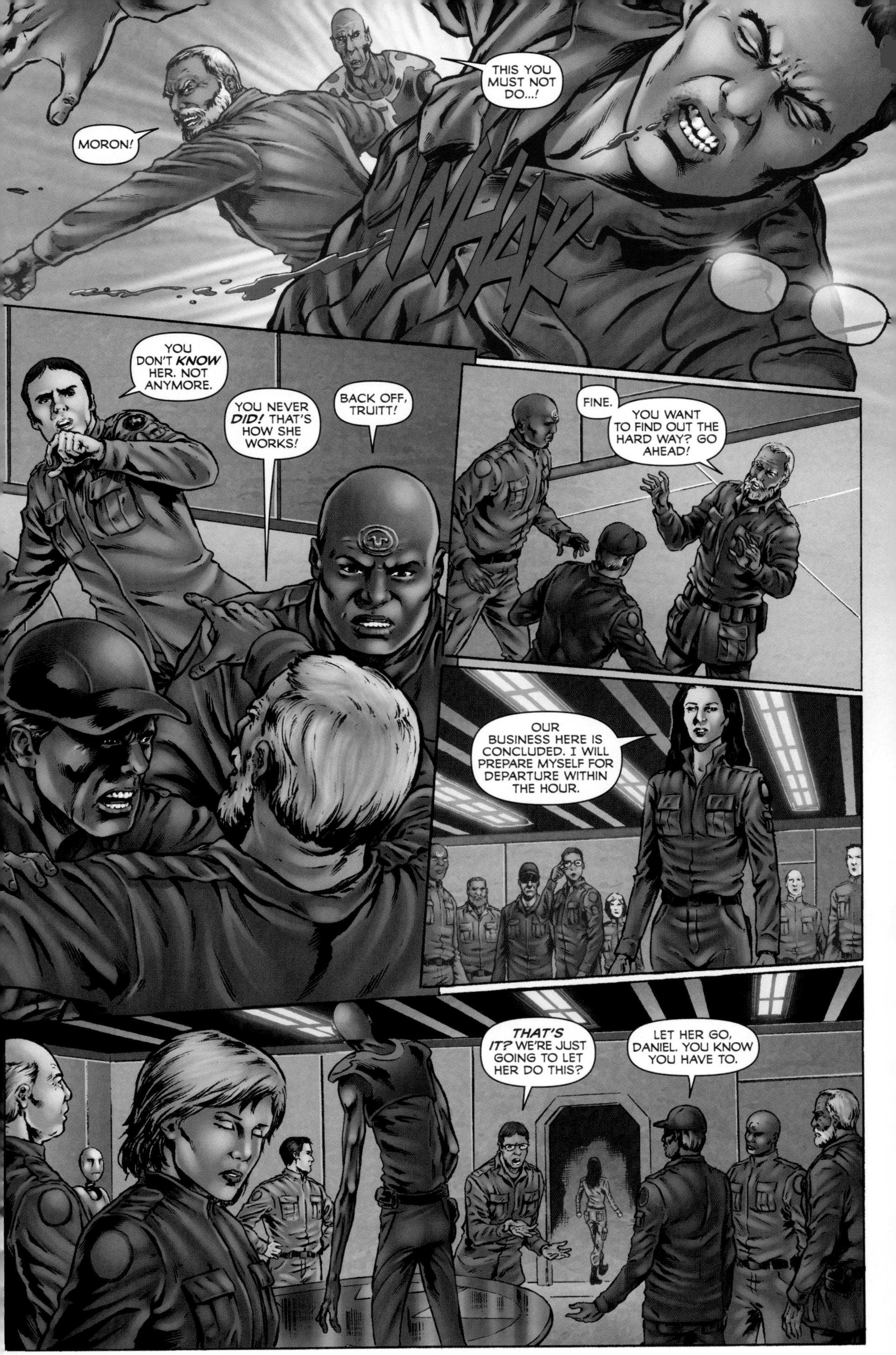
MORON!
THIS YOU MUST NOT DO...!
WHAK
YOU DON'T KNOW HER. NOT ANYMORE.
YOU NEVER DID! THAT'S HOW SHE WORKS!
BACK OFF, TRUITT!
FINE.
YOU WANT TO FIND OUT THE HARD WAY? GO AHEAD!
OUR BUSINESS HERE IS CONCLUDED. I WILL PREPARE MYSELF FOR DEPARTURE WITHIN THE HOUR.
THAT'S IT? WE'RE JUST GOING TO LET HER DO THIS?
LET HER GO, DANIEL. YOU KNOW YOU HAVE TO.

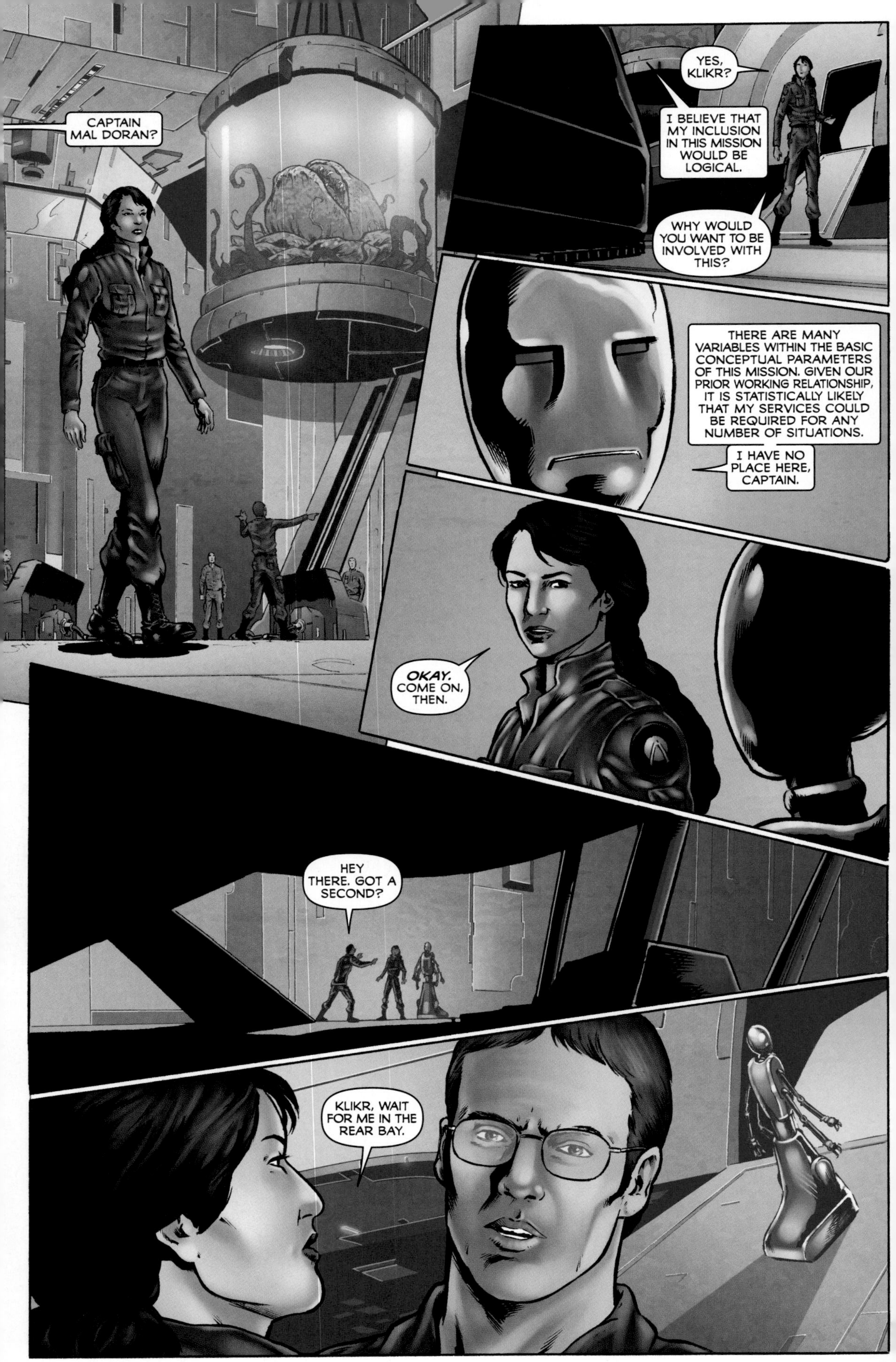
CAPTAIN MAL DORAN?
YES, KLIKR?
I BELIEVE THAT MY INCLUSION IN THIS MISSION WOULD BE LOGICAL.
WHY WOULD YOU WANT TO BE INVOLVED WITH THIS?
THERE ARE MANY VARIABLES WITHIN THE BASIC CONCEPTUAL PARAMETERS OF THIS MISSION. GIVEN OUR PRIOR WORKING RELATIONSHIP, IT IS STATISTICALLY LIKELY THAT MY SERVICES COULD BE REQUIRED FOR ANY NUMBER OF SITUATIONS.
I HAVE NO PLACE HERE, CAPTAIN.
OKAY. COME ON, THEN.
HEY THERE. GOT A SECOND?
KLIKR, WAIT FOR ME IN THE REAR BAY.

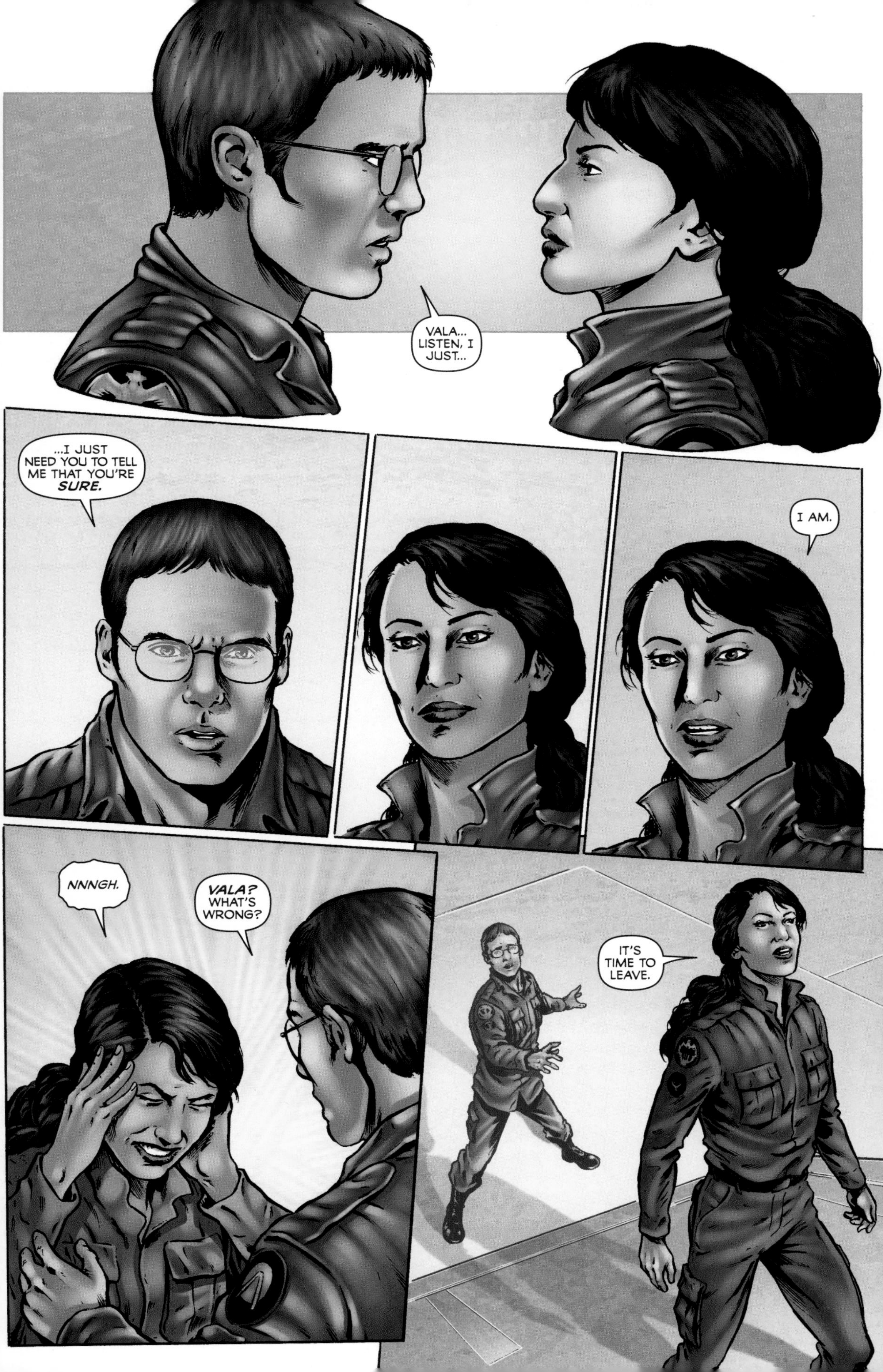
VALA... LISTEN, I JUST...
...I JUST NEED YOU TO TELL ME THAT YOU'RE *SURE.*
I AM.
NNNGH.
VALA? WHAT'S WRONG?
IT'S TIME TO LEAVE.

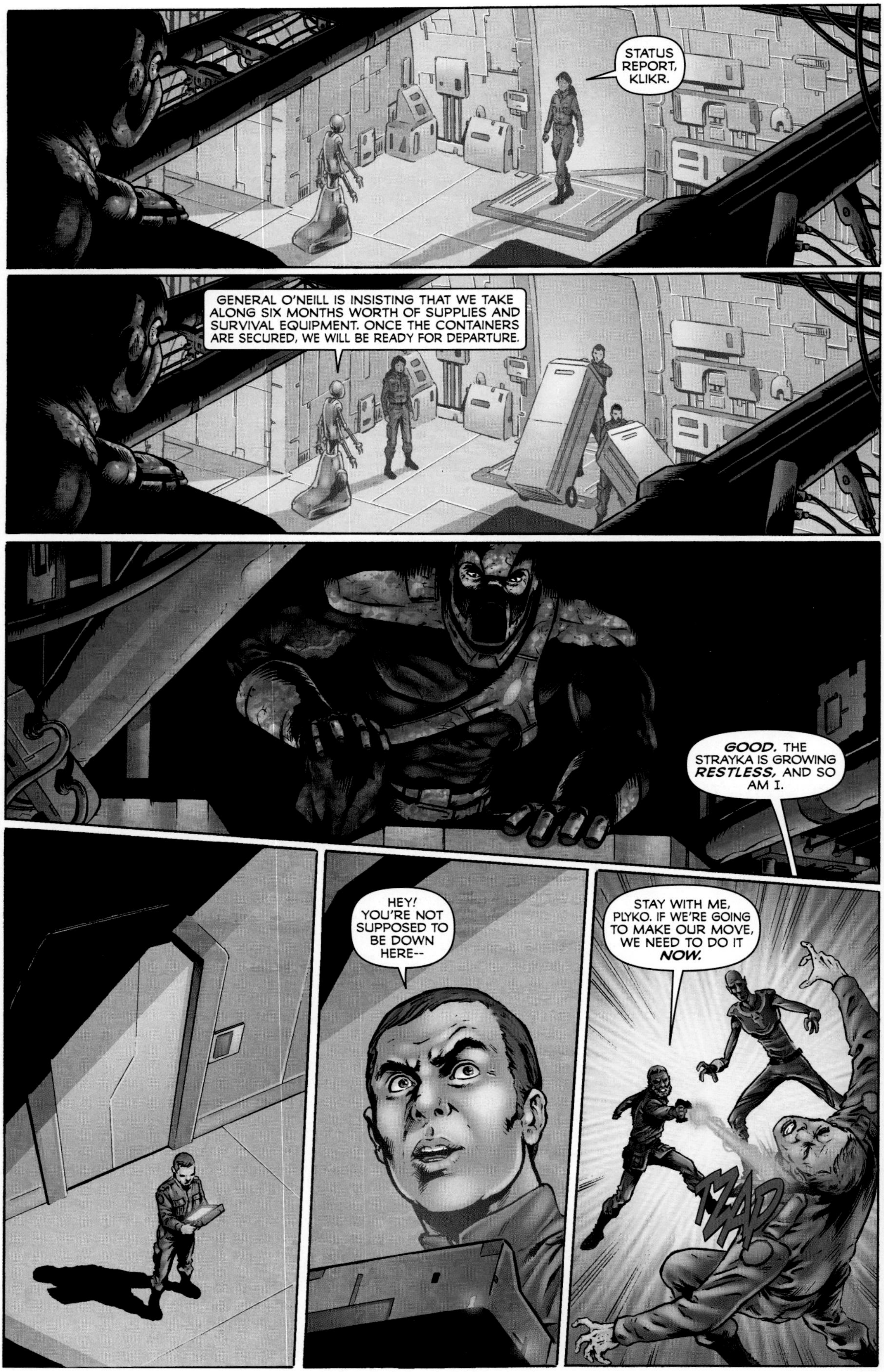

STATUS REPORT, KLIKR.
GENERAL O'NEILL IS INSISTING THAT WE TAKE ALONG SIX MONTHS WORTH OF SUPPLIES AND SURVIVAL EQUIPMENT. ONCE THE CONTAINERS ARE SECURED, WE WILL BE READY FOR DEPARTURE.
GOOD. THE STRAYKA IS GROWING RESTLESS, AND SO AM I.
HEY! YOU'RE NOT SUPPOSED TO BE DOWN HERE--
STAY WITH ME, PLYKO. IF WE'RE GOING TO MAKE OUR MOVE, WE NEED TO DO IT NOW.
TZAP

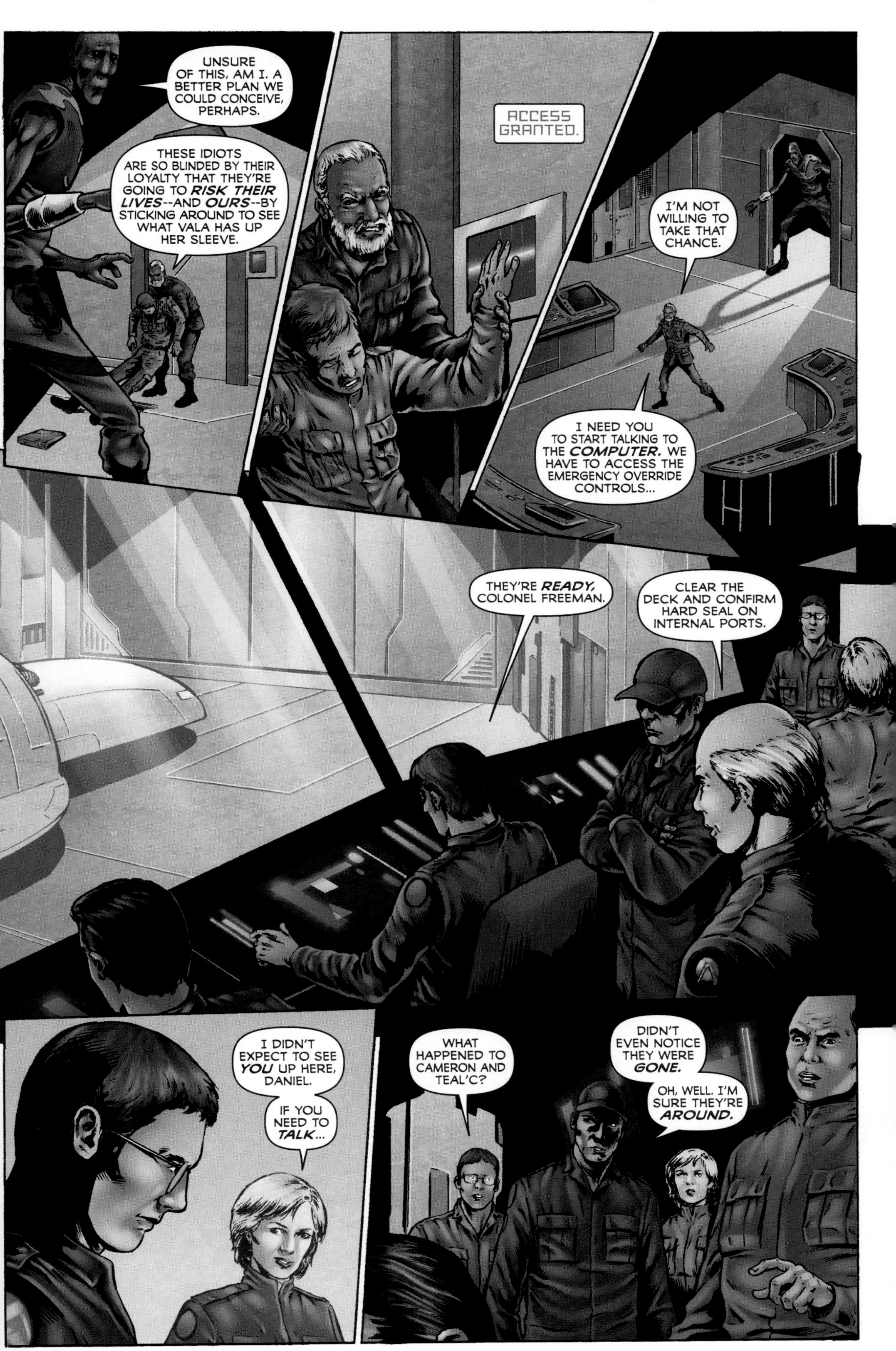
UNSURE OF THIS, AM I. A BETTER PLAN WE COULD CONCEIVE, PERHAPS.
THESE IDIOTS ARE SO BLINDED BY THEIR LOYALTY THAT THEY'RE GOING TO RISK THEIR LIVES--AND OURS--BY STICKING AROUND TO SEE WHAT VALA HAS UP HER SLEEVE.
ACCESS GRANTED.
I'M NOT WILLING TO TAKE THAT CHANCE.
I NEED YOU TO START TALKING TO THE COMPUTER. WE HAVE TO ACCESS THE EMERGENCY OVERRIDE CONTROLS...
THEY'RE READY, COLONEL FREEMAN.
CLEAR THE DECK AND CONFIRM HARD SEAL ON INTERNAL PORTS.
I DIDN'T EXPECT TO SEE YOU UP HERE, DANIEL.
IF YOU NEED TO TALK...
WHAT HAPPENED TO CAMERON AND TEAL'C?
DIDN'T EVEN NOTICE THEY WERE GONE.
OH, WELL. I'M SURE THEY'RE AROUND.

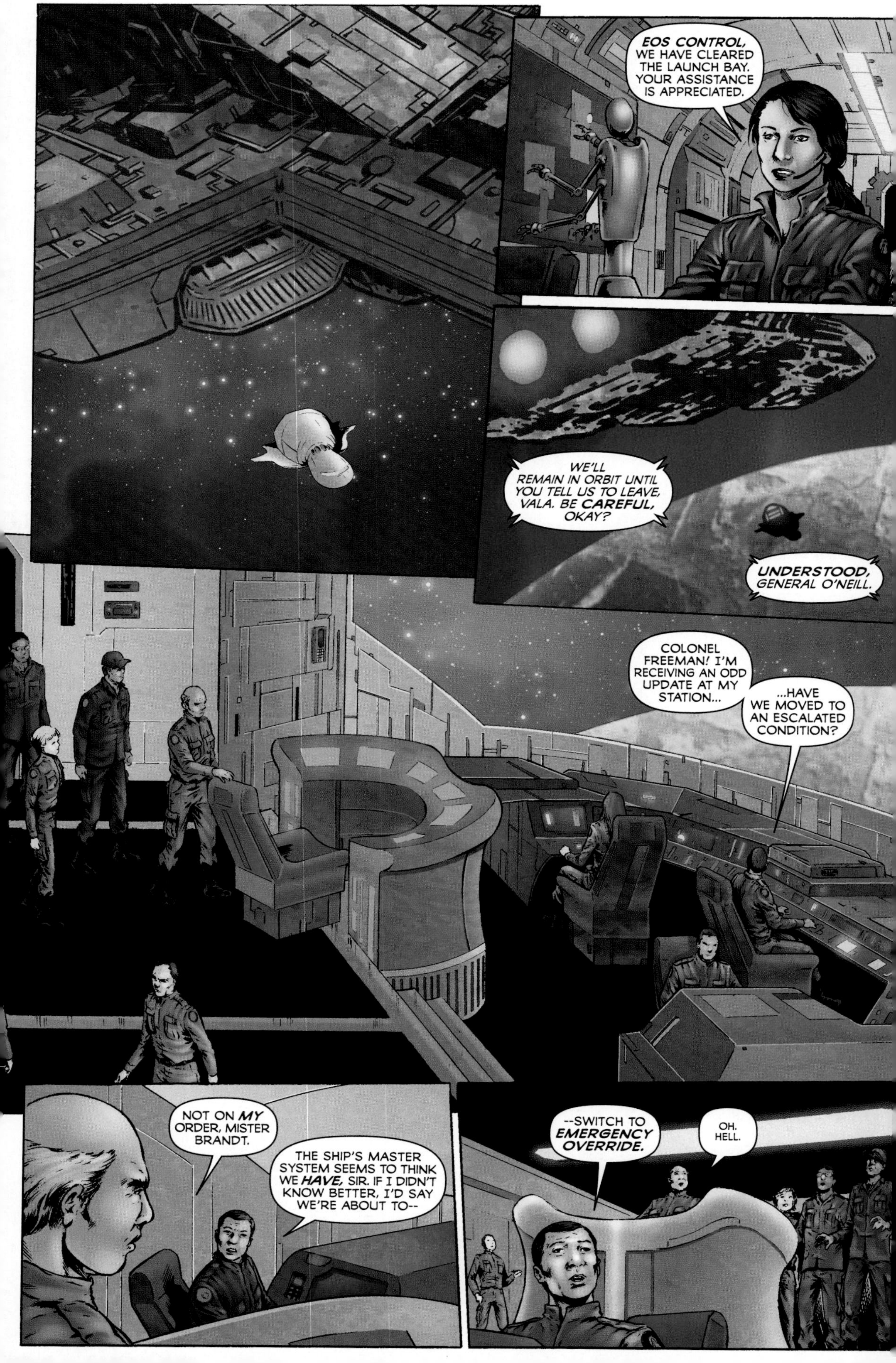
EOS CONTROL, WE HAVE CLEARED THE LAUNCH BAY. YOUR ASSISTANCE IS APPRECIATED.
WE'LL REMAIN IN ORBIT UNTIL YOU TELL US TO LEAVE, VALA. BE CAREFUL, OKAY?
UNDERSTOOD, GENERAL O'NEILL.
COLONEL FREEMAN! I'M RECEIVING AN ODD UPDATE AT MY STATION...
...HAVE WE MOVED TO AN ESCALATED CONDITION?
NOT ON MY ORDER, MISTER BRANDT.
THE SHIP'S MASTER SYSTEM SEEMS TO THINK WE HAVE, SIR. IF I DIDN'T KNOW BETTER, I'D SAY WE'RE ABOUT TO--
--SWITCH TO EMERGENCY OVERRIDE.
OH. HELL.

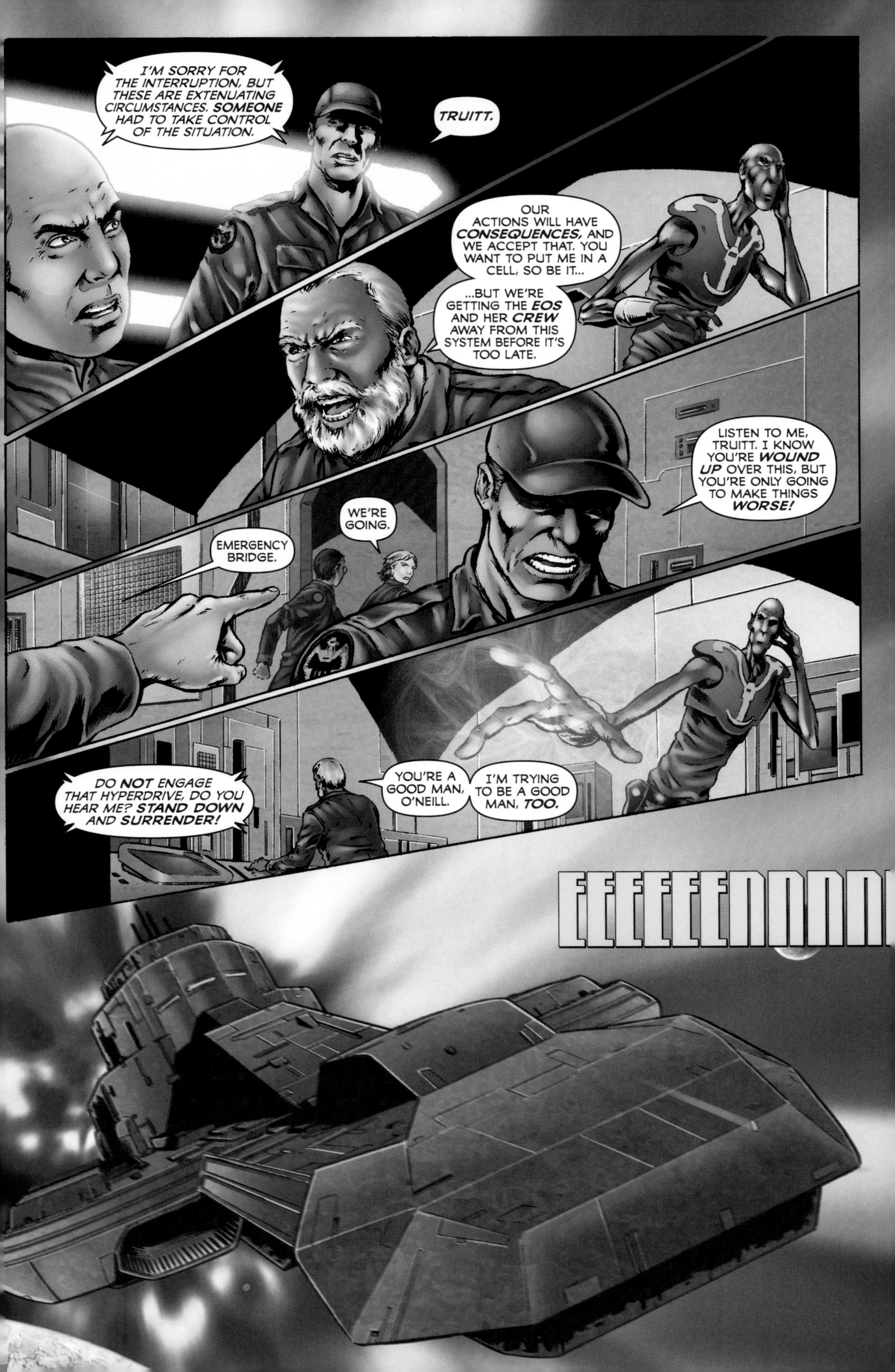
I'M SORRY FOR THE INTERRUPTION, BUT THESE ARE EXTENUATING CIRCUMSTANCES. SOMEONE HAD TO TAKE CONTROL OF THE SITUATION.
TRUITT.
OUR ACTIONS WILL HAVE CONSEQUENCES, AND WE ACCEPT THAT. YOU WANT TO PUT ME IN A CELL, SO BE IT...
...BUT WE'RE GETTING THE EOS AND HER CREW AWAY FROM THIS SYSTEM BEFORE IT'S TOO LATE.
LISTEN TO ME, TRUITT. I KNOW YOU'RE WOUND UP OVER THIS, BUT YOU'RE ONLY GOING TO MAKE THINGS WORSE!
WE'RE GOING.
EMERGENCY BRIDGE.
DO NOT ENGAGE THAT HYPERDRIVE, DO YOU HEAR ME? STAND DOWN AND SURRENDER!
YOU'RE A GOOD MAN, O'NEILL.
I'M TRYING TO BE A GOOD MAN, TOO.
EEEEEENNNNN

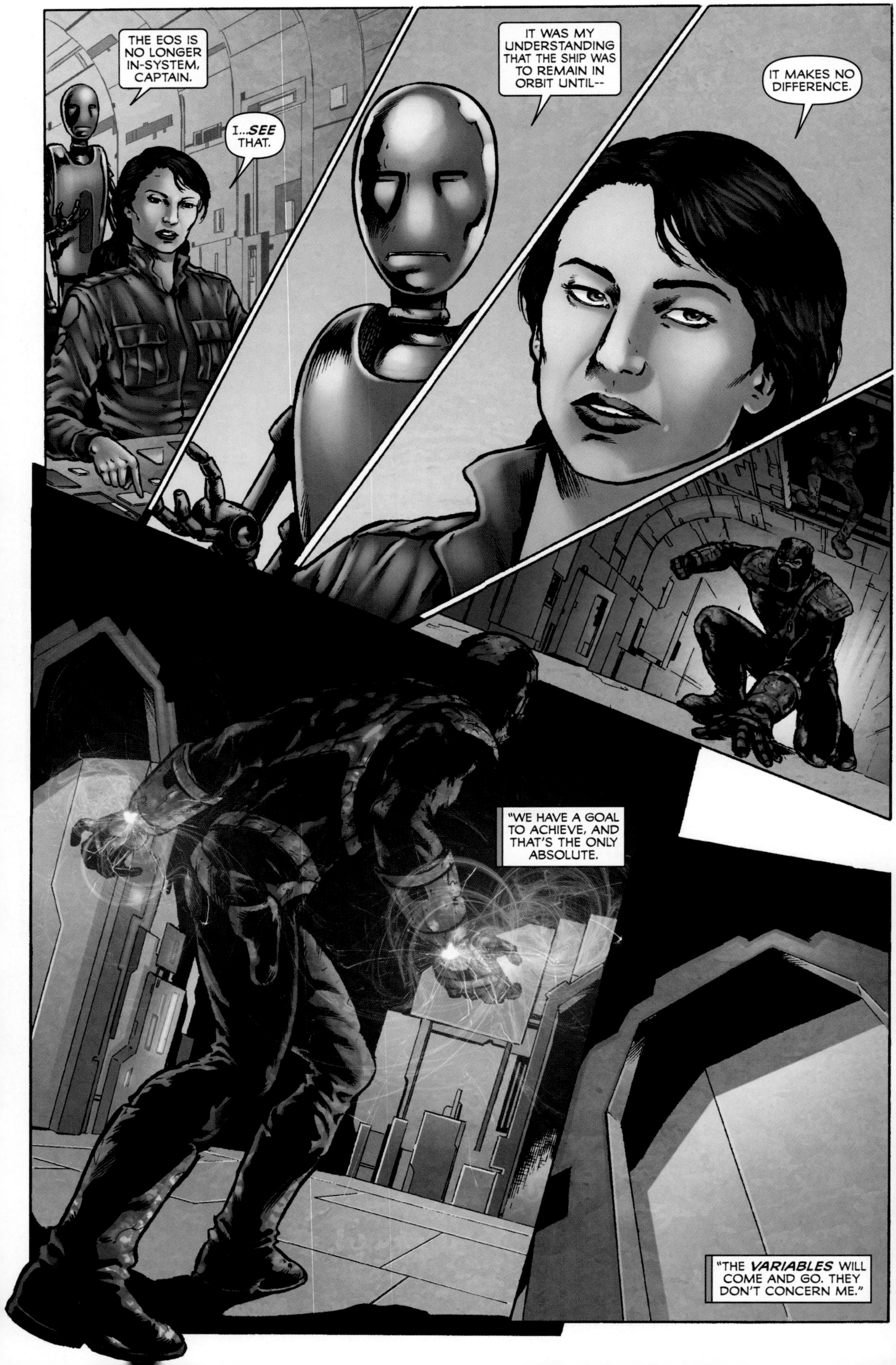
THE EOS IS NO LONGER IN-SYSTEM, CAPTAIN.
I...SEE THAT.
IT WAS MY UNDERSTANDING THAT THE SHIP WAS TO REMAIN IN ORBIT UNTIL--
IT MAKES NO DIFFERENCE.
"WE HAVE A GOAL TO ACHIEVE, AND THAT'S THE ONLY ABSOLUTE.
"THE VARIABLES WILL COME AND GO. THEY DON'T CONCERN ME."

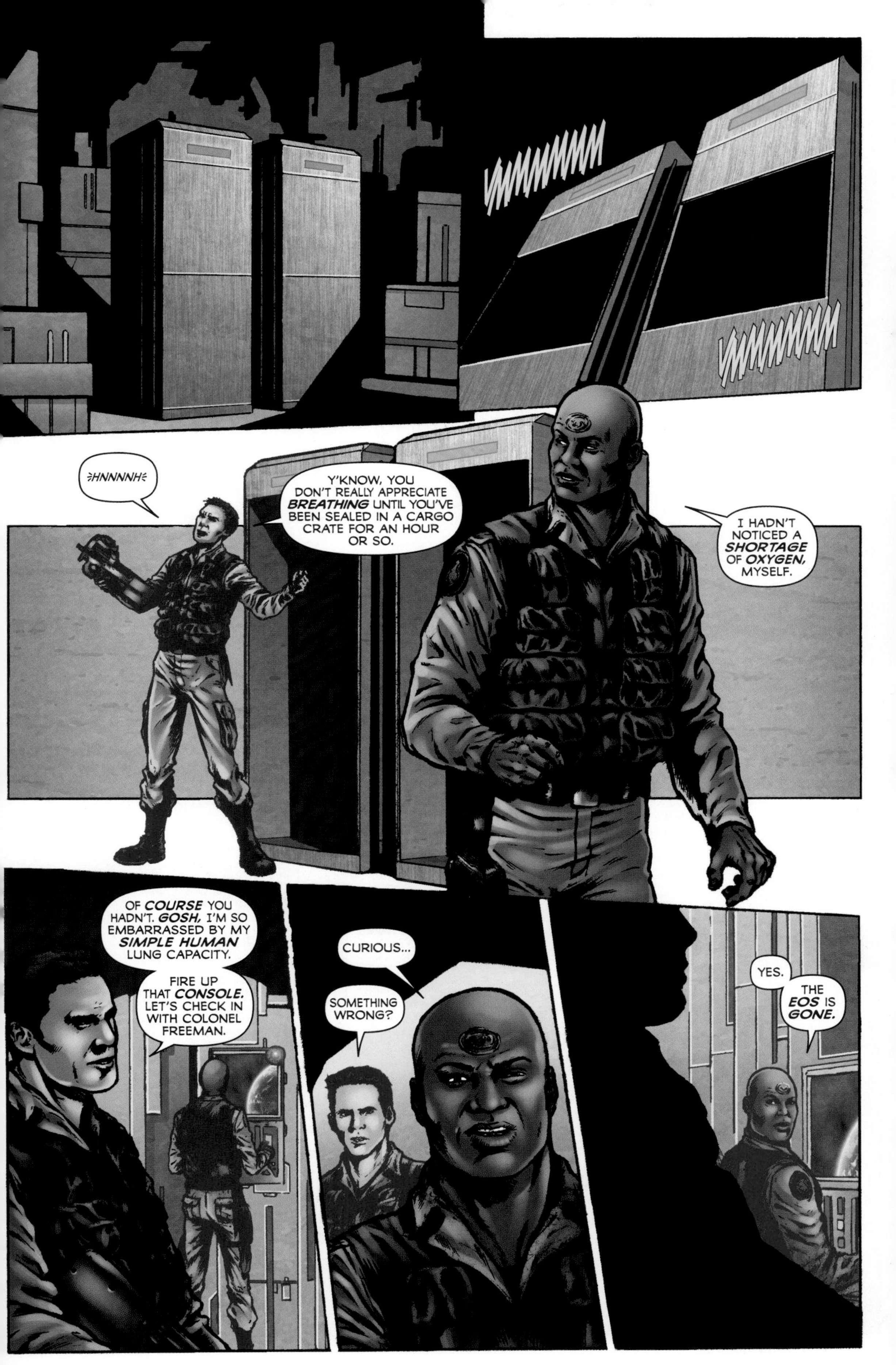
VMMMMMM
VMMMMMM
≈HNNNNH≈
Y'KNOW, YOU DON'T REALLY APPRECIATE BREATHING UNTIL YOU'VE BEEN SEALED IN A CARGO CRATE FOR AN HOUR OR SO.
I HADN'T NOTICED A SHORTAGE OF OXYGEN, MYSELF.
OF COURSE YOU HADN'T. GOSH, I'M SO EMBARRASSED BY MY SIMPLE HUMAN LUNG CAPACITY.
FIRE UP THAT CONSOLE. LET'S CHECK IN WITH COLONEL FREEMAN.
CURIOUS...
SOMETHING WRONG?
YES.
THE EOS IS GONE.

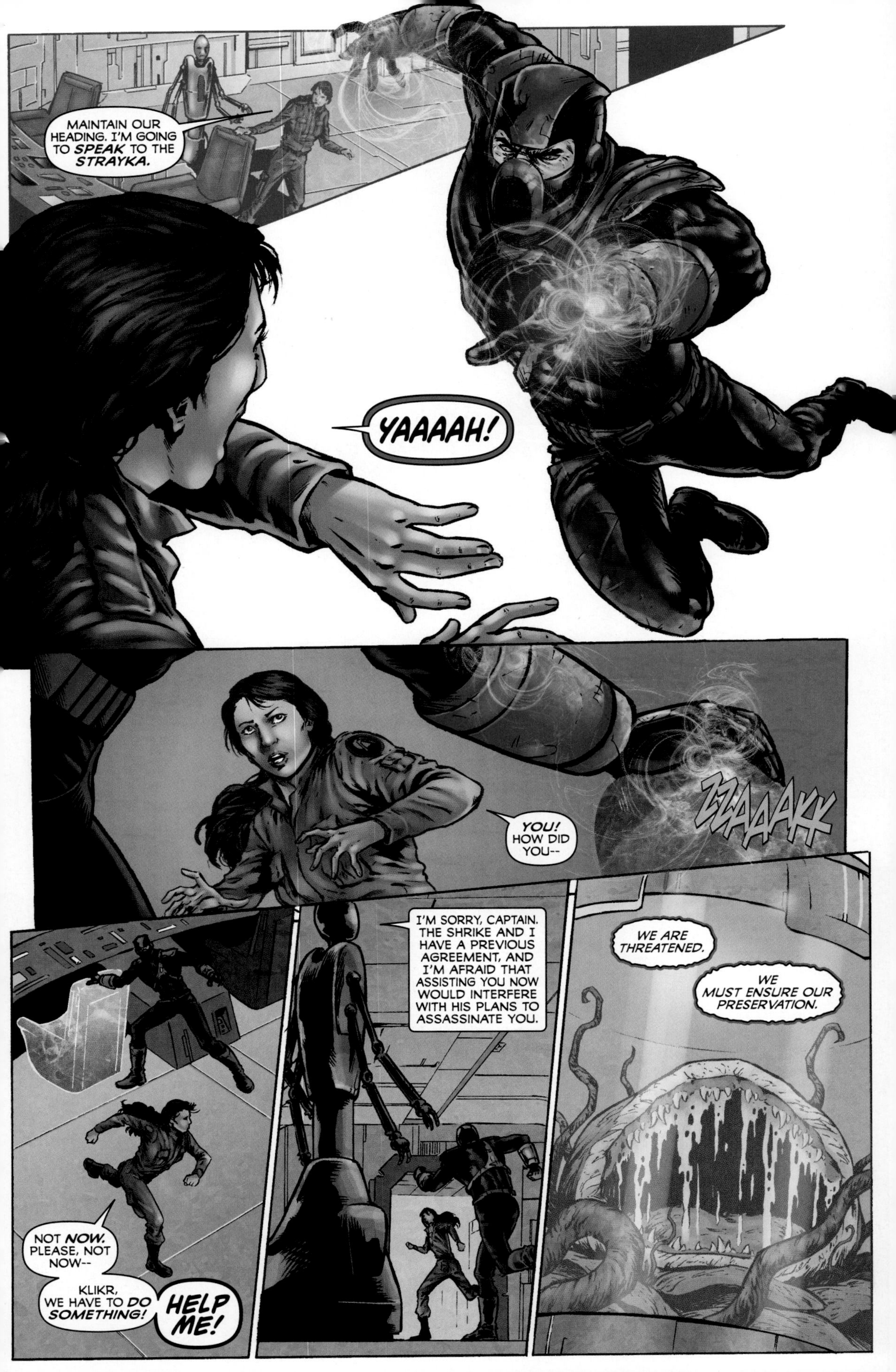
MAINTAIN OUR HEADING. I'M GOING TO SPEAK TO THE STRAYKA.
YAAAAH!
YOU! HOW DID YOU--
ZZAAAKK
NOT NOW. PLEASE, NOT NOW--
KLIKR, WE HAVE TO DO SOMETHING!
HELP ME!
I'M SORRY, CAPTAIN. THE SHRIKE AND I HAVE A PREVIOUS AGREEMENT, AND I'M AFRAID THAT ASSISTING YOU NOW WOULD INTERFERE WITH HIS PLANS TO ASSASSINATE YOU.
WE ARE THREATENED.
WE MUST ENSURE OUR PRESERVATION.

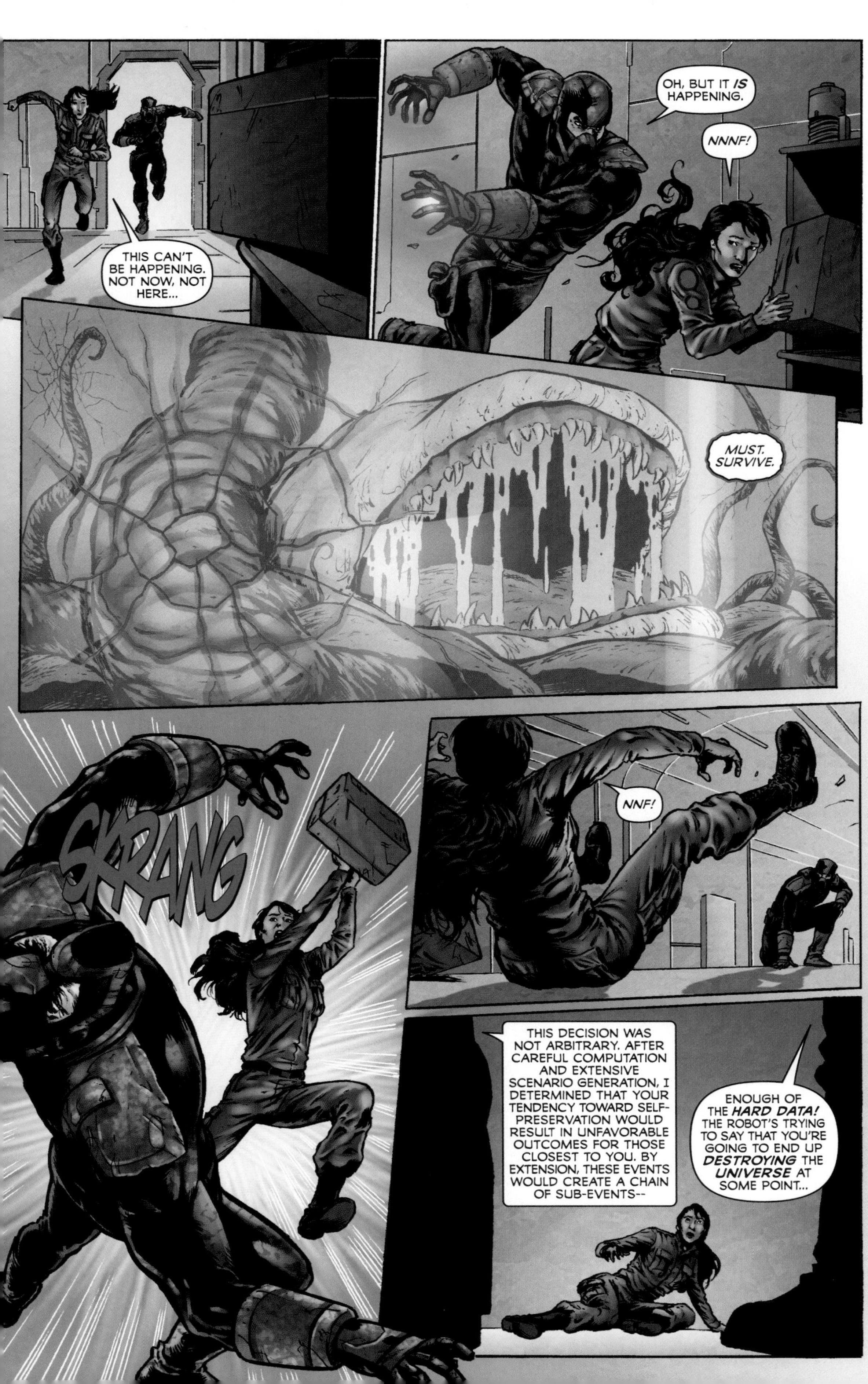
THIS CAN'T BE HAPPENING. NOT NOW, NOT HERE...
OH, BUT IT *IS* HAPPENING.
NNNF!
MUST. SURVIVE.
SKRANG
NNF!
THIS DECISION WAS NOT ARBITRARY. AFTER CAREFUL COMPUTATION AND EXTENSIVE SCENARIO GENERATION, I DETERMINED THAT YOUR TENDENCY TOWARD SELF-PRESERVATION WOULD RESULT IN UNFAVORABLE OUTCOMES FOR THOSE CLOSEST TO YOU. BY EXTENSION, THESE EVENTS WOULD CREATE A CHAIN OF SUB-EVENTS--
ENOUGH OF THE ***HARD DATA!*** THE ROBOT'S TRYING TO SAY THAT YOU'RE GOING TO END UP ***DESTROYING*** THE ***UNIVERSE*** AT SOME POINT...

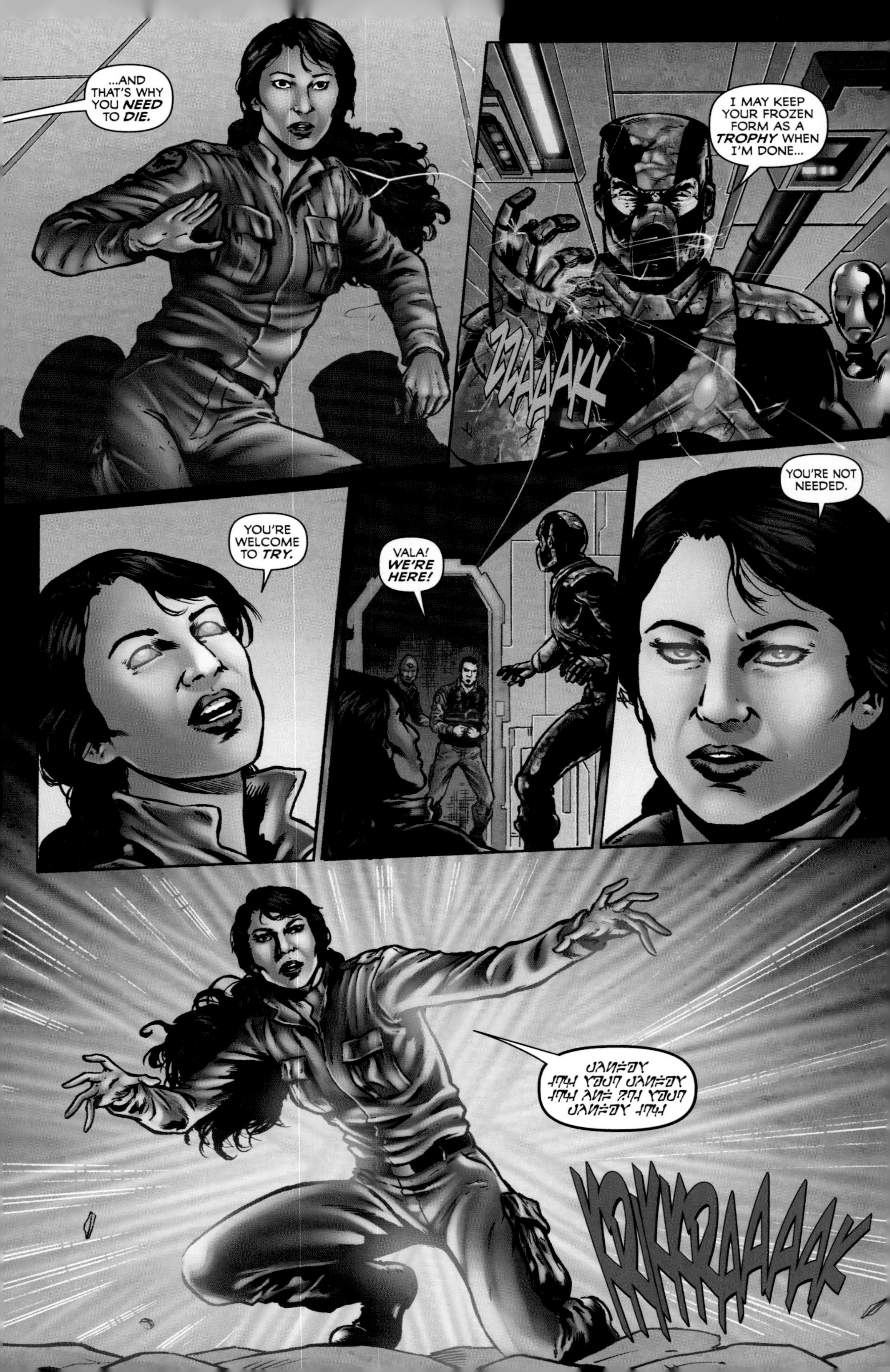
...AND THAT'S WHY YOU *NEED* TO *DIE.*
I MAY KEEP YOUR FROZEN FORM AS A *TROPHY* WHEN I'M DONE...
ZZAAAKK
YOU'RE WELCOME TO *TRY.*
VALA! *WE'RE HERE!*
YOU'RE NOT NEEDED.
VOKKRAAAAK

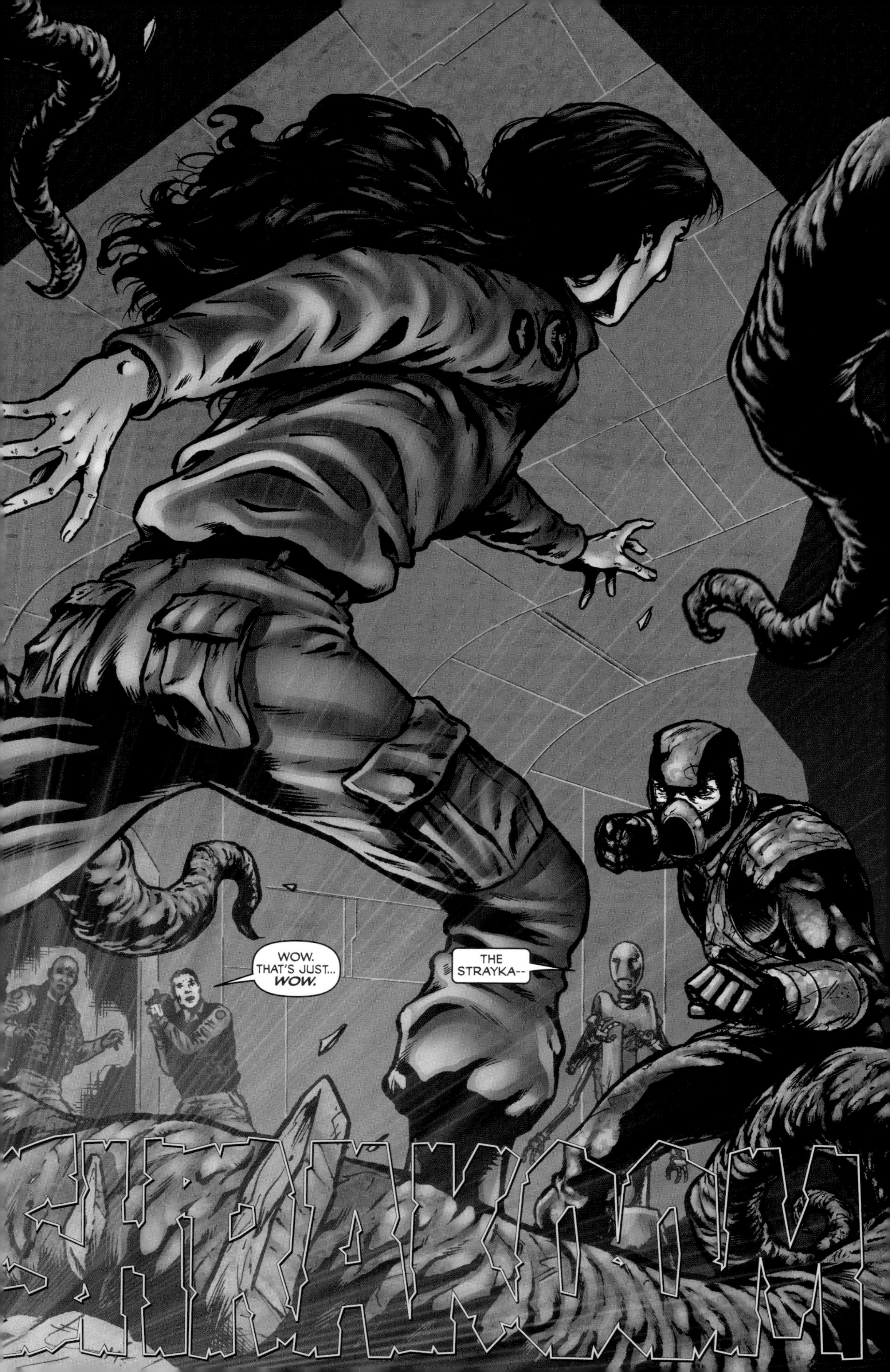
WOW. THAT'S JUST... ***WOW.***
THE STRAYKA--
SHRAKOOM

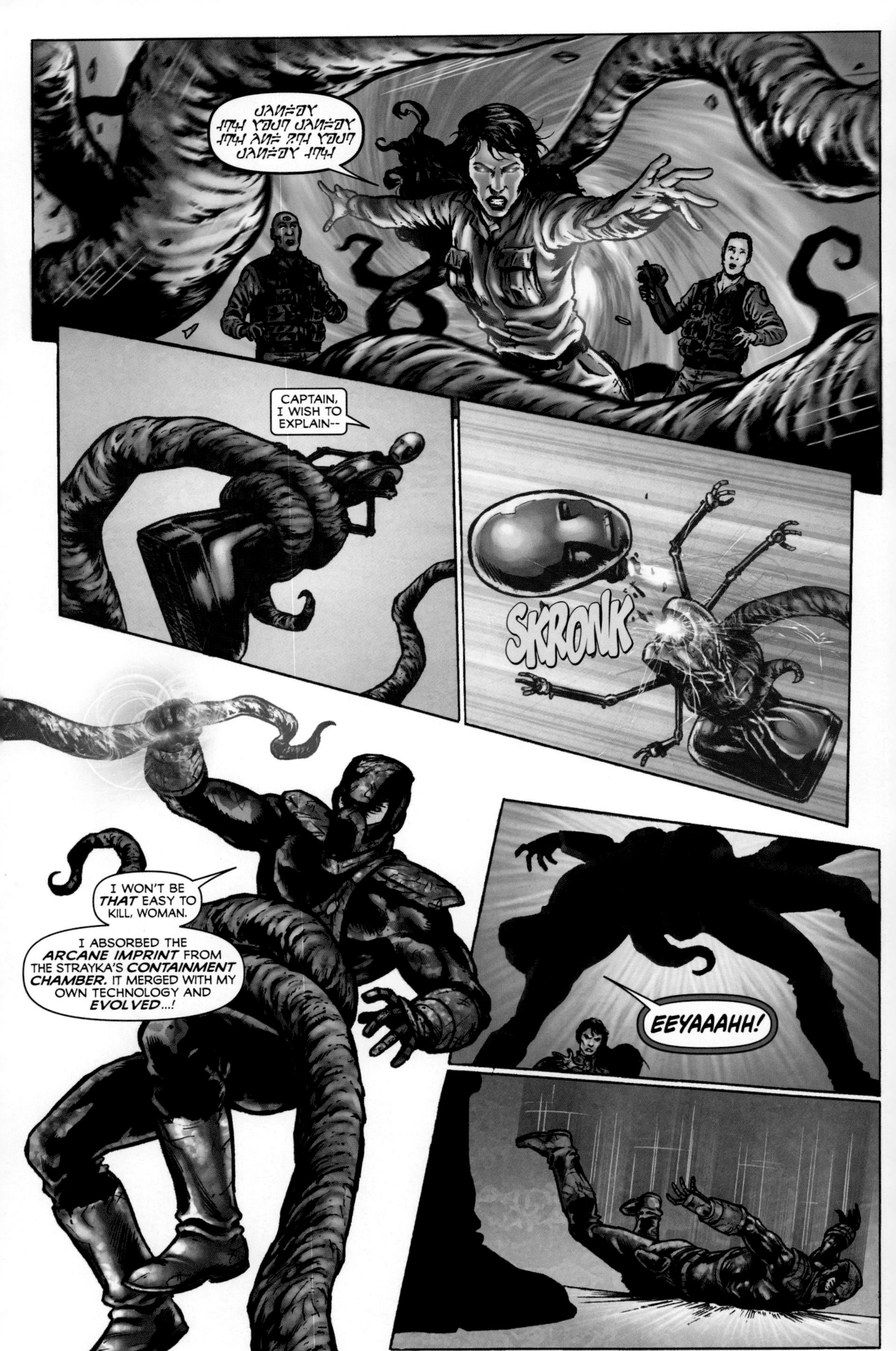
CAPTAIN, I WISH TO EXPLAIN--
SKRONK
I WON'T BE *THAT* EASY TO KILL, WOMAN.
I ABSORBED THE *ARCANE IMPRINT* FROM THE STRAYKA'S *CONTAINMENT CHAMBER.* IT MERGED WITH MY OWN TECHNOLOGY AND *EVOLVED*...!
EEYAAAHH!

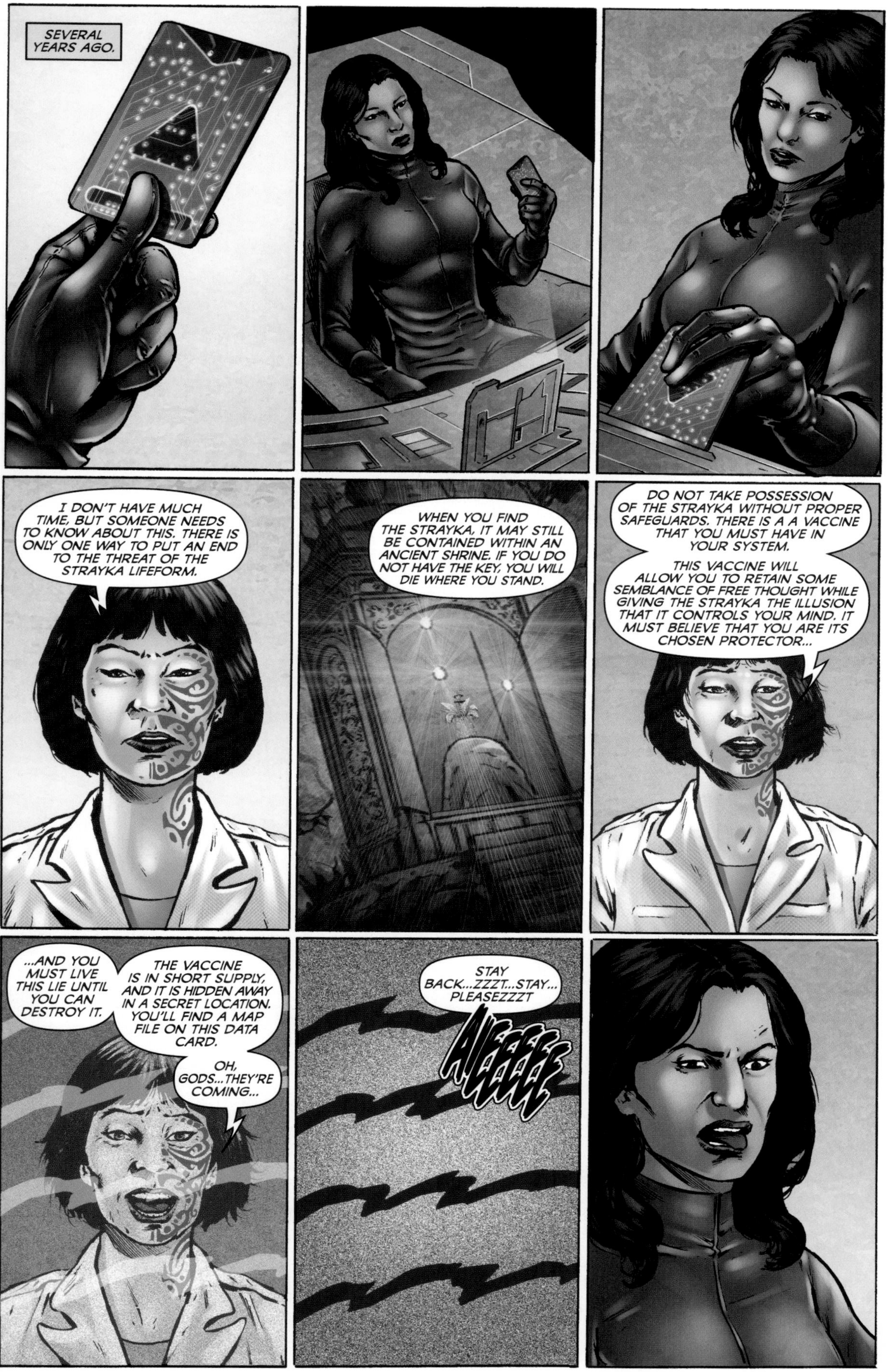
SEVERAL YEARS AGO.
I DON'T HAVE MUCH TIME, BUT SOMEONE NEEDS TO KNOW ABOUT THIS. THERE IS ONLY ONE WAY TO PUT AN END TO THE THREAT OF THE STRAYKA LIFEFORM.
WHEN YOU FIND THE STRAYKA, IT MAY STILL BE CONTAINED WITHIN AN ANCIENT SHRINE. IF YOU DO NOT HAVE THE KEY, YOU WILL DIE WHERE YOU STAND.
DO NOT TAKE POSSESSION OF THE STRAYKA WITHOUT PROPER SAFEGUARDS. THERE IS A A VACCINE THAT YOU MUST HAVE IN YOUR SYSTEM.
THIS VACCINE WILL ALLOW YOU TO RETAIN SOME SEMBLANCE OF FREE THOUGHT WHILE GIVING THE STRAYKA THE ILLUSION THAT IT CONTROLS YOUR MIND. IT MUST BELIEVE THAT YOU ARE ITS CHOSEN PROTECTOR...
...AND YOU MUST LIVE THIS LIE UNTIL YOU CAN DESTROY IT.
THE VACCINE IS IN SHORT SUPPLY, AND IT IS HIDDEN AWAY IN A SECRET LOCATION. YOU'LL FIND A MAP FILE ON THIS DATA CARD.
OH, GODS...THEY'RE COMING...
STAY BACK...ZZZT...STAY... PLEASEZZZT
AIEEEEEE

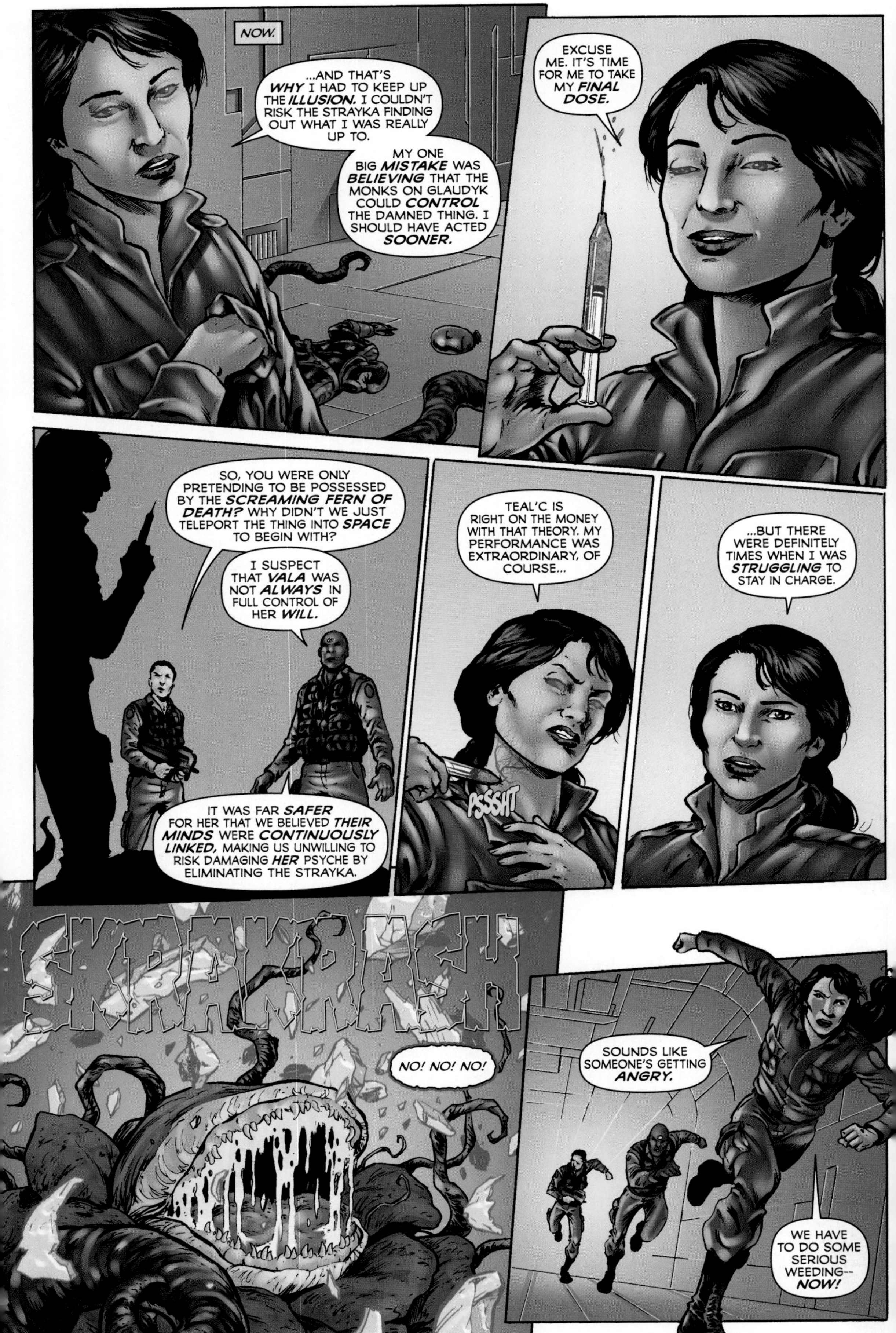
NOW.
...AND THAT'S WHY I HAD TO KEEP UP THE ILLUSION. I COULDN'T RISK THE STRAYKA FINDING OUT WHAT I WAS REALLY UP TO.
MY ONE BIG MISTAKE WAS BELIEVING THAT THE MONKS ON GLAUDYK COULD CONTROL THE DAMNED THING. I SHOULD HAVE ACTED SOONER.
EXCUSE ME. IT'S TIME FOR ME TO TAKE MY FINAL DOSE.
SO, YOU WERE ONLY PRETENDING TO BE POSSESSED BY THE SCREAMING FERN OF DEATH? WHY DIDN'T WE JUST TELEPORT THE THING INTO SPACE TO BEGIN WITH?
I SUSPECT THAT VALA WAS NOT ALWAYS IN FULL CONTROL OF HER WILL.
IT WAS FAR SAFER FOR HER THAT WE BELIEVED THEIR MINDS WERE CONTINUOUSLY LINKED, MAKING US UNWILLING TO RISK DAMAGING HER PSYCHE BY ELIMINATING THE STRAYKA.
TEAL'C IS RIGHT ON THE MONEY WITH THAT THEORY. MY PERFORMANCE WAS EXTRAORDINARY, OF COURSE...
PSSSHT
...BUT THERE WERE DEFINITELY TIMES WHEN I WAS STRUGGLING TO STAY IN CHARGE.
NO! NO! NO!
SOUNDS LIKE SOMEONE'S GETTING ANGRY.
WE HAVE TO DO SOME SERIOUS WEEDING-- NOW!

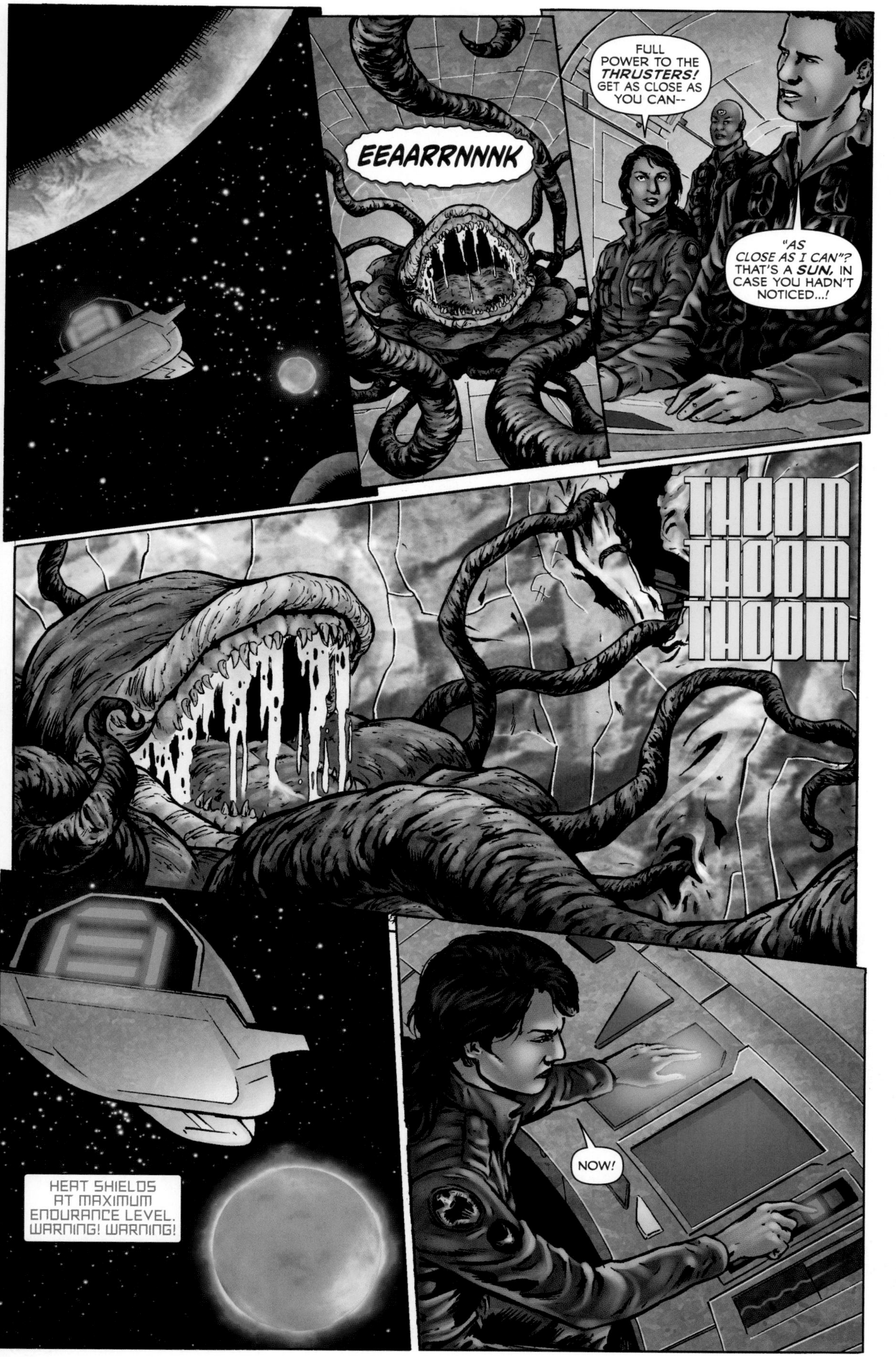
EEAARRNNNK
FULL POWER TO THE THRUSTERS! GET AS CLOSE AS YOU CAN--
"AS CLOSE AS I CAN"? THAT'S A SUN, IN CASE YOU HADN'T NOTICED...!
THOOM THOOM THOOM
HEAT SHIELDS AT MAXIMUM ENDURANCE LEVEL. WARNING! WARNING!
NOW!

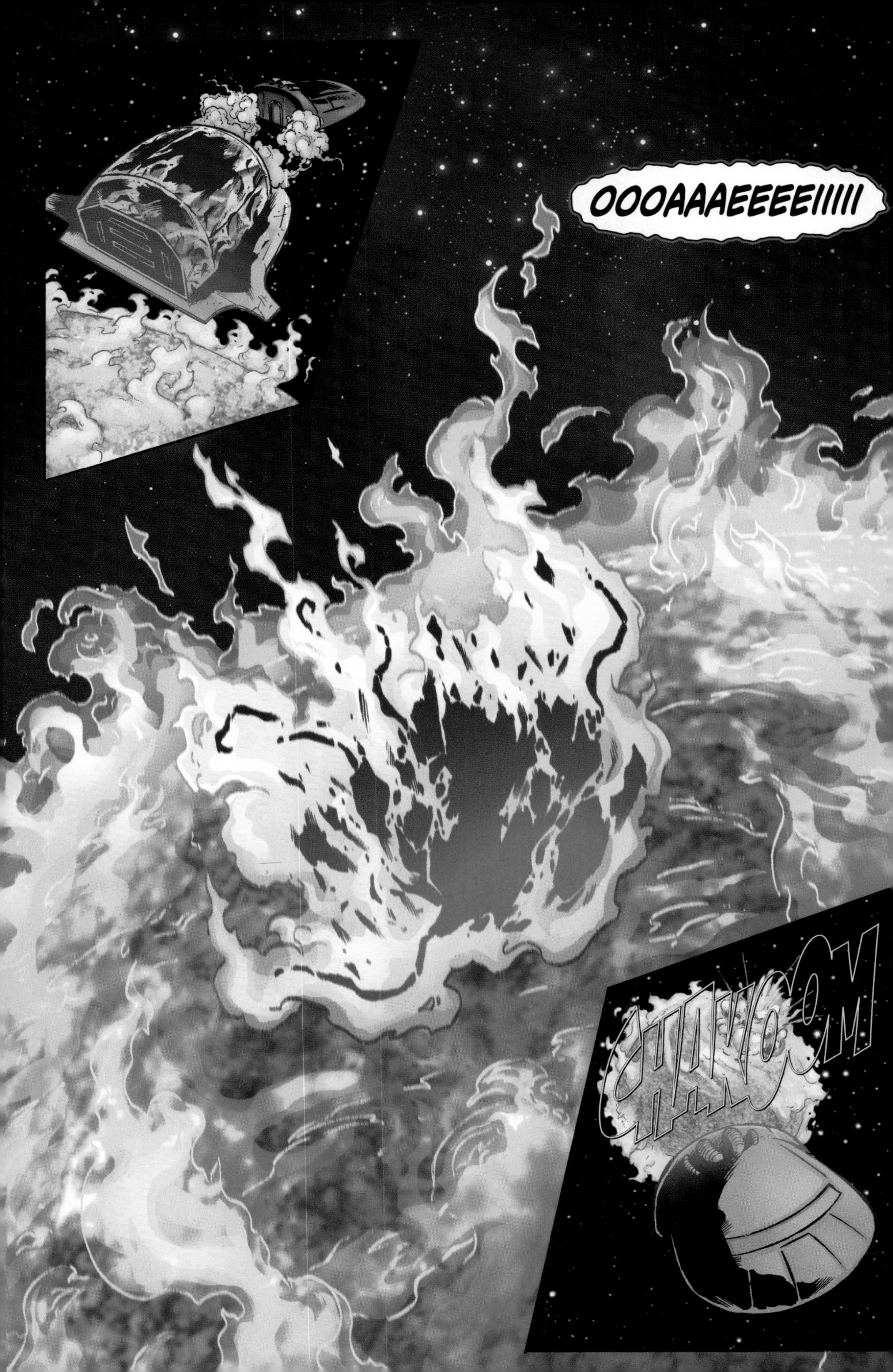
OOOAAAEEEEIIIIII